GCSE Mathematics

GCSE Mathematics

Owen Elbourn

CollinsEducational

An imprint of HarperCollins*Publishers*

Published by
CollinsEducational
77–85 Fulham Palace Road
Hammersmith
London W6 8JB

10 East 53rd Street
New York, NY 10022
USA

First published in 1992

ISBN: 0 00 322267 5

British Library Cataloguing in Publication Data

A catalogue record for this book is available from the
British Library

Typeset in Times roman 9½ point on 12 by
Dorchester Typesetting Group Ltd
and printed in Great Britain by Scotprint Ltd, Musselburgh

Contents

Introduction

This book is intended for use by mature students whose aim is to achieve at least a grade C in the GCSE. Mature students are those over the age of 16; there is no upper limit. The book assumes a background of school mathematics but it is not important how long ago this was or how much it has been forgotten. The book contains all the material necessary to achieve a grade A pass and the advice is to do the work in the order presented.

Throughout the book the text is cut to a minimum and the emphasis is on solving problems. All the questions are answered in full with all the steps of working out shown. This feature makes the book unique. It is important that the book is done in its entirety; a considerable amount of material is introduced in the solutions to the problems.

There are occasions when a question is posed before a full explanation has been given. This is done on purpose to encourage a real feature of the subject: facing the unknown and having to sort it out. This feature also helps to develop the approach to investigations and coursework; having the courage to try, to experiment and see what happens. It is also the best way to learn the subject. Some of the chapters are preceded by assessment tests which can be used as *before and after* exercises: do the test before doing the chapter and again afterwards and compare your results.

Throughout there are suggestions for investigations and coursework and if these are pursued you will build up a good coursework file for presentation at the end of the course. The coursework file is essential because it is a compulsory part of the course and it is worth approximately a quarter of the final mark (the fraction varies a little from board to board).

The best way to study this subject is:

- to aim at doing a modest amount each day rather than a big load once a week
- to work at a controlled steady pace.

At all times be prepared to ponder and reflect, and think deeply about what is being done. If a problem is too difficult leave it and return to it later (a day, a week, a month; it depends on the situation).

The book covers the first two stages of a three-stage course, the whole to be covered in nine months. The suggested programme is:

Stage 1: September to February – Chapters 1–11 which cover the content of the syllabus.

Stage 2: March – Revision papers at the end of the book which provide repeated miscellaneous practice on the whole of the book.

Stage 3: April, May   – Past papers which can be obtained
                              from your examining board.

It is important that the student is aware of the contents of the syllabus for the particular examination being taken. Throughout the book there are indications of the level of the examination that particular text is suited to. These are given by the use of stars (★) before the section heading or question number.

	No star	All levels
	One star	Intermediate and Higher levels D – F
★	One star	Intermediate and Higher levels D – F
★★	Two stars	Higher level A – C

If at the beginning you are unsure of the level of examination to take, don't worry: just work steadily at the book and it will become apparent as you go along which level to enter.

The book, and the suggestions about how to study, are based on the author's experiences, which have been accumulated over 30 years of continuously teaching the subject.

Further notes on study skills and examination preparation

Mathematics is all about developing a high level of logical thinking, about deducing as much as possible from the smallest amount of information and about solving problems in the simplest way. When you take the examination these are the things the examiner is looking for.

The syllabus of a mathematics examination is not very big when compared with other subjects but you are most certainly expected to know all of it. You will not do very well if you rely on the method, which rightly works well in many subjects, of remembering *key facts*. In mathematics, all facts are key facts which you need to know and to be able to use.

By the time you have finished this book you will be ready to tackle past examination papers. At first when you see them you may panic but that won't do any good! If you have done the work in this book properly you should be well on the way to sorting out your approach. There are two main stages to tackling papers:

• actually succeeding in doing the problems
• pacing your work so that the time is used efficiently.

The best way of sorting out the pacing is to be guided by the marks available e.g. if there are 110 marks on a 120 minute paper you should be working at approximately 1 mark per minute to gain full marks. Hence a question worth 10 marks should take approximately 10 minutes, but if you took 12 or 13 minutes you would still be in the over 80% bracket, sufficient for the highest grade.

It goes without saying that you should always have the relevant equipment, including drawing instruments (simple ones, not those required for engineering drawing) and a basic scientific calculator. Throw the correction fluid away, examiners (and teachers) don't like the stuff. Mistakes should be crossed out by a single diagonal line: let the examiner decide whether to give credit.

Believe it or not, the examiners are on your side; they are looking for every opportunity to give you credit so help them to do so.

Study patterns before an examination are obviously very much a personal choice but my advice is always to put away your books two or three days before and rest, take part in your favourite hobby or sport – anything but mathematics. In that way you will enter the examination alert and refreshed. Rugby players don't train hard the day before or on the morning of a big match, and the comparison is valid.

If you have tackled the book, and the past examination papers seriously and as intended, then the examination becomes a challenge you look forward to, it is what you have been working for. When that is the case you will be starting to enjoy the satisfaction that only this subject can give: and who knows what your next mathematics examination may be?

This state of affairs is created by you, and you alone, at the beginning of the course: you are the master who decides that this is how it is going to be. Hard work? Yes! Frustrating? Yes! But the result is well worth it.

1 Number

This chapter is about number. By the time you have completed it you will:

- recognise different **types** and **classes of number**
- be able to solve problems on **number patterns and sequences.**

To get you going, there is an assessment exercise in number. Don't worry if you cannot answer it, this chapter will put things right.

Number assessment test

1   Write down all the prime numbers between 70 and 90.

2   Write down the first triangular number after 40.

3   Which of the following numbers are rational?
$\sqrt{25}$ $\sqrt{23}$ π $\frac{2}{3}$ $-\sqrt{8}$

★ 4   Add the next two numbers to this sequence.
−1   2   7   14   23

5   Find the number missing from this sequence.
1   4   5   □   14   23   37

★ 6   Fill in the empty squares.

3	5	7	2	
19	51		9	3

ANSWERS TO NUMBER ASSESSMENT TEST

1   71   73   79   83   89

2   45

3    $\sqrt{25}$ $\frac{2}{3}$

4   34   47

5   9

6

3	5	7	2	1
19	51	99	9	3

Since the beginning of civilisation human beings have been fascinated with the study of number. At first it was out of a need to count and record. Archeologists have found much evidence of the earliest work in this area. With the advance of civilisation the study of number has continued, going deeper and wider into the subject. The work continues today, aided considerably by the computer, and the subject is vast. It is quite true that without the knowledge of number life as we know it in the civilised world could not be.

Types of numbers

The whole world of number can be split up into an infinite amount of different groups and we shall now look at some of them.

Natural numbers: {1, 2, 3, 4, 5, ...} are represented collectively by the symbol ℕ.

★**Whole numbers:** {0, 1, 2, 3, 4, ...} are represented by ℤ and are more properly called integers.

★**Rational numbers** are those for which the value is known exactly. Their symbol is ℚ; examples are 3, $\frac{1}{2}$, -7.

★**Irrational numbers** are those for which the value is not known exactly; examples are $\sqrt{2} = 1.414213562...$, $\pi = 3.141592654...$

★**Real numbers** are represented by ℝ, and they include integers, rational numbers and irrational numbers.

We need to look at a different range of definitions concerning number and then we can look at some problems.

Odd numbers are whole numbers which cannot be divided by 2 without leaving a remainder; examples are -7, -3, 5, 57.

Even numbers are whole numbers which can be divided by 2 without leaving a remainder; examples are -14, -4, 6, 28.

Prime numbers are whole numbers which cannot be divided by anything (except themselves and 1); examples are 2, 3, 5, 7, 11.

Directed numbers are numbers where the difference between positive and negative is recognised. They can be represented on a number line like this.

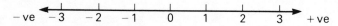

Triangular numbers are numbers which can be represented by equilateral triangles of dots. Examples are shown below.

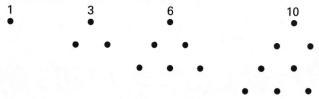

Square numbers are numbers which can be represented by squares of dots and they have square roots which are integers.

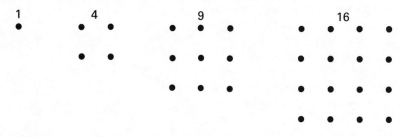

We shall now have a look at some problems.

EXERCISE 1.1

1   Write down all the prime numbers between 40 and 50.

2   How many square numbers are there between the fourth and fifth triangular numbers?

3   How many even numbers are prime?

4   If all the even numbers were divided by 2 would the answers be
    (a) even   (b) odd   (c) evenly divided between even and odd?

5   Which is the larger number, -5 or 3?

★ 6   Which of the following are irrational? (A calculator will help.)
    (a) $\sqrt{3}$ (b) $\sqrt{9}$ (c) $\frac{1}{3}$ (d) $\sqrt{5} \times \sqrt{5}$ (e) $-\sqrt{25}$

7   Find the first square number with digit sum equal to its square root.

8   A triangular number is four times the number of dots along one of its sides. What is the number?

9   Find the first triangular number (other that 1) which is also a square number.

10 Find the first prime number which, when its digits are reversed, gives another, different, prime number.

> **Digit sum**
>
> This is the sum of the digits in a number.
> The digit sum of 53 is
> $5 + 3 = 8$
> The digit sum of 48 is
> $4 + 8 = 12$
> $\Rightarrow 1 + 2 = 3$

Number patterns and sequences

A popular type of puzzle question is the one where you are given a chain of numbers and you have to add the next two.

EXAMPLE

Add the next two numbers to this sequence.
3   7   11   15   □   □

Solution

19, 23

In this section we shall look at questions of this type. There are only a limited number of rules or routines for finding the answer. You have to find them by experiment or *trial and error*. The formal mathematical wording for this is *by inspection*.

EXERCISE 1.2

In each case, add the next two numbers to the sequence.

1	3	−1	−3	−4				
2	26	37	50	65	82			
3	1.9	2.8	3.7	4.6				
4	1	−2	4	−8	16			
5	$\frac{1}{4}$	$\frac{3}{4}$	$\frac{5}{4}$	$\frac{7}{4}$				
6	2	6	12	20				
7	1	1	2	3	5	8	13	
8	53	59	61	67				
★ 9	10	1	12	2	14	4	16	8	18
★ 10	0	7	36	63	124			

Investigation: The method of differences

By the time you have worked through this investigation you will have realised the value of the method of differences. It is used often.

This investigation will help you to find out more about differences. You must expect to use second, third, fourth and higher differences, as necessary.

Using x gives the sequence	1	2	3	4	5
Using x^2 gives the sequence	1	4	9	16	25
Using x^3 gives the sequence	1	8	27	64	125
Using x^4 gives the sequence	1	16	81	256	625

Try to find the connection between the powers of x and the differences – there is one.

Investigation: Fibonacci

In question 7 of **Exercise 1.2** the Fibonacci sequence was introduced.

Find out about Fibonacci.

Find out about uses and applications of the sequence. It is a natural sequence and you will find out more about it from the Biology department.

★Extension

An extension to this work, again, often the substance of recreational puzzles, is in questions of this type.

Fill in the missing number.

1	11	21
3		103

Notation

The usual word for a mathematical exercise of this type is *operation*, or *function*. You will find this work useful because it appears later in the section on algebra.

The implication here is that some mathematical exercise has been done to 1 to produce 3; the same exercise on 21 produces 103. The problem is to find the exercise and use it on 11.

Inspection is the method used. One chain of thought might be:

3 from 1   not very helpful

103 from 21 $5 \times 20 = 100$ $5 \times 21 = 105$ $5 \times 21 - 2 = 103$

Try it on 1: $5 \times 1 - 2 = 3$ It works!

Find missing number: $5 \times 11 - 2 = 53$

Here is another example.

Fill in the missing number.

1	3	5
1		25

By far the greatest number of people will fill in 9, assuming that the operation is squaring the top number – and that answer would be correct. Equally correct, though, would be 13. Why?

Because $6 \times 1 - 5 = 1$ and $6 \times 5 - 5 = 25$

so $6 \times 3 - 5 = 13$

Either answer is correct, as long as the method of obtaining it is justified. The ideas behind this question appear again when we do work on simultaneous equations, later.

EXERCISE 1.3

In each case, fill in the missing number.

1

1	3	5	7	9
	3	15	□	63

2

4	12	16	48
17	147	260	

3

12	23	33	121
2	6		2

4

1	2	3	4
4	15		85

A harder question.

5

2	4	5	10
9	4	3	

Another hard question.

Do not worry if you found the last exercise difficult. This type of work will crop up again, and by then you will find it easier.

Solutions to exercises

SOLUTIONS TO EXERCISE 1.1

1   41   43   47

2 | Rank | Triangular number |

Rank	Triangular number
1st	1
2nd	3
3rd	6
4th	10 ⎫
5th	15 ⎭ ⇒ There are no square numbers between 10 and 15.

3   There is only one even prime number: 2.

4   (c) They will be equally divided.

	2	4	6	8	10	12	14	. . .
Divide by 2	1	2	3	4	5	6	7	. . .

5   3   (Which man is richer, the one with £3 or the one £5 in debt?)

6   **(a)** $\sqrt{3} = 1.7320508$ which is an approximation, so $\sqrt{3}$ is irrational.

   (b) $\sqrt{9} = 3$ so rational.

   (c) $\frac{1}{3}$ is rational.
   But $\frac{1}{3}$ as a decimal is 0.333 333. . . which is an approximation, so irrational.
   $\frac{1}{3}$ of $6 = \frac{1}{3} \times 6 = 2$
   0.333 333... of $6 = 0.333\,333... \times 6 = 1.999\,998$

   (d) $\sqrt{5} \times \sqrt{5} = 5$ so rational.

   (e) $-\sqrt{25} = -5$ so rational.

7
Square numbers	1	4	9	16	25	36	49	64	81
							13	10	
Digit sum	1	4	9	7	7	9	4	1	9

The square number is 81, its square root is 9.

8   List the numbers as below. We need only look for a multiple of 4, since a quarter of it must be a whole number.

Triangular number	1	3	6	10	15	21	28
Quarter of number							7

28 is the number; there are 7 dots in the side of its triangular pattern.

9   None of the numbers in question 8 is a square.
So, continuing   ⇒   36   45
36 is a square number.

10 **Prime numbers** 1   2   3   5   7   11   13
    Digits reversed 1   2   3   5   7   11   31
    31 is the first to give a different number which is also prime.

SOLUTIONS TO EXERCISE 1.2

1 3   −1   −3   −4
        −4   −2   −1   are the differences.
    ⇒ next two differences are $-\frac{1}{2}$ $-\frac{1}{4}$
    ⇒ next two terms are $-4\frac{1}{2}$ $-4\frac{3}{4}$

2 26   37   50   65   82
    ⇒ 11   13   15   17   differences
  ⇒ next terms are $82 + 19 = 101$
                and $101 + 21 = 122$

> A quicker method is to spot that each number is a square number plus 1.
>
> ⇒ $10^2 + 1 = 101$
> and $11^2 + 1 = 122$
>
> Don't be too surprised. There are often alternative methods.

3 1.9 2.8 3.7 4.6
    An easier one – the difference is 0.9, giving   5.5   6.4

4 1 −2 4 −8 16
    The sequence is formed by multiplying each term by −2.
    So the next two terms are $16 \times -2 = -32$
                    and $-32 \times -2 = 64$

> This question can also be answered by looking at the pattern of differences. Try it.

> A sequence of this type is called a **geometric sequence**.

5 $\frac{1}{4}$ $\frac{3}{4}$ $\frac{5}{4}$ $\frac{7}{4}$
    The easiest one! $\frac{9}{4}$ $\frac{11}{4}$

> A sequence of this type is called an **arithmetic sequence**. So is the one in question 3.

6 2 6 12 20
    Again, there are two methods.

    (a) Differences 4 6 8 ⇒ next terms 30 42
    (b) $2 = 2^2 - 2$ $6 = 3^2 - 3$ $12 = 4^2 - 4$ $20 = 5^2 - 5$
        So $6^2 - 6 = 30$ $7^2 - 7 = 42$

7   1   1   2   3   5   8   13

The easiest method: adding the last two terms gives the next one.

$\Rightarrow$ $8 + 13 = 21$ $13 + 21 = 34$

Or again, by differences,

1   1   2   3   5   8   13   21   34
   0   1   1   2   3   5   8   13

which suggests the routine shown by the dotted lines.

8   53   59   61   67

This one is a change in routine; they are primes.

$\Rightarrow$ 71   73

9   10   1   12   2   14   4   16   8   18

There is no obvious link between successive numbers but inspection shows that the sequence can be separated.

10   12   14   16   18
   1   2   4   8

Then it is very easy to see that the next two terms are   16   20.

> This is a mixture of an arithmetic and a geometric sequence, and thus is called an **arithmetico-geometric** progression. Fancy that!

10   0   7   26   63   124

Rapid increase in the numbers suggests cubes, perhaps.

$\Rightarrow$ $6^3 - 1 = 215$ and $7^3 - 1 = 342$

The investigation should reveal an alternative method for this question.

SOLUTIONS TO EXERCISE 1.3

1   35

Multiplying adjacent numbers on the top row gives the number below.

2
$4^2 + 1 = 17$ $4^2 + \frac{1}{4} \times 4 = 17$
$12^2 + 3 = 147$ $\Bigg\}\Rightarrow$ $12^2 + \frac{1}{4} \times 12 = 147$
$16^2 + 4 = 260$ $16^2 + \frac{1}{4} \times 16 = 260$

So $48^2 + \frac{1}{4} \times 48 = 2316$

3
$1 \times 2 = 2$
$2 \times 3 = 6$ i.e. the digit product $\Rightarrow$ $3 \times 3 = 9$
$1 \times 2 \times 1 = 2$

> Always be on the lookout for simple answers.

4
$1^3 + 1^2 + 1 + 1 = 4$
$2^3 + 2^2 + 2 + 1 = 15 \Big\}\Rightarrow$ $3^3 + 3^2 + 3 + 1 = 40$
$4^3 + 4^2 + 4 + 1 = 85$

5
$\frac{20}{2} - 1 = 9$
$\frac{20}{4} - 1 = 4 \Big\}\Rightarrow$ $\frac{20}{10} - 1 = 1$
$\frac{20}{5} - 1 = 3$

2 Ratio

When you have finished this chapter, which isn't as bad as it sounds, you will:

- know what **fractions** are
- be able to **change fractions to decimals**
- be able to **approximate numbers**
- be able to **change a fraction to a percentage**
- be able to find **one quantity as a percentage of another**
- be able to find **a percentage of a quantity**
- be able to **add, subtract, multiply and divide fractions**
- be able to **divide quantities into given ratios**.

Ratio assessment test

1   Express $\frac{7}{13}$ as a decimal correct to (**a**) 1 d.p. (**b**) 2 d.p.

2   Evaluate $1\frac{3}{7} + \frac{2}{3}$ giving your answer correct to 2 d.p.

3   Express £2.90 as a percentage of £18.40.

4   Find 17% of 491.5.

5   Express 75% as a fraction.

6   Evaluate $\frac{1}{2} + \frac{1}{4}$.

7   Evaluate $\frac{11}{12} + \frac{1}{6} - \frac{2}{3}$.

8   Evaluate $2\frac{4}{7} \div \frac{9}{14}$.

9   Divide £80 in the ratio 5 : 3.

10   When £750 is divided in the ratio 7 : 5 : 3 the middle share is £250. What are the other shares?

> The shorthand notation you will need in this chapter includes
> d.p.   decimal place
> s.f.   significant figure
> $\approx$ is approximately equal to
> :   used in a ratio, means *to* or *is to*.

ANSWERS TO RATIO ASSESSMENT TEST

1   (**a**) 0.5   (**b**) 0.54

2   2.10

3   15.8%

4   83.56

5   $\frac{3}{4}$

6   $\frac{3}{4}$

7   $\frac{5}{12}$

8   4

9   £50, £30

10   £350, £150

Introduction

In this chapter there are several sections, all connected by the idea of **ratio**, which means the comparison of numbers. The most common form of work in this area involves fractions. This may be a dreaded word for you, because it reminds you of something you have met before and did not understand, and have come to believe that you never will understand it. This will not do! We cannot make any progress without a working knowledge of fractions. Think about it. Thousands of other people understand fractions, so why shouldn't you?

Wherever we look we see **subdivision** taking place. We divide our **time** into sleeping, eating, working and leisure. We divide our **money** into taxes, home running costs, family costs, car costs, leisure costs. Our **country** is divided into counties, rural and urban areas, hilly land and flat land. We divide our **people** according to age, sex, living accommodation and so on. Subdivision sometimes has to be measured or **quantified**. This is where fractions come in.

Suppose a family consists of mother, father, two boys and two girls. It is easy to see that half the family is male and half is female – but where does the *half* come from? Out of six people, three are female. Mathematically, this is written as

$\underline{3} \rightarrow$ number of females
$6 \rightarrow$ number in family

This can be read as *three out of six*, and is the same rate or ratio as one out of two.

The structure of a fraction

A fraction consists of three parts:

the top	3	the **numerator**	states or **enumerates** how *many* of the type: three
the line in the middle	–	the **solidus**	
the bottom	7	the **denominator**	names or **denotes** the *type* of fraction: sevenths

You must know the words *numerator* and *denominator*, but generally there is nothing wrong with using the words *top* and *bottom*.

Fractions into decimals

One convenient way of dealing with fractions is to convert them into **decimal numbers**. Quite possibly, *decimal* is another word which brings back unpleasant memories. Decimal is from the Latin word *decem* which means ten, and decimal numbers are made up of whole numbers plus decimal parts comprising tenths, hundredths, thousandths and so on, in any combination.

EXAMPLES

$\frac{1}{2} = \frac{5}{10} = 0.5$

$\frac{1}{4} = \frac{25}{100} = 0.25$

$\frac{1}{8} = \frac{125}{1000} = 0.125 \leftarrow$ 3rd figure after point indicates number of thousandths

   2nd figure after point indicates number of hundredths

   1st figure after point indicates number of tenths

i.e. $\dfrac{125}{1000} = \dfrac{1}{100} + \dfrac{2}{1000} + \dfrac{5}{1000}$

Where did 0.125 come from?
Use your calculator and follow the sequence

$\boxed{1}\boxed{\div}\boxed{8}\boxed{=}$

Now let's try changing $\frac{3}{7}$ into decimal form.

$\boxed{3}\boxed{\div}\boxed{7}\boxed{=}\boxed{\quad 0.4285714 \quad}$

This answer is not very practical to use at this stage, so we would approximate.

	$0.428\,571\,4 \approx 0.428\,571$	this is correct to 6 decimal places
	$0.428\,571\,4 \approx 0.428\,57$	this is correct to 5 decimal places
†	$0.428\,571\,4 \approx 0.4286$	this is correct to 4 decimal places
†	$0.428\,571\,4 \approx 0.429$	this is correct to 3 decimal places
†	$0.428\,571\,4 \approx 0.43$	this is correct to 2 decimal places
	$0.428\,571\,4 \approx 0.4$	this is correct to 1 decimal place

In the approximations marked (†) 1 has been added to the last figure. Can you spot the rule?

> **Remember**
>
> When we round to a given number of decimal places we **approximate**.

Rule for approximations
If the *first number after* the cut-off is 5, 6, 7, 8 or 9, then 1 is added to the last number before cut-off. If it is 1, 2, 3 or 4 then there is no change.

Read through the list of approximations and you should be able to see the rule in operation.

EXERCISE 2.1

Convert the following fractions into decimals, correcting them to the number of decimal places indicated.

1 $\frac{2}{9}$ (2 d.p.)   2 $\frac{1}{13}$ (3 d.p.)

3 $\frac{5}{8}$ (1 d.p.)   4 $\frac{5}{12}$ (3 d.p.)

5 $\frac{23}{37}$ (3 d.p.)   6 $\frac{29}{200}$ (2 d.p. and 1 d.p.)

7 $\frac{11}{17}$ (2 d.p. and 1 d.p.)   8 $2\frac{3}{8}$ (3 d.p.)

9 $5\frac{2}{3}$ (1 d.p.)   10 $1\frac{8}{13}$ (1 d.p.)

> **Be careful!**
>
> Source of common mistake in questions 6 and 7!

One reason for converting fractions into decimals is that it makes comparisons, additions and subtractions much easier.

EXAMPLE

Arrange these fractions in order of size, smallest first.

$\frac{3}{7}$ $\frac{2}{5}$ $\frac{5}{13}$ $\frac{5}{9}$

> **Remember**
>
> This is called **ascending order**.

Solution

$\left. \begin{array}{l} \frac{3}{7} = 0.428\,571\,4 \\ \frac{2}{5} = 0.4 \\ \frac{5}{13} = 0.384\,615\,3 \\ \frac{5}{9} = 0.5555 \end{array} \right\} \Rightarrow$ required order is $\frac{5}{13}, \frac{2}{5}, \frac{3}{7}, \frac{5}{9}$

EXAMPLE

Work out $\frac{3}{4} + \frac{2}{5}$.

Solution

$\frac{3}{4} + \frac{2}{5} = 0.75 + 0.4 = 1.15$

> This method is fine if it is OK for the answer to be in decimal form.

The calculator sequence would be

$\boxed{3}\ \boxed{\div}\ \boxed{4}\ \boxed{=}\ \boxed{0.75}\ \boxed{M+}\ \boxed{2}\ \boxed{\div}\ \boxed{5}\ \boxed{=}\ \boxed{0.4}\ \boxed{+}\ \boxed{MR}\ \boxed{=}$

EXERCISE 2.2

1   Evaluate $\frac{2}{7} + \frac{3}{4} - \frac{3}{10}$ giving your answer correct to 2 d.p.

2   Evaluate $\frac{4}{9} \times \frac{3}{5}$ giving your answer correct to 3 d.p.

3   Arrange these numbers in descending order.

  $\frac{7}{11}$ $\frac{2}{3}$ $\frac{3}{5}$ $\frac{9}{13}$ $\frac{5}{9}$

4   Evaluate $\frac{4}{9} + \frac{3}{5}$ giving your answer correct to 3 d.p.

5   Evaluate $\frac{61}{79} + \frac{47}{53} - \frac{17}{19}$ giving your answer correct to 2 d.p.

6   Evaluate $1\frac{2}{7} + 3\frac{3}{4}$ giving your answer correct to 2 d.p.

7   Evaluate $4\frac{2}{3} \times 1\frac{5}{8}$ giving your answer correct to 1 d.p.

8 Find $\frac{3}{7}$ of $\frac{3}{4}$ of 20   giving your answer correct to 2 d.p.

9 How much is $\frac{2}{3}$ of $\frac{5}{9}$ short of 2? Give your answer correct to 2 d.p.

10 Evaluate $\frac{3}{8} \times \frac{1}{5} \times \frac{2}{7}$ giving your answer correct to 2 d.p.

★Percentages

Percentage is another word which causes more anxiety than it should. A percentage is just another form of conversion of a fraction to a decimal. The idea is very useful, especially when two or more quantities have to be compared. Interest rates offered by banks and building societies, rate of inflation, employment statistics, wage claims and so on are all examples of the use of percentages.

A percentage is just a fraction in which the bottom is 100.

EXAMPLES

$$\frac{4}{8} = \frac{6}{12} = \frac{10}{20} = \frac{1}{2} = \frac{45}{90} = \frac{50}{100}$$

All these fractions are equal to $\frac{1}{2}$ but the last one can be read as 'fifty per cent', which means, literally, fifty *per* or *out of* every hundred. The 100 on the bottom is written as % and put on the same line as the 50, to give 50%.

> **Remember**
>
> $\frac{4}{8}$ $\frac{6}{12}$ $\frac{10}{20}$ $\frac{1}{2}$ $\frac{45}{90}$ $\frac{50}{100}$
> These are all equivalent fractions because they all mean the same. These fractions are all equivalent to $\frac{1}{2}$.

> **★Investigation: Fibonacci again**
> As already mentioned, the Fibonacci sequence is
>
> 1 1 2 3 5 8 13 21 34 55 89 . . .
>
> Now write out the fractions formed from consecutive terms
>
> $\frac{1}{1}$ $\frac{2}{1}$ $\frac{3}{2}$ $\frac{5}{3}$ $\frac{8}{5}$ . . .
>
> and convert them to decimals.
>
> Investigate and consider representing your results on a diagram.

Changing to percentages

Here are some examples of fractions being changed to percentages.

$\frac{3}{4} = \frac{75}{100} = 75\%$ $\frac{3}{4} = 0.75$

$\frac{1}{5} = \frac{20}{100} = 20\%$ $\frac{1}{5} = 0.2$

$\frac{3}{10} = \frac{30}{100} = 30\%$ $\frac{3}{10} = 0.3$

Comparing these two columns gives us a simple rule for changing a fraction into a percentage. We just change it to a decimal and move the decimal point two places to the right.

> **Remember**
>
> Some people would say that the decimal point stays where it is and the digits all move two places to the left. It doesn't matter how we remember it, as long as we can do it.

EXERCISE 2.3

Repeat **Exercise 2.1**, converting the fraction in each question into a percentage (%) and giving the answers correct to 1 d.p.

When you have finished and checked the last exercise, think about the answers you found. Look at the answer to question 8, which is 237.5% Does this make sense? It certainly does! Consider this example.

EXAMPLE

A radio is bought for £12.

It is sold for £12   ⇒   no profit
It is sold for £18   ⇒   £6 profit   50% (half its cost)
It is sold for £24   ⇒   £12 profit   100% (the same as it cost)
It is sold for £30   ⇒   £18 profit   150% (1.5 times its cost)
It is sold for £36   ⇒   £24 profit   200% (twice its cost)

So we can see that figures like 237.5% do make sense.

★ One quantity as a percentage of another

When we need to express one quantity as a percentage of another the routine is ordered and simple.

- First, express as a fraction.
- Second, change the fraction to a decimal.
- Third, multiply by 100.

★EXAMPLE

Express 45p as a percentage of £2.70.

Solution

As a fraction: $\frac{45}{270}$
As a decimal: 0.166 666 6 . . .
As a percentage: 16.7%

> **Remember**
>
> Make sure that the units are the same top and bottom – in this case pence.

★EXAMPLE

Find the percentage profit when a bicycle bought for £65 is sold for £87.20.

Solution

Profit = £87.20 − £65 = £22.20
As a fraction: $\frac{22.5}{65}$
As a decimal: 0.341 538 4
As a percentage: 34.2%

> **Remember**
>
> The percentage profit must be worked out as a fraction of the cost, i.e. the *cost* goes on the *bottom*.

Finding a percentage of a quantity

EXAMPLE

Find 17% of 4471.

Solution

This means 'find 0.17×4471'.
$0.17 \times 4471 = 760.07$

EXAMPLE

Find 130% of £52.40.

Solution

$$130\% \text{ of } £52.40 = 1.3 \times £52.40$$
$$= £68.12$$

EXERCISE 2.4

1   A man who weighs 95 kg is told to reduce his weight by 8%. How much must he lose?

2   The recommended maximum towing limit is 75% of the weight of the car. Find the towing limit for a car which weighs 22 cwt.

3   A class of 26 has an average attendance of 22. What is the average absence as a percentage?

4   A workman is to receive a pay rise of 6.5%. His present wage is £135.70 per week. What will his new weekly wage be?

5   Which of the following two savings plans is the more profitable investment for a girl with £800? Account A pays no interest on the first £200 but 9% on the rest. Account B pays 7% on the whole amount. (If you do not understand interest, go straight to the solution.)

6   It is said that one person in five has some hearing loss. What percentage is this?

7   Of 6000 voters, 55% voted for candidate A and 45% voted for candidate B. What percentage swing is required for B to win next time?

8   A darts player hits double 20 seven times in 18 attempts. What is his percentage chance of hitting double 20?

9   A man invests £5000. He puts £4000 into stock which makes 7% and £1000 into stock which loses 8%. What is the percentage gain or loss overall?

10   Out of a class of 30 students, 24 pass in Mathematics. Out of a class
of five students, one passes in Latin.

For Mathematics: fraction pass $= \frac{24}{30} \approx 80\%$

For Latin: fraction pass $= \frac{1}{5} \approx 20\%$

So the overall pass rate is the average $= \dfrac{80\% + 20\%}{2} = 50\%$

Is this reasoning, and the conclusion, valid or not? Investigate.

Fractions: addition, subtraction, multiplication and division

So far, we have made things easier by making use of decimal numbers
and the calculator. This is not always permissible, so the time has come
to work with fractions in fraction form.

Addition

The important thing to remember is that we cannot add fractions
together unless they are of the same type.

> **Remember**
>
> It is the number on the
> *bottom* which indicates
> the type: thirds, twenty-
> ninths, etc.

EXAMPLE

Add $\frac{2}{3} + \frac{1}{5}$.

Solution

These have to be made into fractions of the same type.

$\frac{2}{3} = \frac{4}{6} = \frac{6}{9} = \frac{8}{12} = \frac{10}{15} = \frac{12}{18}$ and

$\frac{1}{5} = \frac{2}{10} = \frac{3}{15} = \frac{4}{20}$

Inspection shows that

$\frac{2}{3} = \frac{10}{15}$ and $\frac{1}{5} = \frac{3}{15}$

both have the same number on the bottom.

$\therefore \frac{2}{3} + \frac{1}{5} = \frac{10}{15} + \frac{3}{15} = \frac{13}{15}$

There has to be a more efficient way of getting the number on the bottom
than writing out the long chains of equivalent fractions. The clue lies in
the fact that $3 \times 5 = 15$. This means that 3 and 5 both go into 15.

EXAMPLE

Add $\frac{1}{4} + \frac{3}{7}$.

Solution

$4 \times 7 = 28$ so 4 and 7 both go into 28.

$\therefore \frac{1}{4} + \frac{3}{7} = \frac{7}{28} + \frac{12}{28} = \frac{19}{28}$

EXAMPLE

Add $\frac{1}{3} + \frac{2}{5} + \frac{1}{4}$.

Solution

$3 \times 5 \times 4 = 60$, so 3, 5 and 4 all go into 60.

$\therefore \frac{1}{3} + \frac{2}{5} + \frac{1}{4} = \frac{20}{60} + \frac{24}{60} + \frac{15}{60}$
$= \frac{59}{60}$

EXAMPLE

Add $\frac{2}{3} + \frac{1}{6}$.

Solution

$3 \times 6 = 18$

$\therefore \frac{2}{3} + \frac{1}{6} = \frac{12}{18} + \frac{3}{18} = \frac{15}{18}$
$= \frac{5}{6}$

The last example was a good case of working without thinking clearly, or going into 'automatic mode'.
It would have been better to say
$\frac{2}{3} + \frac{1}{6} = \frac{4}{6} + \frac{1}{6} = \frac{5}{6}$

Subtraction

This is very similar to addition except that we have a *minus* sign instead of the *plus*. It is a little more complicated when we come to mixed numbers but we shall worry about that later.

Multiplication

This is the easiest operation with fractions, because we can do what we should like to do in addition and subtraction. We simply multiply the tops, and multiply the bottoms.

EXAMPLE

Multiply $\frac{3}{7} \times \frac{2}{5}$.

Solution

$\frac{3}{7} \times \frac{2}{5} = \frac{6}{35}$

Division

This is related to multiplication but we need to remember a fairly easy rule. We turn the fraction we are dividing by upside down, then multiply.

EXAMPLE

Divide $\frac{3}{4} \div \frac{5}{7}$.

Solution

$\frac{3}{4} \div \frac{5}{7} = \frac{3}{4} \times \frac{7}{5} = \frac{21}{20}$

There seems to be a touch of magic in stating a rule in this way. Perhaps we should see why it works.

Consider $\quad \frac{1}{2} \div \frac{1}{6}$ i.e. how many $\frac{1}{6}$s in $\frac{1}{2}$?

$\Rightarrow \quad \frac{3}{6} \div \frac{1}{6}$

$\Rightarrow \quad 3 \div 1$

$\qquad = 3$ We knew the answer all the time!

So if the bottoms are the same, we just need to divide the tops.

Now consider $\quad \frac{2}{7} \div \frac{3}{4}$

$\Rightarrow \quad \frac{8}{28} \div \frac{21}{28} = \frac{8}{21}$

We can look at it again, and fill in some more details.

$$\frac{2}{7} \div \frac{3}{4} = \left(\frac{2}{7} \times \frac{4}{4} \right) \div \left(\frac{3}{4} \times \frac{7}{7} \right)$$

$$= \quad \frac{2 \times 4}{7 \times 4} \div \frac{3 \times 7}{4 \times 7}$$

$$\Rightarrow \quad \frac{2 \times 4}{3 \times 7} = \frac{2 \times 4}{7 \times 3} = \frac{2}{7} \times \frac{4}{3}$$

i.e. $\dfrac{2}{7} \div \dfrac{3}{4} = \dfrac{2}{7} \times \dfrac{4}{3}$

The rule is proved!

Investigation

A purist would say that this proves the rule only for $\frac{2}{7} \div \frac{3}{4}$.

You could take this further and use algebra to consider $\dfrac{p}{q} \div \dfrac{x}{y}$

(Don't worry if you don't feel up to the algebra yet. It will keep.)

EXERCISE 2.5

1 Work out $\quad \frac{3}{4} + \frac{1}{2} - \frac{1}{3}$.

2 Work out $\quad \frac{1}{2} \times \frac{3}{4} \div \frac{3}{8}$.

3 Find the exact value of $\quad \frac{2}{3} + \frac{1}{2}$.

4 Out of 600 ewes, $\frac{1}{30}$ had triplets, $\frac{5}{12}$ had twins and the rest had single lambs. How many lambs were born?

5 Work out $\quad \frac{2}{4} + \frac{4}{5} - \frac{1}{10}$.

6 Work out $\quad 1\frac{3}{4} \times \frac{9}{14}$. (Hint: $1\frac{3}{4} = \frac{7}{4}$)

7 Work out $\quad 3\frac{1}{3} \div \frac{5}{6}$.

8 Three-quarters of the pupils in a school arrive on time and two-thirds of the rest are less than five minutes late. What fraction of the pupils are more than five minutes late?

> Read this carefully and don't be put off by all the words.

9 Work out $\frac{3}{8} + \frac{1}{4} \times \frac{1}{2}$.

> A bit naughty, this one, but not unknown on examination papers.

10 Work out $[\frac{1}{2} + (\frac{1}{4} \times \frac{3}{5})] \div (2 - \frac{1}{5})$.

Ratio problems

Early in this chapter we used the word *ratio* but since then we have used the word *fraction*. The two words mean the same thing but in some cases one is used rather than the other.

Consider this problem.

Divide £30 between two people in the ratio 2 : 1. This means that the first person has twice as much as the second. The answer is that the first person has £20 and the second has £10. Simple!

Now let us look at the work involved.

EXAMPLE

Divide £72 in the ratio 7:2.

Solution

For one person to get seven parts and the other to get two parts, we need a total of nine parts.
We need to find the value of one part first.
£72 = 9 × £8
∴ 1st person: 7 × £8 = £56
　 2nd person: 2 × £8 = £16
So £72 is split into £56 and £16.

EXAMPLE

Share out £65 in the ratio 3 : 4 : 6.

Solution

The total number of shares is 3 + 4 + 6 = 13.
£65 ÷ 13 = £5
∴ 1st share = 3 × £5 = £15
　 2nd share = 4 × £5 = £20
　 3rd share = 6 × £5 = £30

Now let us look back at the example before this one. Would it have been much different – or any different – if it had been put like this?

Divide £72 so that A gets $\frac{7}{9}$ and B gets $\frac{2}{9}$.

It would have been the same question. The same is true for the example above, but using the ratio notation allows for more concise wording.

EXERCISE 2.6

1   In a food factory in one hour, 250 puddings are made, 500 cakes are made and 1250 buns are made. What is the ratio of puddings to cakes to buns?

★★ 2   In the factory in question 1, it takes one hour for one person to pack 100 puddings *or* 250 cakes *or* 600 buns. What is the ratio of the numbers of people employed for packing the different products?

3   Anna, Brian and Chris inherit a sum of money which is divided in the ratio   5 : 4 : 3   among them. Anna received £750. How much did Brian and Chris receive?

★ 4   A man can build 15 metres of dry stone wall in two days. What length of wall could three men build in five days?

5   The average flow of traffic along a particular road is 500 vehicles per hour. The maximum flow is limited to an increase in the average flow of 125%. What is the ratio of the number of vehicles per half-hour at maximum flow to the number of vehicles per hour at normal flow?

6   The chain wheel on a bicycle has 52 teeth and the sprocket on the rear wheel has 24 teeth.

   (a) What is the ratio of teeth on the chain wheel to teeth on the sprocket?

★   (b) How many times does the road wheel turn for one turn of the pedals?

7   A school decides that it wishes to have a pupil : teacher ratio of 24 : 1 in the classroom.

   (a) If there are 864 pupils, how many teachers would be required?

★★   (b) It is then decided that the ratio of teaching to non-teaching time for teachers will be 6 : 1. How many extra teachers will now be required?

8   Concrete is made by mixing aggregate, sand and cement in the ratio of   4 : 2 : 1   by volume. 28 cubic metres of concrete are required.

   (a) What volume of each component is needed?

★   (b) The cost of the components, in the same order as before, is   1 : 1 : 2   and one cubic metre of aggregate costs £6. What is the cost of the concrete?

Solutions to exercises

SOLUTIONS TO EXERCISE 2.1

	Calculator display	Answer	
1	0.2222222	0.22	
2	0.076923	0.077	
3	0.625	0.6	
4	0.4166666	0.417	
5	0.6216216	0.622	
6	0.145	0.15	0.1
7	0.6470588	0.65	0.6
8	$\boxed{3}\ \boxed{\div}\ \boxed{8}\ \boxed{=}\ 0.375$	2.375	
9	$\boxed{2}\ \boxed{\div}\ \boxed{3}\ \boxed{=}\ 0.66666666$	5.7	
10	$\boxed{8}\ \boxed{\div}\ \boxed{13}\ \boxed{=}\ 0.6153846$	1.62	

> Study the answers to questions 6 and 7 carefully. They are correct. A popular mistake is to say 0.15 and 0.2, and 0.65 and 0.7.

Memory buttons on the calculator

In the solutions to questions 6 and 7, study the calculator routines carefully and establish why the buttons need to be pressed in the order shown. Notice the difference between $\boxed{\text{Min}}$ and $\boxed{\text{M+}}$. $\boxed{\text{Min}}$, or $\boxed{\text{STO}}$ on some machines, holds in the memory only the last number shown on the display; $\boxed{\text{M+}}$ builds a running total in the memory.

SOLUTIONS TO EXERCISE 2.2

1. $\boxed{2}\ \boxed{\div}\ \boxed{7}\ \boxed{+}\ \boxed{3}\ \boxed{\div}\ \boxed{4}\ \boxed{-}\ \boxed{3}\ \boxed{\div}\ \boxed{10}\ \boxed{=}\ 0.7357142 \approx 0.74$

2. $\boxed{4}\ \boxed{\div}\ \boxed{9}\ \boxed{\times}\ \boxed{3}\ \boxed{\div}\ \boxed{5}\ \boxed{=}\ 0.2666666 \approx 0.267$

3. $\frac{9}{13}\quad \frac{2}{3}\quad \frac{7}{11}\quad \frac{3}{5}\quad \frac{5}{9}$

4. $\boxed{4}\ \boxed{\div}\ \boxed{9}\ \boxed{+}\ \boxed{3}\ \boxed{\div}\ \boxed{5}\ \boxed{=}\ 1.0444444 \approx 1.044$

5. $\boxed{61}\ \boxed{\div}\ \boxed{79}\ \boxed{+}\ \boxed{47}\ \boxed{\div}\ \boxed{53}\ \boxed{-}\ \boxed{17}\ \boxed{\div}\ \boxed{19}\ \boxed{=}\ 0.7642075 \approx 0.76$

6. $\boxed{2}\ \boxed{\div}\ \boxed{7}\ \boxed{=}\ \boxed{+}\ \boxed{1}\ \boxed{=}\ \boxed{\text{M+}}\ \boxed{3}\ \boxed{\div}\ \boxed{4}\ \boxed{=}\ \boxed{+}\ \boxed{3}\ \boxed{=}\ \boxed{\text{M+}}\ \boxed{\text{MR}}\ 5.0357143 \approx 5.04$

7. $\boxed{2}\ \boxed{\div}\ \boxed{3}\ \boxed{=}\ \boxed{+}\ \boxed{4}\ \boxed{=}\ \boxed{\text{Min}}\ \boxed{5}\ \boxed{\div}\ \boxed{8}\ \boxed{=}\ \boxed{+}\ \boxed{1}\ \boxed{=}\ \boxed{\times}\ \boxed{\text{MR}}\ \boxed{=}\ 7.5833333 \approx 7.6$

8. $\frac{3}{7}$ of $\frac{3}{4}$ of $20 = \frac{3}{7} \times \frac{3}{4} \times 20 = 6.4285714 \approx 6.43$

9. $\boxed{2}\ \boxed{\times}\ \boxed{8}\ \boxed{\div}\ \boxed{3}\ \boxed{\div}\ \boxed{9}\ \boxed{=}\ \boxed{\text{Min}}\ \boxed{2}\ \boxed{-}\ \boxed{\text{MR}}\ \boxed{=}\ 1.4074074 \approx 1.41$

10. $0.0214285 \approx 0.02$

SOLUTIONS TO EXERCISE 2.3

1 22.2%   **2** 7.7%   **3** 62.5%   **4** 41.7%   **5** 62.2%
6 14.5%   **7** 64.7%   **8** 237.5%   **9** 566.7%   **10** 161.5%

SOLUTIONS TO EXERCISE 2.4

1   Reduce 95 kg by 8%   i.e. 0.08 of 95 kg
$\boxed{.08}$ $\boxed{\times}$ $\boxed{95}$ $\boxed{=}$ 7.6 kg

2   75% = 0.75
∴ limit = 0.75 × 22 cwt = 16.5 cwt

3   Average absence = 4
Fraction absent = $\frac{4}{26}$
Percentage absent = 15.4%

4   6.5% = 0.065
Rise = 0.065 × 135.70 = 8.82
∴ new wage = £144.52

5   Interest is amount added by bank etc.
Interest earned in account A = 0.09 × £600 = £54
Interest earned in account B = 0.07 × £800 = £56
Account B is the more profitable.

6 $\frac{1}{5}$ = 0.2 = 20%

7   A received 0.55 × 6000 = 3300 votes
B received 0.45 × 6000 = 2700 votes
∵ B needs 301 voters to change.
⇒ $\frac{301}{6000}$ = 5.02%

8   Chance $= \dfrac{\text{actual hits}}{\text{possible hits}} = \dfrac{7}{18}$
$= 38.9\%$

9   7% of £4000 = £280
8% of £1000 = £80
Total gain = £200   ⇒   percentage gain = $\frac{200}{5000}$ = 4%

10   It definitely is not valid.
This example exposes a fallacy which unfortunately is followed all too often, particularly by the media, politicians and advertisers. Many also do it in ignorance.
The first two lines, i.e. Mathematics 80% and Latin 20%, are OK.
Overall pass rate $= \dfrac{\text{number of passes}}{\text{number of candidates}} = \dfrac{25}{35}$

$= 71.4\%$

NB
301 because
3300 − 2700 = 600.
Half this is 300, but we must add 1 for a majority.

SOLUTIONS TO EXERCISE 2.5

1 $\frac{3}{4} + \frac{1}{2} - \frac{1}{3} = \frac{9}{12} + \frac{6}{12} - \frac{4}{12} = \frac{11}{12}$

You might well have used 24 on the bottom. This is still correct, but you will have needed to cancel.

2 $\frac{1}{2} \times \frac{3}{4} \div \frac{3}{8} = \frac{1}{2} \times \frac{3}{4} \times \frac{8}{3} = \frac{24}{24}$

or $\frac{1}{2_1} \times \frac{1\cancel{3}}{\cancel{4}_1} \times \frac{1\cancel{4}\cancel{8}}{\cancel{3}_1} = \frac{1}{1} = 1$

Remember

Cancelling means dividing top and bottom by the same number. Cancel whenever you can.

3 $\frac{2}{3} + \frac{1}{2} = \frac{4}{6} + \frac{3}{6} = \frac{7}{6}$

$\frac{7}{6}$ is correct but clumsy.

It is better to have $\frac{7}{6} = 1\frac{1}{6}$.

Remember

The word 'exact' is important in that it means you *must not* use the calculator.
∴ $\frac{7}{6}$ is the exact answer.
∵ $\frac{7}{6} = 1.1666667$ by calculator, and is an approximation.

4 $600 \times \frac{1}{30} = 20 \Rightarrow 60$ lambs
$600 \times \frac{5}{12} = 250 \Rightarrow 500$ lambs
$\Rightarrow 330 \Rightarrow 330$ lambs
Total 890 lambs

5 $\frac{3}{4} + \frac{4}{5} - \frac{1}{10} = \frac{15}{20} + \frac{16}{20} - \frac{2}{20} = \frac{29}{20} = 1\frac{9}{20}$

Again, notice that the mixed number $1\frac{9}{20}$ is preferred to the improper fraction $\frac{29}{20}$.

6 $1\frac{3}{4} \times \frac{9}{14} = \frac{1\cancel{7}}{4} \times \frac{9}{\cancel{14}_2}$ cancelling
$= \frac{9}{8}$ improper fraction (top-heavy)
$= 1\frac{1}{8}$ mixed number (whole number plus fraction)

7 $3\frac{1}{3} \div \frac{5}{6} = \frac{2\cancel{10}}{\cancel{3}_1} \times \frac{2\cancel{6}}{\cancel{5}_1} = \frac{4}{1} = 4$

8 $\frac{3}{4}$ on time $\frac{1}{4}$ late
$\Rightarrow \frac{2}{3}$ of $\frac{1}{4}$ are less than 5 minutes late
$\frac{2}{3} \times \frac{1}{4} = \frac{1}{6}$
$\Rightarrow \frac{3}{4} + \frac{1}{6} = \frac{9}{12} + \frac{2}{12} = \frac{11}{12}$ are less than 5 minutes late
∴ $\frac{1}{12}$ of the pupils are more than 5 minutes late.

9 $\frac{3}{8} + \frac{1}{4} \times \frac{1}{2}$

Method 1: $\frac{3}{8} + \frac{2}{8} \times \frac{1}{2} = \frac{5}{8} \times \frac{1}{2} = \frac{5}{16}$ Popular, but WRONG!

Method 2: $\frac{3}{8} + (\frac{1}{4} \times \frac{1}{2}) = \frac{3}{8} + \frac{1}{8} = \frac{4}{8} = \frac{1}{2}$ Correct!

Order of operations

In the absence of any brackets, $\times$ and $\div$ are carried out before $+$ and $-$.
BODMAS: Brackets Of Division Multiplication Addition Subtraction
spells out the order of operations.

Comment

The question would have been much better presented as $\frac{3}{8} + (\frac{1}{4} \times \frac{1}{2})$ because work in brackets is always done first.

10 $[\frac{1}{2} + (\frac{1}{4} \times \frac{3}{5})] \div (2 - \frac{1}{5}) = [\frac{1}{2} + \frac{3}{20}] \div 1\frac{1}{5}$

$$= \frac{13}{20_4} \times \frac{1 \overset{5}{\cancel{5}}}{9}$$

$$= \frac{13}{36}$$

SOLUTIONS TO EXERCISE 2.6

1   Ratio is   250 : 500 : 1250
                    = 1 : 2 : 5

2   Packing needs to be done at the same rate as production.
With one person, packing rate is 100 : 250 : 1250
Number of people needed $2\frac{1}{2}$: 2 : $2\frac{1}{12}$
$\therefore 2\frac{1}{2} \times 100 = 250$ $2 \times 250 = 500$ $2\frac{1}{12} \times 600 = 1250$
$\therefore$ ratio of people needed is $\frac{5}{2} : 2 : \frac{25}{12}$ or $30 : 24 : 25$

3   Anna receives $\dfrac{5}{5 + 4 + 3} = \frac{5}{12}$ of the sum

$\therefore \frac{1}{12}$ the sum is £750 $\div$ 5 = £150
Brian receives $\frac{4}{12}$ of the sum which is $4 \times$ £150 = £600
Chris receives $\frac{3}{12}$ of the sum which is $3 \times$ £150 = £450

4   1 man in 2 days builds 15 metres
1 man in 1 day builds $\frac{15}{2}$ metres
3 men in 1 day build $3 \times \frac{15}{2}$ metres
3 men in 5 days build $5 \times 3 \times \frac{15}{2}$ metres = $\frac{225}{2} = 112.5$ metres

Follow each line carefully and note how the answer is built up.

5   Flow of 500 vehicles.

Increase of 150% $\Rightarrow \dfrac{125}{100} \times 500 = 625$ vehicles

$\therefore$ maximum flow = 500 + 625 = 1125 vehicles per hour
                              = 562.5 vehicles per half hour
The required ratio is   562.5 : 500
                    = 5625 : 5000 $\times$ 10
                    = 1125 : 1000 $\div$ 5
                    =   45 :   40 $\div$ 25
                    =   9 :   8 $\div$ 5

6   **(a)** Ratio chain wheel : sprocket = 52 : 24
                              = 13 : 6

(b) One turn of the pedals $\Rightarrow$ 52 teeth i.e. 52 links of the chain
   $\therefore$ number of turns of the sprocket = $\frac{52}{24} = \frac{13}{6}$

$\Rightarrow$ 1 turn of chain wheel = $\frac{13}{6} = 2\frac{1}{6}$ turns of the road wheel

7   (a) $864 : n = 24 : 1$

$$\frac{n}{864} = \frac{1}{24} \Rightarrow n = \frac{864}{24} = 36$$

(b) Teaching time reduced in ratio $1 : 6$ i.e. by $\frac{1}{7}$.

Teachers now teach for $\frac{6}{7}$ of the time.

∴ number of teachers teaching $\frac{6}{7}$ of the time

= 36 teachers teaching full time

$$n \times \frac{6}{7} = 36 \times \frac{7}{7}$$

$\Rightarrow \quad n = 42$

So 6 extra teachers are needed.

8   (a) Aggregate = $\dfrac{4}{4 + 2 + 1} \times 28 = \dfrac{4}{7} \times 28 = 16 \text{ m}^3$

Sand = $\dfrac{2}{4 + 2 + 1} \times 28 = \dfrac{2}{7} \times 28 = 8 \text{ m}^2$

Cement = $\dfrac{1}{4 + 2 + 1} \times 28 = \dfrac{1}{7} \times 28 = 4 \text{ m}^2$

(b) Cost ratio is $1 : 1 : 2$.

∴ aggregate costs £6 per m^3

sand costs £6 per m^3

cement costs £12 per m^3

Total cost = £6 × 16 + £6 × 8 + £12 × 4

= £192

3 Statistics

'There are lies, damned lies, and statistics.'

There are many words to be learnt in the study of statistics, and there are many problems associated with them. By the end of this chapter you will know the words and be able to do the problems. You will study these topics:

- **tally, frequency**
- **pictograms**
- **bar charts, line charts**
- **pie charts**
- **cumulative frequency** and **cumulative frequency curves**
- **mode, median**
- **mean**
- **grouped data**
- **modal class**
- **histogram**
- **frequency polygon**
- **quartiles**
- **scatter diagrams.**

Introduction

Statistics is the branch of mathematics which is concerned with the collection and handling of large quantities of numerical information. It is particularly important as a section of mathematics with applications in other areas: the sciences generally, industry, business, politics and sport – none of these could function properly without the use of statistics. There are thousands of people who earn their living by processing large amounts of numbers: they are using statistics.

We shall start by considering a set of figures and looking at methods of recording and presenting them. The figures we shall use are a record of the numbers of eggs laid by 100 hens over a period of ten days. You may wonder why we are going to use hens and eggs. A good question, but we have to start somewhere, and the argument over the chicken and the egg rumbles on...

Recording information
★★ Cumulative frequency table
The best way to show our information is in a table like this.

Number of eggs n	Tally	Frequency f	Cumulative frequency c.f.
0	//	2	2
1	////	5	7
2	//// ////	10	17
3	//// //// ////	14	31
4	//// //// //// //// //// ////	29	60
5	//// //// //// //// //// //	27	87
6	//// ////	9	96
7	////	4	100

The section headed *Tally* is used for counting. Notice the method of using blocks of five marks. Done neatly, it gives an instant visual display of the information.

The section headed *Frequency* means *number of*, for example, five hens laid just one egg each.

The section headed *Cumulative frequency* gives a running total for all the frequencies; the frequencies are added up as we come down the table, so we know that 60 hens laid four or fewer eggs.

The final number in the 'Cumulative frequency' column should always give the total number of hens, or students, or cars – or whatever else we are studying at the time.

There are different diagrams which can be drawn to represent this information and these are described in detail in the following sections.

Pictograms

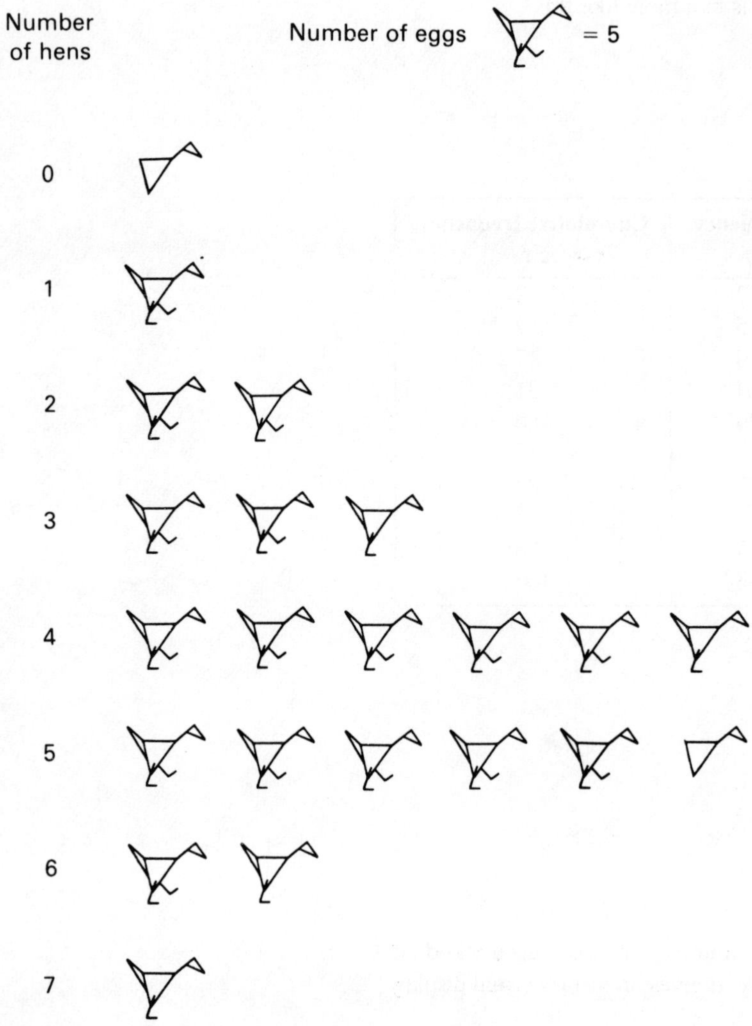

Number of hens

Number of eggs = 5

0	
1	
2	
3	
4	
5	
6	
7	

This is a pictogram. The information is displayed using little pictures, which are usually related to the type of information being shown. This is a popular type of diagram, used often by the media.

Notice how numbers less than five are shown by leaving out parts of the symbol.

Bar charts and line charts

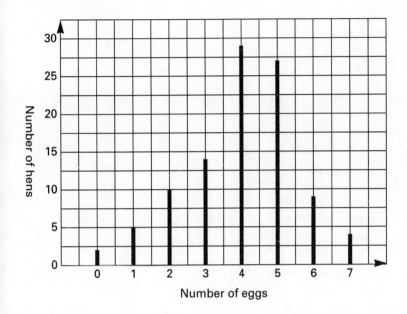

In this bar chart, the length of the bar represents the number of hens laying that number of eggs, in each case. If we had used a straight line instead of each bar, it would have been a line chart.

30	25	20	15	10	5	0
0	1	2	3	4	5	6	7

Number of hens

Number of eggs

Pie charts

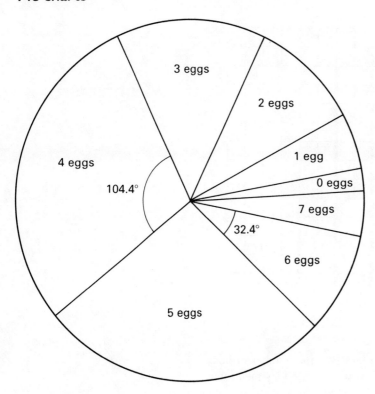

In this pie chart, the area of each sector represents the corresponding number of hens. The main purpose of a pie chart is to give a quick visual comparison. Pie charts are popular with the media and in advertising. It is easy, though, to give wrong impressions if a pie chart is drawn inaccurately, but not obviously so.

To draw a pie chart, we need to work out the angles at the centre.

For 4 eggs: number of hens laying 4 eggs = 29
total number of hens in survey = 100
angle at centre = $\frac{29}{100} \times 360°$
= 104.4°

For 6 eggs: number of hens laying 6 eggs = 9
total number of hens in survey = 100
angle at centre = $\frac{9}{100} \times 360°$
= 32.4°

The angle is found by working out $\dfrac{\text{frequency}}{\text{number in survey}} \times 360°$

★★ Cumulative frequency curves

When the cumulative frequency curve is drawn, the characteristic shape shown in this diagram is obtained.

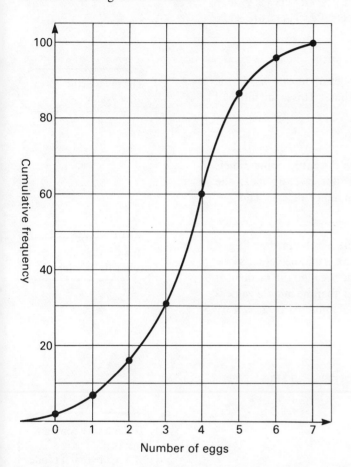

> The cumulative frequency curve is also called the **ogive** (pronounced o-jive).

This curve is particularly useful, as we shall see shortly. However, the cumulative frequency curve has limited value in a case like this, because eggs only come in whole numbers. Anyway, we have established the idea.

Investigation
The ogive features in architecture.

Find out how it is used.

Three averages

We have looked at ways of displaying a set of values, and now we need to think about what we can do with the information. A frequent need is to compare one set of figures with another, and that is not very easy when they are presented in tables like the one on page 27. There are some characteristics which we can work out, to help us.

★The mode

The easiest value to look at is the one which occurs *most often* in the range. In this case it is '4 eggs' which occurs 29 times. This is the mode of the range.

> The **mode** is the 'most often' value.

★Population and median

Another useful idea is to find the *middle value*, if the entire population is arranged in numerical order. By *population*, in this case, we mean the 100 hens. If they were arranged in order of number of eggs laid, we should have

0 0 1 1 1 1 1 2 2 2 2 2 2 2 2 2 2 . . .

By inspection, we can see that the middle value will be in the '4 eggs' section. Out of 100 (an even number) there is not a middle value, so we take the average of the 50th and 51st. This value is called the **median**. If we look at the cumulative frequency curve we see that the middle value is 3.75, purely a theoretical number, but theoretical numbers are necessary in statistics.

> The middle value is called the **median**.

Average or mean

The last characteristic we shall work out is the **average** – and this is where mistakes are made, like the one below.

$$\text{Average} = \frac{\text{total}}{\text{number of}}$$
$$= \frac{0 + 1 + 2 + 3 + 4 + 5 + 6 + 7}{8}$$
$$= \frac{28}{8}$$
$$= 3.5 \qquad \text{What a load of rubbish!}$$

> This is a very common mistake.
> Make sure that it is one that you don't make.

This takes no account of the fact that only two hens laid no eggs but 29 laid four. Indeed, the number of hens does not even appear in the silly calculation above, yet we are supposed to be finding the average number of eggs laid per hen. The correct way to find out average is like this.

$$\text{Average} = \frac{\text{total number of eggs}}{\text{total number of hens}}$$

We need to extend our table.

Number of eggs n	Frequency f	n × f
0	2	0
1	5	5
2	10	20
3	14	42
4	29	116
5	27	135
6	9	54
7	4	28
Totals	100	400

The column we have added gives the total number of eggs laid by all the hens. For example, 10 hens laid 2 eggs each, so that gives 20 eggs. Also, 27 hens laid 5 eggs each, giving 135.

Taking the total for the whole column, we can find the total number of eggs laid by all the hens together.

$$\text{Average} = \frac{400}{100} = 4$$

> This average is usually called the **mean**.

The mean can easily be worked out by calculator, without drawing up a table.

Calculator sequence	Display
C	0
0	0
×	0
2	2
=	0
M+	0
1	1
×	1
5	5
=	5
M+	5
2	2
×	2
10	10
=	20
M+	20

and so on.
Finally, mean = $\boxed{\text{MR}}$ $\boxed{\div}$ $\boxed{100}$ $\boxed{=}$ $\boxed{4}$

EXERCISE 3.1

1   The tally chart shows the number of people, including the driver, in
      each of 50 cars being driven into town between 8.00 a.m. and 9.00
      a.m. on an average weekday.

Number of people, n	Tally
1	HHH HHH HHH HHH HHH ///
2	HHH HHH ////
3	HHH
4	//
5	/

Pay particular attention
to the solution to this
question. You will need
it for question 2.

      Copy the table and add two columns, one for the frequency, f, and
      one for $n \times f$.
      Find the totals.
      Draw the line chart.
      Calculate the mean and state the mode.

2   This is a similar table to the one in question 1, but on this occasion
      the 50 cars are in a queue approaching an air show at 11.00 a.m. on
      a Saturday.

Number of people, n	Tally
1	////
2	HHH HHH
3	HHH HHH //
4	HHH HHH HHH HHH
5	////

      Copy the table and add two columns, one for the frequency, f, and
      one for $n \times f$.
      Find the totals.
      Draw the frequency polygon.
      Calculate the mean and state the mode.

3   Compare the results for questions 1 and 2.
      Suggest reasons for the differences.

4   An analysis of the opening paragraphs in the lead article of a newspaper one day produced the following results.

Number of letters in word n	Frequency f
1	8
2	38
3	49
4	27
5	23
6	21
7	18
8	16
9	6
10	4
11	1
12	1

State the mode. Find the mean and show the results on a frequency polygon.

Investigation

Question 4 provides the starting point for a coursework project. Collect similar data from a French and a German newspaper and compare the results. Alternatively, compare the same passage written in the three different languages, in the same way.

5   Thirty families were asked how many children they had. The results were as shown below.

Number of children, n	0	1	2	3	4	5 or more
Number of families, f	2	7	13	6	1	1

Show this information on (**a**) a bar chart (**b**) a pie chart.

★ Grouped data

Now we consider the percentage marks scored by a group of 30 people in a mathematics exam.

30	27	39	9	54	37	49	71	55	19
34	46	45	41	58	17	42	51	59	53
52	61	82	32	63	48	73	64	57	65

As individual figures, a collection like this is awkward to deal with. If we drew a bar chart it would have 30 bars. If the population were much larger, we could possibly have every mark from 0 to 100 represented, which would give a bar chart with 100 bars – unthinkable!

To overcome this problem, we group the data together into **classes**. One way would be like this.

Mark	Tally	Frequency
0–10	/	1
11–20	//	2
21–30	//	2
31–40	////	4
41–50	### /	6
51–60	### ///	8
61–70	////	4
71–80	//	2
81–90	/	1

We now have something which we can represent on a chart.
The **modal class** or **modal group** is 51–60.

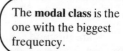

The **modal class** is the one with the biggest frequency.

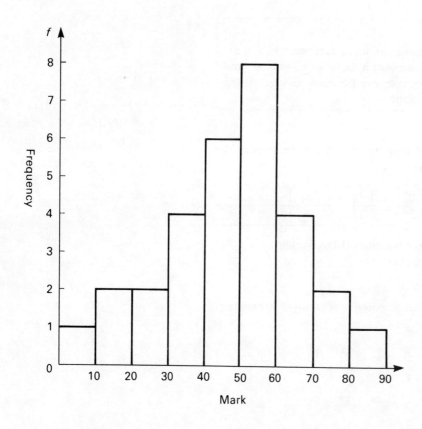

The diagram on page 36 is a bar chart. It is also a **histogram**, though. Often, bar charts and histograms look the same but there is an important difference. In a bar chart, the important quantity is the length, and only the length, of the bar. The length represents the quantity. In a histogram the important quantity is the area of the rectangle making up the bar. The area represents the quantity.

> **Histograms v bar charts**
> In a bar chart, the **length** or height of the bar is important, as it represents the quantity. In a histogram it is the **area** of the bar that represents the quantity.

★★ Using a histogram

In the frequency chart we have just considered, the categories could have been slightly different. The last three lines could have been:

61–70	////	4
71–80	//	2
81–90	/	1

Then the histogram would have looked like this.

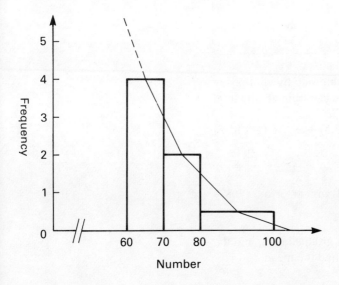

> Notice that the frequency polygon is anchored by joining it to the axis a further half-class along.

The **frequency polygon** is drawn by joining the midpoints of the tops of the bars, in sequence, and then anchoring them to the axis, to close the polygon.

We shall now work out the mean, using two methods.

First method:
We shall use the well-known system of summing up all the scores and dividing by 30.
The result is 47.8.

Second method:
Let us suppose, as often happens, that we do not know the individual scores and we only have the information as presented in the grouped frequency table.

We have to make some assumptions (the same one, repeatedly!). We assume that in any group the marks are evenly distributed and the average for the group is the midgroup value.

> By **midgroup value**, we mean the middle value in the group.

The table is extended to look like this.

Mark	Midvalue m.v.	Frequency f	Cumulative frequency c.f.
0–10	5	1	1
11–20	15.5	2	3
21–30	25.5	2	5
31–40	31.5	4	9
41–50	45.5	6	15
51–60	55.5	8	23
61–70	65.5	4	27
71–80	75.5	2	29
81–90	85.5	1	30

We now work out the total marks scored for each group by multiplying the frequency f by the midvalue. For example, we can estimate the total marks scored by the 41–50 group as $6 \times 45.5 = 273$.

$\Rightarrow$ total marks $= (1 \times 5) + (2 \times 15.5) + (2 \times 25.5) + \ldots + (1 \times 85.5)$
$= 1445.5$

$\Rightarrow$ mean $= \dfrac{1445.5}{30} = 48.2$

This result is very near the accurate result of 47.8, with an error of 0.8% (check this).

When data is presented in this way it is known as grouped data, and the second method just covered is the one we use to find the mean.

The calculator sequence is $\boxed{f}\ \boxed{\times}\ \boxed{\text{m.v.}}\ \boxed{=}\ \boxed{\text{M+}}$

repeated for each group.

Finally, $\boxed{\text{MR}}\ \boxed{\div}\ \boxed{\text{total } f}\ \boxed{=}$ mean.

Notes on drawing the cumulative frequency curve for grouped data

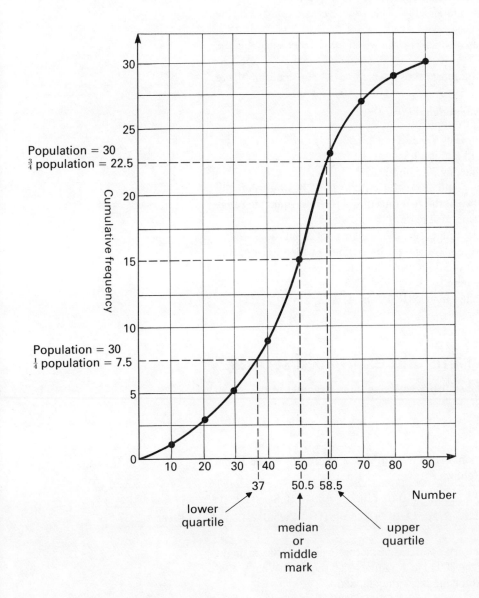

Note that the points are plotted for the upper limit of each group or class; i.e. class 21–30 has c.f. 5, and the point (30, 5) is plotted.

★★Quartiles

The **quartiles** correspond to points on the c.f. axis which, with the median, divide the total cumulative frequency into quarters.

The **lower quartile** is the mark below which there is one quarter of the population.

The **median** is halfway up – which is what we should expect since it is the middle value.

The **upper quartile** is the mark above which is the top quarter of the population.

For the curve shown above, population = 30

quarter of population = 7.5

Lower quartile is at frequency 7.5 and is 37.

Median is at frequency 15 and is 50.5

Upper quartile is at frequency 22.5 and is 58.5.

It follows that half the population, the middle half, lies between the quartiles. The range between the two quartiles – the **inter-quartile range** – is an indicator of the type of spread of the population.

A small inter-quartile range for the weights of adult dogs might indicate that the dogs were all of similar breed, but a wide inter-quartile range would indicate that the dogs were of varied breeds.

The inter-quartile range here is $58.5 - 37 = 21.5$
and the semi inter-quartile range (SIR for short) is $\frac{21.5}{2} = 10.75$.

★Scatter diagrams and estimated scores

We finish the section on statistics with one more example of the use of the mean of a set of values.

★EXAMPLE

In an athletics competition involving 10 athletes, the results of the 100 m and the 800 m were as follows.

100 m (seconds)	10.5	10.5	10.6	10.7	10.8	10.8	11.1	11.2	11.3	11.5
800 m (min : sec)	2:9.0	2:17.5	2:10.0	2:16.0	2:15.0	2:25.0	2:12.5	2:25.0	2:17.5	2:27.5

Bill and Ben are the reserve athletes. Bill runs only the 100 m in 11 seconds, Ben runs only the 800 m in 2 minutes 22.5 seconds. What would be their estimated times for the races they missed?

Solution

To answer this question we draw a graph and try to find a link or **correlation** between the 100 m and the 800 m times. The diagram we shall draw is a scatter diagram.

- First, the points are plotted as shown below, each point representing one athlete.
- Second, the mean 100 m time and mean 800 m time are worked out. These are 10.9 seconds and 2 minutes 17.5 seconds respectively. The point representing these two values is plotted.
- Finally, a straight line is drawn through the points representing the means and with the other points distributed as evenly as possible on either side of it.
  Using this line, the estimated times are read.

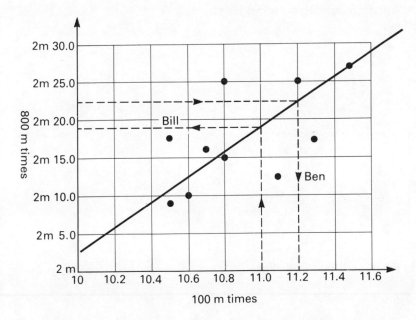

Bill ran 100 m in 11 seconds which corresponds to a time of 2 minutes 19.0 seconds for the 800 m.
Similarly, by relating Ben's 800 m time to the line, we get a time of 11.21 seconds for him to run 100 m.

EXERCISE 3.2

1   At a meeting a survey of the ages of members present produced the following results.

Age	40–49	50–59	60–64	65–69	70+
Frequency	22	38	48	40	38

Show these figures on a histogram.
Calculate the mean.

2   The goals scored by a netball team in 50 matches are listed below.

2 2 2 0 4 2 3 1 2 2
0 1 3 1 0 2 2 1 3 3
1 4 2 1 1 2 4 2 0 2
3 0 2 3 5 4 2 3 2 1
2 3 3 2 3 1 0 2 1 0

Find the mean, the mode and the median.

3   During the season, a cricket scorer records the scores of all the players and the table is as follows.

Score	Frequency
0– 9	9
10–19	13
20–29	20
30–39	22
40–49	30
50–59	27
60–69	20
70–79	17
80–89	11
90–99	2
100+	7

Find **(a)** the modal class   **(b)** the mean   **(c)** the median.

Solutions to exercises

SOLUTIONS TO EXERCISE 3.1

1

n	f	$n \times f$
1	28	28
2	14	28
3	5	15
4	2	8
5	1	5
Totals	50	84

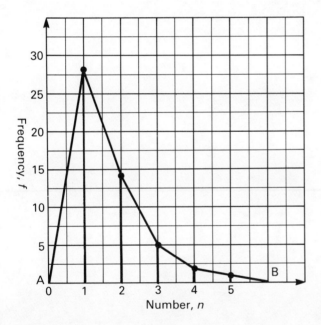

NB: Frequency polygon

This is the polygon formed by connecting, with straight lines, the tops of all the lines in the line chart. Note that the polygon is closed by joining it to the axes at the points A and B.

$$\text{Mean} = \frac{84}{50} = 1.68$$

This is a theoretical figure because we cannot have 0.68 of a person.

Mode = 1

2

n	f	$n \times f$
1	4	4
2	10	20
3	12	36
4	20	80
5	4	20
Totals	50	160

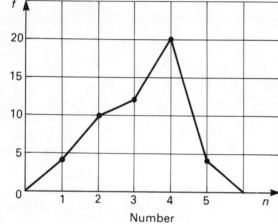

$$\text{Mean} = \frac{160}{50}$$

$$= 3.2 \text{ people per car}$$

$$\text{Mode} = 4$$

3   Most people travelling between 8.00 and 9.00 a.m. on weekdays are going to work or school. Hence the large number of cars with just one person inside, and the significant numbers with only two inside. These may also include people having lifts to work.

Traffic at 11.00 a.m. on Saturday to an air show is mostly family groups. All the people are going to the same place. Cost per passenger per mile is halved in the second case.

> You may be able to add more points in the comparison in this question. This is one of the important aspects of statistics: using the figures, once you have got them, to draw conclusions.

4

n	f	$n \times f$
1	8	8
2	38	76
3	49	147
4	27	108
5	23	115
6	21	126
7	18	126
8	16	128
9	6	54
10	4	40
11	1	11
12	1	12
Totals	212	951

Mode = 3

$$\text{Mean} = \frac{951}{212}$$

$$= \frac{\text{number of letters}}{\text{number of words}}$$

$$= 4.5$$

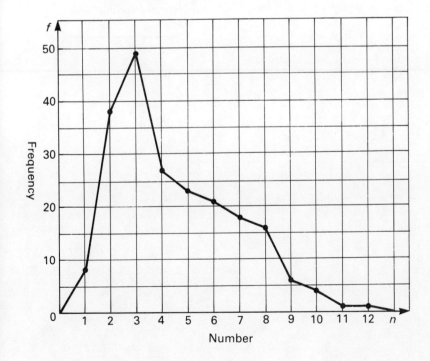

5　**(a)**

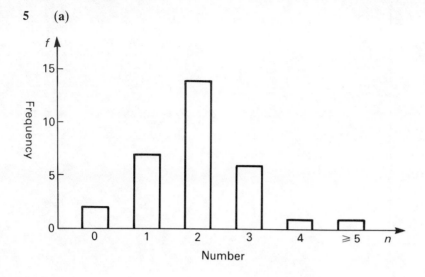

(b) Angles required

$n = 0$　$\theta = \dfrac{2}{30} \times 360° = 24°$

$n = 1$　$\theta = \dfrac{7}{30} \times 360° = 84°$

$n = 2$　$\theta = \dfrac{13}{30} \times 360° = 156°$

$n = 3$　$\theta = \dfrac{6}{30} \times 360° = 72°$

$n = 4$　$\theta = \dfrac{1}{30} \times 360° = 12°$

$n \geqslant 5$　$\theta = \dfrac{1}{30} \times 360° = 12°$

θ is a Greek letter (theta) often used for angles.

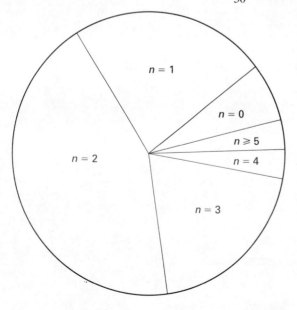

SOLUTIONS TO EXERCISE 3.2

1 Care is needed because the group intervals are not all the same.
Remember that it is the area that matters in a histogram.
Frequency = width of class × height.
Since height is the usual unknown, it is better to remember

$$\text{height} = \frac{\text{frequency}}{\text{width of class}}$$

The table then looks like this.

Age	40–49	50–59	60–64	65–69	70+
Frequency	22	38	48	40	38
Height	22/10 = 2.2	38/10 = 3.8	48/5 = 9.6	40/5 = 8	38/20 = 1.8

> An upper class limit of 89 has been assumed here.

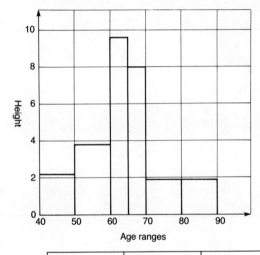

	Goals	**Tally** n	**Frequency** f	$n \times f$	**Cumulative frequency** c.f.
2	0	⅂⅂⅂⅂ //	7	0	7
	1	⅂⅂⅂⅂ ⅂⅂⅂⅂ /	11	11	18
	2	⅂⅂⅂⅂ ⅂⅂⅂⅂ ⅂⅂⅂⅂ //	17	34	35
	3	⅂⅂⅂⅂ ⅂⅂⅂⅂	10	30	45
	4	////	4	16	49
	5	/	1	5	50
	Totals		50	105	

$$\text{Mean} = \frac{\Sigma\, n \times f}{\Sigma\, f} = \frac{105}{50} = 2.1$$

Mode = 2
Median = 2

> Σ is the Greek capital letter sigma, and is used throughout mathematics to mean *the sum of*.

3

Score	Frequency	Cumulative frequency	Mid-class value
0– 9	9	9	4.5
10–19	13	22	14.5
20–29	20	42	24.5
30–39	22	64	34.5
40–49	30	94	44.5
50–59	27	121	54.5
60–69	20	141	64.5
70–79	17	158	74.5
80–89	11	169	84.5
90–99	2	171	94.5
100+	7	178	120

The mid-class value of 120 for the 100+ class is obviously a guess. In the absence of any further initial information, this is all that can be done.

(a) Modal class = 40–49

(b) Mean $= \dfrac{\Sigma (f \times \text{m.v.})}{\Sigma f} = 49.5$

(c) Median: this could be found by drawing the ogive, or like this.

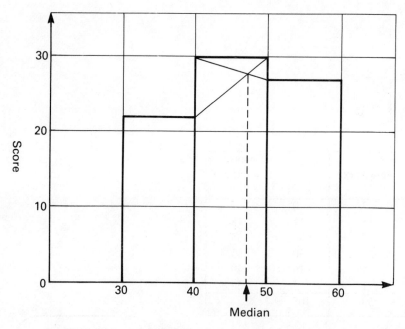

The diagram almost explains itself. It is part of the bar chart which would represent the table above. This part of the bar chart is used because, looking at the cumulative frequency column, we can see that the 89th value is in the 40–49 class.

4 Probability

By the end of this chapter you may not be able to challenge the Las Vegas Moguls but you almost certainly will:
- know what **probability** is
- be able to deal with **combined probability**
- know about **sample spaces** and **tree diagrams**.

In this short chapter we shall have a look at some of the mathematics concerned with chance. The element of chance features largely in our lives: sport, gambling, everyday accidents, life insurance, card playing and so on; the list is endless. The mathematical name for this is **probability** and we shall start by defining it.

In everyday language a question which might be asked is, 'What is my chance of getting heads when I spin a coin?' The answer might be given as 2 to 1, or 1 to 2, or 50−50, or evens.

In mathematical terms we would ask, 'What is the probability that I shall get heads when I spin a coin?' The answer is:
probability of heads is $\frac{1}{2}$
written as P(heads) $= \frac{1}{2}$

The definition of probability is:

$$\text{probability} = \frac{\text{number of ways of obtaining wanted result}}{\text{total number of possible results}}$$

When a coin is spun the list of possible results is:

heads, tails   − total 2
We want heads   − total 1

∴ P(heads) $= \frac{1}{2}$

> This list is called a **sample space**.

Throwing a die

If we throw a die the sample space is:
$\{1, 2, 3, 4, 5, 6\}$
with a total of six possible numbers or outcomes.

P(odd number) $= \dfrac{\text{number of odd numbers}}{\text{number of numbers}}$
                    $= \frac{3}{6} = \frac{1}{2}$

P(square number) $= \frac{2}{6}$
                       $= \frac{1}{3}$

∵ there are two square numbers, 1 and 4.

★Throwing two dice

If we throw two dice and add the scores the sample space looks like this:

		Second die					
		1	2	3	4	5	6
	1	2	3	4	5	6	7
	2	3	4	5	6	7	8
First	3	4	5	6	7	⑧	9
die	4	5	6	7	8	9	10
	5	6	⑦	8	⑨	10	⑪
	6	7	8	9	10	11	12

It is easy to see that there are 36 possible outcomes if we consider one die followed by the other, but obviously there are only 11 different totals. It is important that we do not confuse the two situations.

★EXAMPLE

What is the probability of scoring (**a**) 5 (**b**) 8?

Solution

(**a**) $P(5) = \frac{4}{36} = \frac{1}{9}$

(**b**) $P(8) = \frac{5}{36}$

> Here there are 4 fives in the sample space.

Combined probability

A harder question might be, 'What is the probability of throwing
(**a**) a 3 followed by a 5
(**b**) a 5 followed by an even number?'

(**a**) First die:　$P(3) = \frac{1}{6}$

Second die: $P(5) = \frac{1}{6}$ ⎱ ⇒ $P(3, 5) = \frac{1}{6} \times \frac{1}{6} = \frac{1}{36}$

(**b**) First die:　$P(5) = \frac{1}{6}$

Second die: $P(\text{even}) = \frac{3}{6} = \frac{1}{2}$ ⎱ ⇒ $P(5, \text{even}) = \frac{1}{6} \times \frac{1}{2} = \frac{1}{12}$

The answers to (**a**) and (**b**) can also be checked using the sample space diagram.
(**a**) $P(3, 5)$ is shown as ⑧ ⇒ $\frac{1}{36}$
(**b**) $P(5, \text{even})$ is shown as ⑦⑨⑪ ⇒ $\frac{3}{36} = \frac{1}{12}$
These are examples of combined probabilities.

Tree diagrams

To win a game a girl has to throw a 3 or a 5 on the die, followed by tails on a coin spin. Another way of showing the sample space is in a tree diagram.

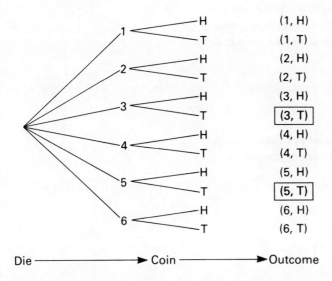

Die ⟶ Coin ⟶ Outcome

A diagram like this clearly shows all the possibilities.
The only ones which satisfy the conditions are framed □.
$\therefore$ P(win) $= \frac{2}{12} = \frac{1}{6}$
Alternatively,
P(3 or 5) $= \frac{2}{6} = \frac{1}{3}$

P(T) $= \frac{1}{2}$

P(3 or 5, T) $= \frac{1}{3} \times \frac{1}{2} = \frac{1}{6}$

EXERCISE 4.1

1   A workman has the letters to make the name ROCHDALE in his bag. He is fastening them to a wall as part of a sign. He draws out the letters without looking. Calculate:
    (a) P(vowel) on his first letter
    (b) P(letter with at least one axis of symmetry) on his first letter
    (c) P(drawing out the first three letters in the right order).

2   In a football match the result may be a win (for the home side) W, a loss L, a 0–0 draw N, or a score draw S. All results are equally likely. Find:
    (a) P(W)   (b) P(N or S)
    Three matches are played. Find:
    (c) P(W, W, L in that order)   (d) P(S, S, S)   (e) P(W or L, S, S).

3 S is a set of numbers where $S = \{3, 4, 5, 6, 7\}$.
One number is selected at random. Find:
(a) P(prime number)   **(b)** P(number > 5).
A second number is selected, the first one being kept out. Find:
(c) P(total $\geqslant 11$)   **(d)** P(product < 30).

More about sets in Chapter 5.

4   In the cutlery drawer in the kitchen there are, in one compartment, 9 plain knives and 6 engraved knives. In a second compartment there are 8 plain forks and 7 engraved forks. Brian selects a knife and a fork without looking. Find:
(a) P(plain knife)   **(b)** P(engraved fork).
Draw a tree diagram to show all the possible outcomes.
(c) Work out the probability in each case.
(d) Find the total of all the answers in part **(c)**.

5   John and Gill each throw a die. Find the probability that:
(a) they both throw a 2   **(b)** they throw different numbers
(c) one throws a 3 and the other throws a 5.

Investigations

Probability is a topic which lends itself to coursework of a practical nature.

1   If you can spin a coin, throw a die, ask other people to draw a card from a pack – make up your own conditions and carry out an investigation! One possible condition, for example, could be that one of the cards must be a picture. Your aim is to compare the actual result with the theoretical. How often must the experiment be repeated before actual and theoretical results do compare?

2   Survey the colours of cars passing a particular point. Investigate whether successive samples of, say, 20 cars contain similar proportions of each colour.

3   If you have access to a statistical sampling bottle, investigate how the actual sample compares with the population.

4   More complicated work can be done on:
- birthdays
- right/left-handed people
- weather.

5   Think of something original and research that.

Solutions to exercises

SOLUTIONS TO EXERCISE 4.1

1 (a) The vowels are O, A, E.
∴ P(vowel) = $\frac{3}{8}$

(b) Letters with symmetry are O, C, H, D, A, E.
∴ P(symmetrical letter) = $\frac{6}{8}$ = $\frac{3}{4}$

(c) $\left.\begin{array}{l} P(R) = \frac{1}{8} \\ P(O) = \frac{1}{7} \\ P(C) = \frac{1}{6} \end{array}\right\}$ ⇒ P(R, O, C) = $\frac{1}{8} \times \frac{1}{7} \times \frac{1}{6}$ = $\frac{1}{336}$

2 (a) P(W) = $\frac{1}{4}$

(b) P(N or S) = $\frac{2}{4}$ = $\frac{1}{2}$

(c) P(W, W, L) = $\frac{1}{4} \times \frac{1}{4} \times \frac{1}{4}$
   = $\frac{1}{64}$

(d) P(S, S, S) = $\frac{1}{4} \times \frac{1}{4} \times \frac{1}{4}$
   = $\frac{1}{64}$

(e) P(W or L, S, S) = $\frac{2}{4} \times \frac{1}{4} \times \frac{1}{4}$
   = $\frac{1}{32}$

3 (a) P(prime) = $\frac{3}{5}$ (Prime numbers are 3, 5, 7)

(b) P(>5) = $\frac{2}{5}$

(c) P(total $\geqslant 11$) = $\frac{8}{20}$
   = $\frac{2}{5}$

+	3	4	5	6	7
3	□	7	8	9	10
4	7	□	9	10	11
5	8	9	□	11	12
6	9	10	11	□	13
7	10	11	12	13	□

(d) P(product < 30) = $\frac{14}{20}$
   = $\frac{7}{10}$

×	3	4	5	6	7
3	□	12	15	18	21
4	12	□	20	24	28
5	15	20	□	30	35
6	18	24	30	□	42
7	21	28	35	42	□

4 (a) $P(pk) = \frac{9}{15} = \frac{3}{5}$

(b) $P(ef) = \frac{7}{15}$

(c)

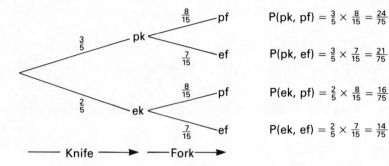

$P(pk, pf) = \frac{3}{5} \times \frac{8}{15} = \frac{24}{75}$

$P(pk, ef) = \frac{3}{5} \times \frac{7}{15} = \frac{21}{75}$

$P(ek, pf) = \frac{2}{5} \times \frac{8}{15} = \frac{16}{75}$

$P(ek, ef) = \frac{2}{5} \times \frac{7}{15} = \frac{14}{75}$

(d) Sum of probabilities $= \dfrac{24 + 21 + 16 + 14}{75}$

$$= \frac{75}{75}$$
$$= 1$$

1 is the maximum value that any probability can have. It means that an event is certain. In this case, the certainty is that Brian can select a knife and a fork.

5 (a) $P(2, 2) = \frac{1}{6} \times \frac{1}{6} = \frac{1}{36}$

(b) When you think about this one it seems complicated, but there is an easy approach.

It is easiest to calculate P(both the same number).

If John throws n then P(Gill throwing n) $= \frac{1}{6}$

P(both the same) $= \frac{1}{6}$

P(different) $= 1 - $ P(both the same)

$= 1 - \frac{1}{6}$

$= \frac{5}{6}$

(c) $P(3, 5) = \frac{1}{6}$ P(one 3, one 5) $= \frac{1}{6} + \frac{1}{6}$

$P(5, 3) = \frac{1}{6}$ $= \frac{1}{3}$

Previous combinations have involved multiplying because, like part (a), they were 'and' conditions, e.g. a 2 and a 2. In this case, either will do, (3, 5) *or* (5, 3), and in the case of 'or' we add the probabilities.

> **Remember**
>
> This technique is often used in probability work.

5 Algebra

Algebra is a form of mathematical shorthand. It is a branch of mathematics in which generalisations are made, using letters to represent numbers.

This is a long chapter and it will take a good deal of time, but by the end of it you will be efficient in the work listed below. It is essential that you go through the assessment exercise and solutions first, and use this as a guide to the areas you need to concentrate on. Don't worry if that means all of them. If you are going to do the whole chapter, you are advised to do it in the order in which it is presented. The work covered includes:

- assessment exercise and answers
- introduction
- **words into algebra**
- **substitution**
- **brackets**
- **factorising** – common
- **linear equations**
- **simultaneous equations**
- **quadratic expressions**
- **factorising quadratic expressions**
- **quadratic equations**
- **equations**, the **quadratic formula**
- **inequalities**
- **sets**
- **indices**

Algebra assessment test

1 Express the following statement as a formula:
   The total weight of a lorry, T, is made up of its empty weight, W, together with the number of boxes, n, on board, each of which weighs w.

2 Write the formula $v^2 = u^2 + 2as$ where v is the final velocity, u is the initial velocity, a is the acceleration and s is the distance covered, as an ordinary sentence.

3 From the formula $s = ut + \frac{1}{2}at^2$ find the value of s when $u = 5, t = 3$ and $a = 10$.

4 Remove the brackets from the following expression.
   $(a + c)(x + y) + f(x - y)$

5 Factorise this expression. $5st - 15tu$

6 Solve this equation. $5 - 4x = 3$

7 Remove the brackets from the following expression.
   $(x + 6)(x - 2)$

8   Factorise this expression.
$x^2 - x - 20$

9   Solve this equation.
$x^2 - x - 20 = 0$

10 Use iteration to solve the equation $x^2 - 6x + 6 = 0$, finding the root between 1 and 2 correct to 2 d.p.

11 Use the quadratic formula to solve this equation.
$3x^2 + 4x - 2 = 0$

12 Solve the inequality $-1 < x + 2 \leqslant 5$,   showing your answer on a number line.

13 Out of 20 girls, nine play hockey, 15 play rounders and three play neither. Use a Venn diagram to find out how many girls play both games.

14 Write down, without using a calculator, the value of   **(a)** $27^{\frac{1}{3}}$
(b) 4^{-2}.

ANSWERS TO ASSESSMENT TEST

1 $T = W + nw$ Substitution, page 59

2   The square of the final velocity is the sum of the square of the initial velocity and twice the product of the acceleration and the distance.   Substitution, page 59

3 $s = 5 \times 3 + \frac{1}{2} \times 10 \times 3^2 = 60$ Substitution, page 59

4 $ax + ay + cx + cy + fx - fy$ Brackets, page 61

5 $5t(s - u)$ Factorising, page 62

6 $x = \frac{1}{2}$ Linear equations, page 64

7 $x^2 + 4x - 12$ Factorising quadratics, page 70

8 $(x - 5)(x + 4)$

9 $x = 5, x = -4$ Quadratic equations, page 73

10 $x = 1.27$ Quadratic equations, page 73
(ensure you have used the correct method)

11 $x = 0.39, x = -1.72$ Quadratic formula, page 76

12 $-3 < x \leqslant 3$ Inequalities, page 77

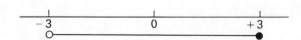

13 7 play both

Sets, page 79

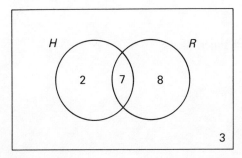

14 (a) 3 (b) $\frac{1}{16}$

Indices, page 82

Introduction

We shall now proceed to look at algebra, that branch of mathematics which frightens so many people, but which is so important. Without algebra, progress in almost any other branch of mathematics would be impossible. In this chapter we shall start by looking at some mistakes people make.

Even after studying algebra for several years, students have been heard to say, 'I still don't see how you can multiply letters together.' Agreed! Nobody can possibly multiply letters together. Let's try to make sense of it.

If 2 and 3 are multiplied together, we get 6.

If a and b are multiplied together we get $a \times b$, which has no real meaning until we give values to a and b, and put numbers in place of the letters.

If we put $a = 2$ and $b = 3$, then $a \times b$ becomes 2×3, which has the answer 6, but until numbers are substituted for a and b, $a \times b$ remains $a \times b$.

When multiplying letters that represent numbers, it is common practice to leave out the multiplication sign so that $a \times b$ is written as ab. This is the only sign that can be left out in this way.

Now go through this argument again, but this time consider addition, i.e. $a + b$.

> **Remember**
>
> $a \times b = ab$

Words into symbols and vice versa

Question 1 in the assessment exercise highlights the area where many people come unstuck with algebra, i.e. the transformation from the words of ordinary English into symbols or letters which form mathematical language.

EXAMPLES

Area equals length times breadth is clumsy, compared with $A = l \times b$ or $A = lb$.

Volume equals one third times π times the radius squared times the height can be written much more briefly as $V = \frac{1}{3}\pi r^2 h$.

It is important to develop the ability to work and think both ways, from words to symbols and back again.

EXERCISE 5.1

Make up formulae for, or write mathematically, the statements in these questions. Use the letters which are given.

1 The perimeter (p) of a rectangle of length l and breadth b is the distance round the edge.

2 The weight of a box containing a number n tins of cat food, each of weight k, is W.

3 The cost of five bags of sugar, at n pence per bag, and two packs of butter at q pence each, is C.

4 The time of swing (T) of a simple pendulum is 2π divided by a constant, w.

★ 5 The total amount payable (E) on an electricity bill is made up of a fixed charge, £F, plus the cost of the number (n) of units used, at 6p each.

★ 6 The volume, V, of a rectangular brick is equal to the product of the length (l), the breadth (b) and the height (h).

★ 7 The rule for converting a temperature C in degrees centigrade to F in degrees Fahrenheit is to multiply by 9, divide by 5 and add 32.

★ 8 The income tax (T) paid is 25% of the income (I) after allowances (A) have been taken off.

★ 9 The cost (C) of surfacing a road is £100 per metre for the first 20 metres, then £40 for every additional metre. Use n for the total number of metres.

★ 10 The heat (h) developed in an electric wire is a constant, k, times the square of the current, A, times the resistance, R, times the time, t.

In the next exercise, what is required is the opposite of what was done in **Exercise 5.1**. Formulae are stated and they have to be put into ordinary English. Don't worry if you don't understand the terms being used. It's the technique that matters.

★ EXERCISE 5.2

1. $V = \frac{4}{3}\pi r^3$ V = volume and r = radius of sphere

2. $v = u + at$ v = final velocity, u = initial velocity, a = acceleration, t = time

3. $\dfrac{1}{v} + \dfrac{1}{u} = \dfrac{1}{f}$ v = image distance, u = object distance, f = focal length of a lens

4. $A = \frac{1}{2}(a + b)h$ A = area of trapezium, a and b = lengths of parallel sides, h = height

5. $s = vt$ s = distance, v = constant speed, t = time

6. $p = \dfrac{nS}{80}$ p = pension, n = number of years service, S = final salary

7. $d = \dfrac{m}{v}$ d = density, m = mass, v = volume

8. $E_k = \frac{1}{2}mv^2$ E_k = kinetic energy, m = mass, v = velocity

9. $C = 2 + \dfrac{n}{2}$ C = cost (in £) to pitch a caravan, n = number of people in caravan

10. $pV = c$ p = pressure, V = volume of gas at constant temperature, c = constant

Substitution

We have spent some time, now, making up and interpreting equations. If you have followed carefully, this should help as we go on to the next section, which is about using formulae.

Using formulae means substituting numbers for some of the quantities or unknowns, and so calculating the value of another quantity.

> **Remember**
>
> A formula is a rule, expressed in symbols, connecting related variables.

EXAMPLE

Using $W = \sqrt{\dfrac{2 + 3x}{5 - x}}$ find W when $x = 2$.

Solution

When $x = 2$ $W = \sqrt{\dfrac{2 + 3 \times 2}{5 - 2}}$

$$= \sqrt{\dfrac{2 + 6}{3}}$$

$$= \sqrt{\dfrac{8}{3}} = 1.6$$

Calculator sequence: $\boxed{8}\,\boxed{\div}\,\boxed{3}$ $\boxed{=}$ $\boxed{\sqrt{}}$

Display: 8   8   3   2.6666667   1.6329932

EXERCISE 5.3

Using the answers to **Exercise 5.1**, find the values indicated.

1 Find p when $l = 7$ and $b = 4$.

2 Find W when $A = 48$ and $k = 750$ g.

3 Find the cost of butter, given that sugar is 71p per bag and the total cost is £4.71.

4 Find T when $w = 3$.

5 Given $F = 11.50$ and $n = 2340$, find the total cost.

6 Find h given $V = 29$, $l = 5.5$ and $b = 3.5$.

7 Find the Fahrenheit temperature equivalent to 20°C.

8 A man earns £17 000 per annum and has allowances of £6250. Find how much tax he pays.

9 Find the cost of surfacing 90 metres of road.

10 Find h when $k = 0.24$, $A = 1.7$, $R = 9.8$ and $t = 80$.

EXERCISE 5.4

This is similar to **Exercise 5.3**, and you should do it only if you feel you need the practice. If you got 7 or more correct in **Exercise 5.3**, you can leave this one out for now and use it later for revision.

Using the formulae given in **Exercise 5.2**, answer the following.

1 Calculate the volume of a sphere of radius 5 cm.

2 Given that $v = 20$, $a = 2$ and $t = 5$, find u.

3 Find f when $v = 3$ and $u = 2$.

4 Find A when $a = 7.5$, $b = 11.25$ and $h = 4.5$.

5 Find how long it takes to go 45 km at 30 km/h.

6 Work out the pension of a teacher who has worked for 38 years and whose salary at retirement was £18 000.

7 Which occupies the greater space: 15 g of substance A with density 3.2 g/cm^3 , or 11 g of substance B with density 2.7 g/cm^3.

8 Find the velocity of a particle of mass 20 units, and kinetic energy 810 units.

9 How much would it cost to pitch a caravan for a family of four?

10 As V increases, what happens to p?

Question 10 is a bit different.

★Brackets

We now move on to the area of manipulation of algebra and we start by considering this diagram.

	x	y	z
a	ax	ay	az
b	bx	by	bz

The length of the rectangle is $x + y + z$

The width of the rectangle is $a + b$

So the total area is $x + y + z \times a + b$ but written like this, it leads to mistakes. The obvious answer is $x + y + az + b$, which is wrong.
When we write $x + y + z \times a + b$ what we mean is the whole of $x + y + z$ multiplied by the whole of $a + b$ and this is made clear by writing $(x + y + z) \times (a + b)$. In algebra, we can leave out the multiplication sign, so we get $(x + y + z)(a + b)$.
From the diagram we can see that the area is $ax + ay + az + bx + by + bz$, and it seems clear that
$(x + y + z)(a + b) = ax + ay + az + bx + by + bz$
because both sides of this equation are expressions for the same area.
So what is the rule for multiplying brackets?

> **Remember**
>
> When multiplying brackets, the rule is 'everything in one bracket multiplied by everything in the other'.

Every term inside the first bracket must be multiplied by every term inside the other bracket.

★EXERCISE 5.5

In this exercise, questions and answers are given but some are incorrect. Find which they are, and correct them.

1 $(p + q)(s + t) = ps + qs + pt + qt$

2 $a(x + 3) = ax + 3a$

3 $(x + 2)(y + 1) = xy + 2$

4 $(x + 3)(x + 5) = x^2 + 3x + 5x + 15 = x^2 + 8x + 15$

5 $(k + l)w = k + lw$

6 $(p - q)(s + t) = ps - qt$

7 $x(a + x) = xa + a$

8 $x(a + c)(p + q) = xap + xaq + xcp$

9 $(a - 7)(a + 3) = a^2 - 7a + 3a - 21 = a^2 - 4a - 21$

10 $(a + c)(p + q)(x + y) = apx + apy + aqx + aqy + cpx + cpy + cqx + cqy$

Helpful tips

If you are missing out terms or otherwise having difficulty with 'everything in one bracket multiplied by everything in the other', the following may help.

The diagram on page 61 may be set out as:

	x	y	z
a	ax	ay	az
b	bx	by	bz

and this way none of the terms are missed out.

★Factorising

Many operations in mathematics are reversible, and the one we have just been doing is one of them. In a statement like

$2 \times 3 = 6$

the LHS is in factorised form, because 2 and 3 are factors of 6 and the RHS is the product or multiple of the factors 2 and 3.

> **Remember**
>
> LHS means left-hand side
> RHS means right-hand side

> **Remember**
>
> Factors of a number are multiplied together, not added.
> $2 \times 3 = 6$
> 2 and 3 are factors.
> $2 + 3 = 5$ $2 + 4 = 6$
> are addition statements.

We shall now look at some algebraic expressions and change them into factorised form, by finding their **factors**.

Product	Factorised	Factors
21	3×7	3, 7
55	5×11	5, 11
25	5×5	5, 5
27	3×9	3, 9
29	1×29	1, 29
pq	$p \times q$	p, q
$6x$	$6 \times x$	$6, x$

1 is a factor of all numbers, and we do not usually bother to write it down unless it is essential, as we shall see later.

★EXAMPLE

Factorise $px + py$.

Solution

px and py both have factor p.
$px + py = p \times (x + y)$ which is written, using brackets, as
$px + py = p(x + y)$

★EXAMPLE

Factorise $3x + 12$.

Solution

$3x + 12 = 3 \times x + 3 \times 4$

$\qquad = 3(x + 4)$

★EXAMPLE

Factorise $5a + 5$.

Solution

$5a + 5 = 5a + 5 \times 1$
$\qquad = 5(a + 1)$

> This is a case where it is necessary to write down the factor 1. Not recognising it, in questions like this, is a common mistake.

★EXAMPLE

Factorise 30.

Solution

$$30 = \begin{matrix} 6 \times 5 \\ 2 \times 15 \\ 3 \times 10 \end{matrix} \quad = \quad \begin{matrix} 2 \times 3 \times 5 \\ 2 \times 3 \times 5 \\ 3 \times 2 \times 5 \end{matrix}$$

Partially factorised   Fully factorised

★EXAMPLE

Factorise $2a^2 + 6ac$.

Solution

$2a^2 + 6ac = 2(a^2 + 3ac)$ $\qquad$ partially factorised
$\qquad\quad = 2a(a + 3c)$ $\qquad$ fully factorised

★EXERCISE 5.6

Factorise these as fully as possible.

A 1   18
    2   $ax + ay$
    3   $3pq + 9pr$
    4   $xy^2 + xz^2 + 2xyz$
    5   $p^2q - pq^2$

B 1   42
    2   $7x - 14y$
    3   $4ab - b$
    4   $x^3 - 2x^2y + 3xy^2$ Hint: $x^3 = x \times x \times x$
    5   $2a^2b + 6ab^2 - 4ac^2 + 8a^2c$

C 1   91
    2   $pa + pb - pc$
    3   $2kl - 8km$
    4   $abc^2 + ab^2c + a^2bc$
    5   $3(a + b) + x(a + b)$

D 1   132
    2   $kx + 2ky + 3kz$
    3   $10tu + 5uv - 15uw$
    4   $8abc + 6a^2b - 3b^2c$
    5   $6c^3 - 4c^2 + 2c$

★EQUATIONS

When we relax with friends, we often find that someone will present a problem or puzzle for the rest of the group to try solving. One such puzzle could be, 'I think of a number, double it, add seven and the result is 19. What is my number?' Try it.

You probably thought along these lines:
19 take off 7   result 12
half of 12   result 6
∴ number is 6.
Not very difficult, was it? Most people would get it right.
Now think about this:
Solve the equation $2x + 7 = 19$.

Many people may panic, including a good number of those who solved the puzzle. The two problems are exactly the same, though, and there is nothing wrong with applying the same techniques to the *mathematical* form as we did to the *puzzle*. Try it out on the next exercise.

★EXERCISE 5.7

Solve these equations, by finding what number the letter stands for.

A 1 $5x + 1 = 21$
    2   $3a - 5 = 13$
    3   $\frac{1}{2}c + 1 = 7$
    4   $2x - 14 = 0$
    5   $5 = 8 - \frac{1}{3}k$

B 1 $4t + 3 = 51$
    2   $3 - 5a = 8$
    3   $\frac{1}{3}q - 4 = 9\frac{1}{2}$
    4   $4 - 5x = 3$
    5   $7 - x = 3 + x$

Question B2 is harder.

Helpful tips

You may have thought that question 5 in part B was a stinker! However, a little thought, should soon have produced the answer 2. You could have looked at it like this.

$7 - x = 3 + x$ Add x to both sides of the equation
$\Rightarrow 7 = 3 + 2x$

Then it is just like the earlier questions, which you can solve quite easily.

Remember

It is important to do the same operation to both sides of an equation: adding x on both sides retains the balance, just like on a seesaw.

Now try these.

★EXERCISE 5.8

1   Solve the equation $3(x + 1) = 12$.

2   Solve the equation $\dfrac{12}{x} + 3 = 7$.

3   A man is seven times as old as his son. If the son is n years old, how old is the man? The sum of their ages is 32 years. Form an equation and solve it to find their ages.

4   Solve the equation $2(x - 1) = 13 - x$.

5   Solve the equation $7x + 3(7 - 2x) = 23.5$.

6   Two maths books and a physics book together cost £10.00. The physics book costs £3.60 and one of the maths books costs three times as much as the other. Form an equation and solve it to find how much each maths book costs.

7   Solve the equation $\frac{3}{4}x + \frac{1}{6} = \frac{5}{12}$ and give the exact value of x.

8   In a triangle, the angles are $x°$, $(2x + 10)°$ and $(3x + 20)°$. Form an equation for x and solve it to find the three angles of the triangle.

9   Find x from this equation.

$$\frac{3}{x + 2} + \frac{2}{5} = \frac{7}{10}$$

Remember

The angle sum of a triangle is 180°.

10   Kim buys five blouses. Three are priced at £4.50 each, but the other two have been marked down to give a 20% reduction of their original price. She spent £21.50 altogether. Form an equation to find how much she paid for the two blouses on offer. They both cost the same, so find the reduced price and the original price of one blouse.

★Simultaneous equations

We often meet problems which seem very similar to some of those that we have just been doing, but are, in fact, a bit different. Consider this.

Two numbers have a sum of 11 and a difference of 5. What are they?
It doesn't take a genius to see that they are 8 and 3.

Now look at this one.

Three times a number, added to twice a second number, gives 21. Three times the second number, subtracted from twice the first, gives 1. Find the numbers.

This looks a bit mind-boggling, and we really do need to find some organised way to approach it. Let's go back to the first one. We are talking about two numbers, so we can choose two letters to represent them, one for each.

. . . sum is 11 $\Rightarrow$ $a + c = 11$
. . . difference is 5 $\Rightarrow$ $a - c = 5$

$$a + a + c - c = 11 + 5$$
$$\Rightarrow \qquad\qquad 2a = 16$$
$$\Rightarrow \qquad\qquad a = 8$$

We can now substitute the value of a back into one of the original equations.

$\Rightarrow$ $8 + c = 11$
$\qquad c = 3$

To sum up:

1 Form the equations.

2 Remove one of the unknowns by adding or subtracting.

3 Find the value of the remaining unknown.

4 Substitute to find the other unknown.

We have just solved a pair of **simultaneous equations**, or solved a pair of equations simultaneously. We had *two* equations, because we had *two* unknowns. If we have *three* unknowns then we need *three* equations, and so on. The good news is that in this course we shall deal only with equations in two unknowns, so we shall only ever have to deal with two equations.

Now we are ready to look at the second problem.

Three times a number, added to twice a second number, gives 21.

$\Rightarrow$ $3 \times p$ $+$ $2 \times q$ $=$ 21
$\Rightarrow$ $3p + 2q = 21$

Three times the second number, subtracted from twice the first, gives 1.

$2 \times p$ $-$ $3 \times q$ $=$ 1

$\Rightarrow$ $2p - 3q = 1$
$3p + 2q = 21$
$2p - 3q = 1$

We can see a problem – the numbers multiplying p and q are both different in both equations.

Don't panic.

Comment

Note that there are now two equations, with the letters lining up, in the same order.
Now we can add these two equations together.

Comment

If we remember that both sides of an equation have the same value, we can add two equations together because what we are adding on both sides is equal in value, even though it looks different.

Comment

Why add the equations? We can get rid of the term in c, to get an equation in a which we can solve.

$$3p + 2q = 21 \quad \Rightarrow \quad 9p + 6q = 63$$
$$2p - 3q = 1 \quad \Rightarrow \quad 4p - 6q = 2$$
$$\bigg\} \quad \text{add} \quad \Rightarrow \quad 13p = 65$$

Why did we change the equations to the form in the second column?
We needed to reach equations with $+6q$ and $-6q$ so that they would balance each other out when we added.

$$13p = 65$$
$$p = 5$$

Substituting back in the second equation, we get
$$2 \times 5 - 3q = 1 \quad \Rightarrow \quad 3q = 9 \quad \Rightarrow \quad q = 3$$
We have used the second equation to find q, and we can check that our solutions are correct by substituting in the first equation.

$$\text{LHS} = 3p + 2q$$
$$= 3 \times 5 + 2 \times 3$$
$$= 15 + 6$$
$$= 21$$
$$= \text{RHS}$$

$\text{LHS} = \text{RHS} \quad \Rightarrow \quad$ the solution is correct.

★EXERCISE 5.9

1 Solve these equations.
$$x + y = 22$$
$$x - y = 4$$

2 Solve these equations.
$$x + y = 5$$
$$x - y = 11$$

3 Solve these equations.
$$x + 2y = 9$$
$$3x + 4y = 20$$

4 Solve these equations.
$$3x + 2y = 27.3$$
$$4x - 3y = 22.8$$

5 Five eggs and two pints of milk cost 98p at the corner shop. Twelve eggs and five pints of milk cost £2.41. Find the cost of an egg and the cost of a pint of milk.

6 In a hardware shop, five catches and two handles cost £3.45, and four catches and one handle cost £2.40. Find how much three catches and three handles would cost. (Think carefully as you answer this one.)

7 A fountain pen costs 12p more than eight ball pens. A fountain pen and a ball pen together cost £1.56. Find the price of a fountain pen.

8 The sum of two numbers is 27. Five times the smaller number exceeds the larger number by 2. Find the numbers.

Hint
You can subtract equations, as well as add them.

Don't let the awkward numbers put you off.

9 The equation of a line is $y = mx + c$. It is satisfied by $x = 2$, $y = 8$ and by $x = -1$, $y = -7$. Find m and c.

10 The lengths of the three sides of a triangle are x, x and y. The sides of length x are double the side of length y, and the perimeter of the triangle is 75 cm. Find the lengths of the sides.

> **Remember**
>
> The perimeter is the total length of all the sides together.

★★Quadratic expressions

It is surprising how often expressions such as $x^2 + 3x + 2$ occur in mathematics, and how much work is generated from them. These are quadratic expressions, and we shall start our study of them by considering the following.

★★Expanding

Let's look through this list of products, and try to find a pattern connecting the numbers on the left-hand side with those on the right.

(a) $(x + 1)(x + 3)$ $= x^2 + x + 3x + 3$ $= x^2 + 4x + 3$

(b) $(x + 5)(x + 2)$ $= x^2 + 5x + 2x + 10$ $= x^2 + 7x + 10$

(c) $(x + 6)(x + 4)$ $= x^2 + 10x + 24$

> **Remember**
>
> If you have forgotten how to do these, look back to page 61.

In these examples, we are looking for a connection between:
in **(a)** the 1 and 3 on the LHS and the 4 and 3 on the RHS
in **(b)** the 5 and 2 on the LHS and the 7 and 10 on the RHS
in **(c)** the 6 and 4 on the LHS and the 10 and 24 on the RHS.

Can you see the link?

> Look at the sums and the products.

In **(a)** $1 + 3 = 4$ $1 \times 3 = 3$

(b) $5 + 2 = 7$ $5 \times 2 = 10$

(c) $6 + 4 = 10$ $6 \times 4 = 24$.

Now that we have found the connection, try this exercise.

★★EXERCISE 5.10

Work out these products, removing the brackets, without the in-between step used in **(a)** and **(b)** above.

A **1** $(x + 5)(x + 3)$

2 $(x + 2)(x + 3)$

3 $(x + 10)(x + 1)$

4 $(x + 7)(x + 8)$

5 $(x + 6)(x - 2)$ No, not a misprint. The minus sign is intended.

> **Comment**
>
> The word for multiplying out brackets is **expanding**. In this exercise you are expanding the brackets.

Signs in multiplying
When multiplying, remember this rule:
- if the signs are the same, the product is positive $(+)$
- if the signs are different, the product is negative $(-)$

For example,
$-3 \times -3 = 9$
$-3 \times -3 \times -3 = +9 \times -3 = -27$
$-3 \times -3 \times 3 = +9 \times 3 = 27$

B
1. $(x + 4)(x - 2)$
2. $(x - 1)(x - 3)$
3. $(x - 2)(x + 5)$
4. $(x - 7)(x - 2)$
5. $(x - 5)(x + 5)$

C
1. $(x - 11)(x + 10)$
2. $(x - 7)(x + 7)$
3. $(x + 2)(x - 3)$
4. $(x + a)(x - a)$
5. $(x + 1)(x - 1)$

A special case
In question **B5**, we finished up with only two terms.
Working through, we find that
$(x - 5)(x + 5) = x^2 + 5x - 5x - 25 = x^2 - 25$

This can only happen if the numbers in the brackets are the same but the signs are different. Then the answer will always have this pattern.

x^2	$-$	25
The first term is a square	The sign is a minus or difference	The last term is a square

Such an expression is called the **difference of two squares.**

★★Definition
Any algebraic expression in which the highest power is 2, for example x^2, and this must be included, and the lowest power is 0, which means a constant term which may be just a number or zero, is called a **quadratic expression**.

Investigation
It was stated above that when multiplying positive and negative numbers,
- if the signs are the same, the product is positive
- if the signs are different, the product is negative.

Investigate why this should be so.

★★EXERCISE 5.11

Complete the following list.

1   $2x^2 + 3x + 1$ is quadratic

2   $5x - 1$ is not quadratic because there is no term in x^2

3   $x^2 - 3$ is quadratic

4   $x^3 + x^2 - 2x + 1$ is not quadratic because it has an x^3 term

5   $5x - 2x^2$ is quadratic

6   $3 - 7x$

7   $2x^2$

8   $1 - x - x^2$

9   $x^4 + 2x^2 + 2$

10 $5 - 6x^2 - 3x$

★★Factorising

So far, we have spent some time removing brackets from expressions, which is called expanding. Now we shall look at the reverse process, which is factorising.

★★EXAMPLE

Factorise $x^2 + 5x + 6$.

Solution

From what we have done so far, we assume that this means we have to put $x^2 + 5x + 6$ into two brackets which are multiplied together.
We need two numbers so that we can write
$x^2 + 5x + 6 = (x \ \ \Box)(x \ \ \Box)$
and the numbers in the boxes will add up to give 5
                                        multiply to give 6.
Looking at the problem, and thinking about it (which means *by inspection*) we see that the numbers we need are 2 and 3 $2 + 3 = 5$
                                        $2 \times 3 = 6$

  $x^2 + 5x + 6 = (x + 2)(x + 3)$
or $x^2 + 5x + 6 = (x + 3)(x + 2)$

> It does not matter which way round the brackets are written.

★★EXERCISE 5.12

Factorise the following expressions.

1   $x^2 + 7x + 6$

2   $x^2 + 7x + 12$

3   $x^2 + 7x + 10$

4 $x^2 + 25x + 24$

5 $x^2 + 14x + 24$

6 $x^2 + 11x + 24$

7 $x^2 + 10x + 24$

8 $x^2 - 7x + 10$

9 $x^2 - 4x - 12$

10 $x^2 - 9$

★★An alternative method

For those who find the inspection method of finding the factors difficult, there is another way. It seems complicated at first, but it does eventually guarantee results.

Consider again the expression $x^2 + 5x + 6$.

$$x^2 \quad + \quad 5x \quad + \quad 6$$

$$\downarrow \qquad\qquad\qquad \downarrow$$

$$x \qquad\qquad\quad 1 \quad 2$$

$$x \qquad\qquad\quad 6 \quad 3$$

The table is set up, and the first column (under x^2) comes from $x^2 = x \times x$

the last column comes from all combinations of

factors of 6: 1×6 and 2×3.

Now we work along the diagonals.

$$x \underset{\qquad x \times 6 = 6x \qquad\qquad x \times 1 = 1x}{\diagdown} \; 1$$

$$x \underset{}{} \; 6$$

We need to decide what we are looking for.

$x^2 + 5x + 6$

The sign before the last term (6) is $+$, so we are looking for an addition to give the second term ($5x$).

Looking back to the diagonal we see that we have $6x + x = 7x$, which will not do.

Now we need to try the other possibility.

$$x \underset{\qquad x \times 3 = 3x \qquad\qquad x \times 2 = 2x}{\diagdown} \; 2 \qquad\qquad \text{row 1}$$

$$x \underset{}{} \; 3 \qquad\qquad \text{row 2}$$

$3x + 2x = 5$ which is what we are looking for.

We put the number from row 1 in the first bracket and the number from row 2 in the second.

$\Rightarrow \quad x^2 + 5x + 6 = (x + 2)(x + 3)$

Read that through again, then look at this example, which is question **A9**.

$$x^2 - 4x - 12$$

Step 1

x	1	2	3
x	12	6	4

Step 2 What are we looking for?

$$x^2 - 4x - 12$$

— a substraction
to give $-4x$

Step 3 Back to the table.

x	1	2	3
x	12	6	4

$12x$ and $1x$ give a difference of $11x$, so won't do.
$2x$ and $6x$ give a difference of $4x$, so will do.
We can write down the brackets.
$(x \quad 2)(x \quad 6)$
To get $-4x$ we must have $-6x + 2x$ ($+6x - 2x$ gives $+4x$, which won't do).
$(x - 2)(x + 6)$

If you found part A of **Exercise 5.12** difficult, work through it again using this method.
You can set the questions out more simply, like this.

		×	√	
$x^2 - 4x - 12$	x	1	2	3
$= (x - 2)(x + 6)$	x	12	6	4

Then go on to the remaining parts of the exercise.

★★**EXERCISE 5.12 (continued)**

B
1. $x^2 + 5x - 6$
2. $x^2 + x - 12$
3. $x^2 - 3x - 10$
4. $x^2 - 14x + 24$
5. $x^2 - 4x - 21$
6. $x^2 + 5x$
7. $x^2 - 4$
8. $x^2 - 2x - 35$
9. $x^2 - 49$
10. $x^2 + 6x + 9$

C
1. $x^2 + 6x - 16$
2. $x^2 + 2x + 1$
3. $36 - x^2$
4. $x^2 + x - 30$
5. $x^2 - x - 56$
6. $x^2 - 14x + 49$
7. $x^2 + 25$
8. $x^2 + 20x + 100$
9. $x^2 - 81$
10. $x^2 + 6x - 40$

> Notice that there are three possible sets of factors of 12.

> Be careful!

There is still a bit more to learn about factorising these expressions, but we shall leave it for now and return to it later.

★★Equations again

Earlier, on page 64, we had a brief look at simple equations. We shall now look at some more equations and see how the work on factorising that we have just done can be useful.

Look at this equation.
$x^2 = 25$
Not too difficult, but beware the common mistake. Many people would give the answer as $x = 5$ but that is only partly correct. There are two answers, the other one is $x = -5$.
The solution would be written $x = \pm 5$

A slightly harder problem would be
$$(x + 2)^2 = 16$$
but taking the square root of each side gives
$$x + 2 = \pm 4$$
$$\Rightarrow \quad x = -2 \pm 4$$
$$\Rightarrow \quad x = -2 + 4 \quad \text{or} \quad x = -2 - 4$$
$$x = 2 \qquad\qquad x = -6$$

Another, slightly harder still, would be
$$x^2 + 5x + 6 = 0$$
$$\Rightarrow \quad (x + 2)(x + 3) = 0$$
which we factorised on page 70.

Now one thing is certain, and that is if the answer to a multiplication is zero, then one of the factors being multiplied must be zero. We are trying to find values of x for which $\quad x^2 + 5x + 6 = 0$, $\quad$ which means
$(x + 2)(x + 3) = 0$
so we need values which make $x + 2 = 0$
$$\text{or } x + 3 = 0$$
and these are $x = -2$ and $x = -3$.
So there are two values of x, namely -2 and -3, which make
$x^2 + 5x + 6 = 0$, $\quad$ and there are no others.

We have **solved** a quadratic equation.

★★EXERCISE 5.13

A   Take the quadratic expressions of **Exercise 5.12A**, convert them into quadratic equations by putting each one equal to zero, then solve them.

B   Do the same for **Exercise 5.12B**.

C   Do the same for **Exercise 5.12C**.

Remember

The sign $\pm$ is read as *plus or minus*, so this solution is 'x equals plus or minus five'.

★★Finding solutions by iteration

Just when we think we have got the hang of quadratic equations, we come up with an awkward one.

★★EXAMPLE

Solve the quadratic equation $x^2 - x - 5 = 0$.

We can see that the left-hand side will not factorise. We need to look at a different way of finding an answer. Our calculators will now be well used. First, we make up a table of values.

x	-4	-3	-2	-1	0	1	2	3	4
$x^2 - x - 5$	15	7	1	-3	-5	-5	-3	1	15

Our interest will centre on the two areas inside the dotted lines. Why should this be? Substituting a value of -2 for x gives a positive value for $x^2 - x - 5$, substituting a value of -1 gives a negative value for $x^2 - x - 5$. So the value of x which gives $x^2 - x - 5 = 0$ must lie between $x = -2$ and $x = -1$.

Similarly, by looking at the change from negative to positive, we can see that the other solution for $x^2 - x - 5 = 0$ is somewhere between $x = 2$ and $x = 3$.

We now proceed with a trial and error method, at the same time applying a measure of common sense.

x	$x^2 - x - 5$
-2	1
-1	-3
try -1.75	-0.1875
try -1.8	0.04
try -1.78	-0.0516
try -1.79	-0.0059

This last value, -0.0059, is very close to zero, so the value of x which produced it, -1.79, is a very close approximation to one solution of the equation.

How do we know which values of x to try?

Remember that we are trying to find a value of x in the left-hand column which gives zero in the right-hand column. The first two values were

	-2	$\Rightarrow$ 1	Of these, 1 is nearer to 0 than -3 is.
and	-1	$\Rightarrow$ -3	Try something nearer to -2, such as -1.75.

We now have

	-2	$\Rightarrow$ 1	-0.1875 is nearer to zero than 1 is.
and	-1.75	$\Rightarrow$ -0.1875	Try something near -1.75, such as -1.8.

We now have

	-1.8	$\Rightarrow$ 0.04	0.04 is nearer to zero than 1 is.
and	-1.75	$\Rightarrow$ -0.1875	Try something near -1.8, such as -1.78.

We now have

$-1.8 \Rightarrow 0.04$ These two values are almost equally near zero.

$-1.78 \Rightarrow -0.0516$ Try -1.79.

Finally, we have

$-1.79 \Rightarrow -0.0059$

which, as we said, is very close to zero, hence $x = -1.79$ is a very close approximation to the root.

From the original table, the other root lies between $x = 2$ and $x = 3$. Try to find it before going on.

You should find that it is $x = 2.79$, a result which fits the symmetry of the original table. Using $x = 2.79$, the calculator sequence would be

Algebra	Calculator sequence	Display
x	2.79	2.79
x^2	x^2	7.7841
$-x$	$-$	7.7841
	2.79	2.79
-5	$-$	4.9941
	5	5
	$=$	$-5.9 \quad -0.3 = -0.0059$

★★EXERCISE 5.14

1   The equation $x^3 - 3x^2 + 2x - 1 = 0$ has only one solution.
Find it, given that it is positive, giving your answer correct to 2 d.p.

Remember

Root is another word for solution.

Comment

This is a cubic equation, not a quadratic.

You will need to follow through the solution to this one before proceeding.

2   Use iteration to solve the equation $x - x^3 + 2 = 0$.
Find the solution correct to 2 d.p., given that it is between $x = 1$ and $x = 2$.

3   There is a solution to the equation $x^2 + 2x - 2 = 0$ between $x = -2$ and $x = -3$.
Use an iterative method to find it, correct to 2 d.p.

4   Find the value of the positive root of $5 - x - x^2 = 0$ by an iterative method, giving your answer correct to 2 d.p.

5   Find two negative integers between which the equation $2x^2 + 9x + 8 = 0$ has a solution.
Find the solution correct to 1 d.p.

Comment

This is another cubic equation.

Iteration is the method used in this section to solve quadratic equations.

★★The quadratic formula

There is a formula which can be used to solve quadratic equations which will not factorise. It is beyond the scope of this book to prove the formula, but we can go ahead and use it anyway.

Any quadratic equation can be rearranged and expressed in the form
$ax^2 + bx + c = 0$ where

a is the number of x^2 and is called the **coefficient of x^2**

b is the number of x and is called the **coefficient of x**

c is the **constant term**.

The formula we can use is

$$x = \frac{-b \pm \sqrt{b^2 - 4ac}}{2a}$$

> Learn to recognise this quadratic formula.

★★EXERCISE 5.15

Use the quadratic formula to solve the following equations.

1   $x^2 + 2x - 2 = 0$
    Find both solutions.

2   $2x^2 + 9x + 8 = 0$
    Find both solutions.

3   $x^2 + 7x + 6 = 0$
    Find both solutions.

★★EXERCISE 5.16

Solve the following quadratic equations by using the quadratic formula, giving all answers to 2 d.p.

1   $x^2 + 5x - 3 = 0$

2   $2x^2 - 3x - 3 = 0$

3   $x^2 + 1 = 3x$

4   $2x^2 = 5x + 2$

5   $\frac{1}{2}x^2 + 2\frac{1}{2}x - 3\frac{1}{2} = 0$

6   $2.3x^2 + 4.7x - 1.8 = 0$

7   $x + 2 - 3x^2 = 0$

8   $x^4 + 4x^2 - 2 = 0$

> A little different, question 8, but look carefully at it.

★★Inequalities

We have spent a considerable amount of time now looking at equations, and there is more to come. However, we shall break here to look at statements which say that two expressions are **not** equal. If two quantities are not equal, then:

one is *larger* than the other, written using the > symbol, for example 5 > 3 or

one is *smaller* than the other, written using the < symbol, for example 2 < 7.

If we say $x < 7$ we mean that x can take any value we like as long as it is less than seven.

This can be shown on a number line.

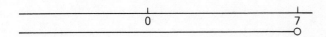

> This is the number line. This represents $x < 7$.

If 7 is to be included in the possible values of x we write $x \leq 7$, read 'x is less than or equal to seven'.

On the number line, it looks like this.

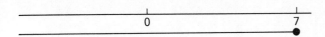

> Note the use of open and closed circles.
> - ● the value is included
> - ○ the value is not included.

> When we have an inequality such as $x > 3$, we are stating the range of possible values of x.

Some of the rules we applied to equations may be applied to inequalities, but some may not.

		Equation		Inequality	Rule valid/not valid
1		$x + 2 = 5$		$x + 2 > 5$	
	⇒	$x = 5 - 2$	⇒	$x > 5 - 2$	
	⇒	$x = 3$	⇒	$x > 3$	valid
2		$7 - x = 2$		$7 - x < 2$	
	⇒	$7 - 2 = x$	⇒	$7 - 2 < x$	
	⇒	$5 = x$	⇒	$5 > x$	valid
3		$\dfrac{x}{3} = 7$		$\dfrac{x}{3} > 7$	
	⇒	$3 \times \dfrac{x}{3} = 3 \times 7$	⇒	$3 \times \dfrac{x}{3} > 3 \times 7$	
	⇒	$x = 21$	⇒	$x > 21$	valid – but look carefully at the next one

4

$$-\frac{x}{3} = 7 \qquad\qquad -\frac{x}{3} > 7$$

$$\Rightarrow \quad -3 \times -\frac{x}{3} = -3 \times 7 \Rightarrow -3 \times -\frac{x}{3} > -3 \times 7$$

$$\Rightarrow \qquad x = 21 \qquad \Rightarrow \qquad x > -21 \qquad \text{not valid}$$

★★Investigation

Look at rules 3 and 4 more thoroughly. Experiment with some numbers and finally combine both into one rule. The result you should obtain is at the end of the solutions to **Exercise 5.17**.

★★EXERCISE 5.17

1   Find the range of values of x if $2x + 5 > 13$.

2   The number, n, of passengers on a bus must not exceed 56. Write this mathematically.

3   The weight of a wagon, when empty, is 8 tonnes and it must not carry more than 15 tonnes of goods. Write this mathematically, as concisely as you can, using W for the total weight.

4   If $x > 5$, write down an inequality for $\dfrac{1}{x}$.

5   Solve the inequality $11 - x > 2$ and show your answer on a number line.

6   Solve the inequality $2(3 - x) < 7$.

7   The tyre pressure on a car should be 24 lb per square inch. The tyre is OK provided that the pressure is within 2% of this value. Using p for the pressure, write down this statement mathematically, **(a)** using percentages   **(b)** using absolute values.

8   The width of a piece of wood is represented by w.
    Write $3 \text{ cm} \leqslant w \leqslant 24 \text{ cm}$ as a full sentence.

9   Solve the inequality $-3 \leqslant (x + 1) \leqslant 7$ and represent the answers on a number line.

10   Find the range of values of x for which $-6 \leqslant 2(x - 1) < 5$ and show the answer on a number line.

★Sets

If we look at a range of numbers, say between -4 and $+6$, they could be considered as a block or a group or a collection or a pack or a set of numbers. In mathematics we use the word **set**. We could call this range of numbers the **set** A and, if we take just the whole numbers or integers, we could write

$A = \{-4, -3, -2, -1, 0, 1, 2, 3, 4, 5, 6\}$

The brackets or braces { } are the standard ones always used when a set is written out in full. The separate bits inside the set, in this case the numbers from -4 to $+6$, are called the **members** or **elements** of the set. There are other symbols we use.

'3 is a member of the set A' is written $3 \in A$

'7 is not a member of the set A' is written $7 \notin A$.

> **Remember**
>
> $\in$ means 'is a member of' or 'is an element of', or even 'is in'
> $\notin$ means 'is not a member of' or 'is not an element of' or 'is not in'.

The numbers -3, 1, 2 and 6 form a set within A, which is called a **subset** of A. This is written

$\{-3, 1, 2, 6\} \subset A$

whilst another set, $\{-5, 53, 71\}$ is clearly not in A, so we write

$\{-5, 53, 71\} \not\subset A$

In our set A there are 11 elements, and we write

$n(A) = 11$

All the numbers which are not in set A form the set 'not in A' and this is written as A'.

> **Remember**
>
> The set of elements not in set A is also called the **complement** of A.

Work on sets is not confined to lists of numbers or anything else purely mathematical. For example, {cars} is a subset of {vehicles}, and {sports cars} is a subset of {cars}; another subset could be {three-wheeled cars}, and so on.

As written, {vehicles} describes all the vehicles which exist, or the total population of vehicles. A set which describes a total population is called a **universal set** and this is written as ε.

If we talked about the set of cows which climb trees, it would have no members. This is written as { } or $\emptyset$, and is called the **empty set** or the **null set**.

> **Remember**
>
> When describing the empty set, take care with notation.
> The empty set is { } or $\emptyset$.
> The set {0} is the set with only zero as a member.

If we now consider the set of cars which were made in Japan but have British number plates, we are talking about cars which belong to two sets: {Japanese cars} and {cars with British number plates}.

Is {cars with British number plates} a subset of {Japanese cars}? No, because there are some cars with British number plates which are not Japanese. Is {Japanese cars} a subset of {cars with British number plates}? Again, no.

A diagram shows the true situation.

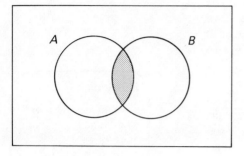

ε = {cars}
A = {cars with British number plates}
B = {Japanese cars}
A and B are both subsets of ε.
The shaded area is {Japanese cars with British number plates} and it is called the **intersection** of sets A and B, denoted $A \cap B$.

The set {Japanese cars and cars with British number plates} would include all the cars in A and all the cars in B. This is called the **union** of sets A and B and is denoted $A \cup B$.

The diagram above is called a **Venn diagram.**

★Investigation
Find out all you can about Venn who developed Venn diagrams.

All should fall into place as we tackle the next exercise.

★EXERCISE 5.18

1 List the set of vowels.

2 List the set of British monarchs of the 20th century.

3 List the set of prime numbers between 30 and 50.

4 If A = {palindromic numbers} and B = {years between 1950 and 2050}, list $A \cap B$.

> **Reminder**
>
> A palindromic word or number reads the same backwards as it does forwards, for example level and 1234321.

5 Find n(P) where P = {diagonals of a pentagon}.

6 In a class of 40 students 21 read the *Independent* and 18 read the *Express*. Six read neither. How many read both?

> **Reminder**
>
> A pentagon is a five-sided closed figure.

★★ 7   One hundred people were asked whether they kept a dog, a cat or a budgie. The results were:

budgie	25
cat	47
dog	51
cat and budgie	11
dog and budgie	8
cat and dog	22
all three	3

Represent this information on a Venn diagram and find how many of the people asked kept none of these pets.

★★ 8   Use your Venn diagram for question 7 to describe each of the following, if

B = {people who kept budgies}
C = {people who kept cats}
D = {people who kept dogs}.
(a) $n(D \cap C \cap B)$ (b) $n(D \cap C \cap B')$ (c) $n(D \cup C \cup B)$
(d) $n(D \cup C \cup B')$ (e) $n(C \cup B)$ (f) $n(B \cap D' \cap C')$

9   Look at the Venn diagram in the solution for question 7. Define mathematically the following sets.
(a) the area with 11 members
(b) the areas with 17 members
(c) the area with 25 members
(d) the area with 68 members

★★ 10   On a day when the weather forecast is for showers, members of a group of 50 people take at least a coat or an umbrella. If 35 take a coat and 21 take an umbrella, how many people take both?

★★ 11   Out of 36 students, all of whom study at least one subject, 22 study mathematics, 28 study physics and 27 study chemistry. Four study mathematics and physics only, six do physics and chemistry only and one does mathematics and chemistry only. How many students take mathematics, physics and chemistry, and how many do only mathematics?

★Indices

We already know that $x \times x$ is written as x^2 and in a similar way $x \times x \times x \times x \times x \times x \times x$ is written as x^6. The small 2 in x^2 is the **index**, or **power**, or **exponent** of x. All three names mean the same and they are all used. Also, x is known as the **base**.

★The first rule of indices

When multiplying numbers which are all powers of the same base, we can simply *add* the indices.

When dividing one number by another, and they are both powers of the same base, we *subtract* the indices. These two statements make up the first rule of indices.

> **Remember**
>
> x^n — index, base
>
> x is the base, n is the index.

EXAMPLES

(a) $x^2 \times x^3 = x^{2+3} = x^5$

(b) $x^7 \div x^4 = x^{7-4} = x^3$

(c) $x^{10} \times x^4 \div x^5 = x^{10+4-5} = x^9$

(d) $x^5 \times x^0 = x^{5+0} = x^5$

(e) $x^5 \div x^0 = x^{5-0} = x^5$

(f) $x^7 \times x^{-3} = x^{7-3} = x^4$

(g) $x^7 \times \dfrac{1}{x^3} = x^{7-3} = x^4$

★The second rule of indices

Compare (**f**) and (**g**) in the example above.

$$x^7 \qquad \times \qquad x^{-3} \qquad = \qquad x^{7-3} \qquad = \qquad x^4$$

$$x^7 \qquad \times \qquad \frac{1}{x^3} \qquad = \qquad x^{7-3} \qquad = \qquad x^4$$

the same   the same   the same   the same   the same   the same

must be the same

$$x^{-3} = \frac{1}{x^3}$$

At first, we may think that an expression such as x^{-3} is meaningless, but the last example shows that it isn't.

$$x^{-3} = \frac{1}{x^3}$$

is the second rule of indices.

To remove a negative (−) sign from an index, take the term across the solidus.

$$5^{-2} = \frac{1}{5^2} = \frac{1}{25}$$

$$\frac{1}{3^{-3}} = 3^3 = 27$$

★★The third rule of indices

The third and last rule of indices involves fractions.

It does not seem possible that $9^{\frac{1}{2}}$ could have any meaning, but it does.

By the first rule: $9^{\frac{1}{2}} \times 9^{\frac{1}{2}} = 9^{\frac{1}{2}+\frac{1}{2}} = 9^1 = 9$

$\Rightarrow \qquad\qquad 9^{\frac{1}{2}} \times 9^{\frac{1}{2}} = 9$ or $9^{\frac{1}{2}} = \sqrt{9} = 3$

Another one: $\quad 8^{\frac{1}{3}} \times 8^{\frac{1}{3}} \times 8^{\frac{1}{3}} = 8^{\frac{1}{3}+\frac{1}{3}+\frac{1}{3}} = 8$

$\Rightarrow \qquad\qquad 8^{\frac{1}{3}} = \sqrt[3]{8} = 2$

And another: $\quad 27^{\frac{2}{3}} \times 27^{\frac{2}{3}} \times 27^{\frac{2}{3}} = 27^2$

$\Rightarrow \qquad\qquad 27^{\frac{2}{3}} = \sqrt[3]{27^2} = 3^2 = 9$

In case you have not recognised the rule, one more should clarify it.

$$32^{\frac{3}{5}} \times 32^{\frac{3}{5}} \times 32^{\frac{3}{5}} \times 32^{\frac{3}{5}} \times 32^{\frac{3}{5}} = 32^{\frac{15}{5}} = 32^3$$

$\Rightarrow \qquad\qquad 32^{\frac{3}{5}} = \sqrt[5]{32^3} = 2^3 = 8$

Written in symbols, the third law of indices states:

$$x^{p/q} = \sqrt[q]{x^p}$$

The denominator indicates the root and the numerator the power, or the power is at the top, like the sun, and the root is at the bottom, like a tree.

★EXERCISE 5.19

1 Simplify $\dfrac{x^3 \times x^7}{x^6}$

2 Simplify $2x^2 \times 5x^5$

3 Evaluate $\dfrac{2^3 \times 3^2}{6^2}$

Simplify, and evaluate where possible.

★★ **4** $36^{\frac{1}{2}} \times 27^{\frac{1}{3}}$

5 $x^2 \times y^5$

6 $2^6 \times 4^{-2}$

★★ **7** $81^{\frac{1}{2}} \times 3^{-2}$

8 $(5^7 \times 3^5)^0$

9 $3x^3 \times 2y^2 \times 2x^{-2} \times y$

★★ **10** $27^{-\frac{2}{3}} \times 6^2$

Remember

Ensure you write indices correctly:

$x^4 = x \times x \times x \times x$

$x4 = x + x + x + x$

$x4$ is more usually written as $4x$.

Comment

The only number you can multiply and divide by without altering the value is 1.

The conclusion is that $x^0 = 1$.

★★Warning – a common mistake

Many people would write $\quad 5^{-2} = -10 \quad$ and they would be wrong! We **never** combine the index with the base directly.

Solutions to exercises

SOLUTIONS TO EXERCISE 5.1

1 $p = l + b + l + b = 2l + 2b$

2   Weight = number of tins × weight of each tin.
$W = nk$

3 $C = 5n + 2q$

4 $T = \dfrac{2\pi}{w}$

5   Cost of n units at 5.5p each is $5.5n$ pence $= £\dfrac{5.5n}{100}$

Then $C = F + \dfrac{5.5n}{100}$

6 $V = l \times b \times h = lbh$

7 $C \times \dfrac{9}{5} \quad \Rightarrow \quad \dfrac{9C}{5} + 32 \qquad\qquad \Rightarrow \dfrac{9C}{5} + 32$

$F = \dfrac{9C}{5} + 32$

8
Income $\Rightarrow I$
Take off allowances $\Rightarrow I - A$
25% $\Rightarrow \frac{25}{100}(I - A) = \frac{1}{4}(I - A)$
$\therefore T = \frac{1}{4}(I - A)$

9
First 20 metres $\Rightarrow 20 \times 100 = 2000$
Distance left $= n - 20 \quad \Rightarrow (n - 20)40 = 40(n - 20)$
$\therefore C = 2000 + 40(n - 20)$
        $= 2000 + 40n - 800$
$\therefore C = 1200 + 40n$

> **Hint** This answers the question, but we can continue.

10 $h = k \times A^2 \times R \times t$
$h = kA^2Rt$

SOLUTIONS TO EXERCISE 5.2

1   The volume of a sphere is four thirds times pi times the radius cubed.

2   The final velocity is equal to the initial velocity plus the product of the acceleration and the time.

> An equation from mechanics.

3   One over image distance plus one over object distance is equal to one over focal length. **Or** The reciprocal of the image distance plus the reciprocal of the object distance is equal to the reciprocal of the focal length.

> The rule for a curved mirror or lens, from physics.

4   The area of a trapezium is half the sum of the parallel sides multiplied by the distance between them.

5 Distance travelled at constant speed is the product of the time and the speed.

6 The pension is equal to the number of years worked, multiplied by the salary at retirement, divided by 80.

> This is an approximation to the rule as it applies to teachers and civil servants.

7 Density is equal to mass divided by volume.

8 Kinetic energy is equal to half the mass multiplied by the square of the velocity.

> Questions 7, 8 and 10 are all borrowed from physics and mechanics.

9 The cost of pitching a caravan is £2 plus 50p for each person camping.

10 For a gas at constant temperature, the product of the pressure and the volume is constant.

SOLUTIONS TO EXERCISE 5.3

1 $p = 2 \times 7 + 2 \times 4 = 14 + 8 = 22$

2 $W = 48 \times 750 = 36\,000$ g $= 36$ kg

3
$$471 = 5 \times 71 + 2q$$
$$\therefore 471 = 355 + 2q$$
$$\therefore 2q = 471 - 355 = 116$$
$$\therefore q = 58\text{p}$$

> Note all prices put into pence.

4 $T = \dfrac{2\pi}{w} = \dfrac{2\pi}{3} = 2.1$

Calculator sequence: $\boxed{\pi}$ $\boxed{\times}$ $\boxed{2}$ $\boxed{=}$ $\boxed{\div}$ $\boxed{3}$ $\boxed{=}$

Display: 3.1415927 2 6.2831853 3 2.094395

5 $C = 11.5 + \dfrac{5.5 \times 2340}{100}$

$\therefore C = £140.20$

Calculator sequence: $\boxed{5.5}$ $\boxed{\times}$ $\boxed{2340}$ $\boxed{=}$ $\boxed{\div}$ $\boxed{100}$ $\boxed{=}$ $\boxed{+}$ $\boxed{11.5}$ $\boxed{=}$

Display: 5.5 2340 12870 $\boxed{100}$ $\boxed{128.7}$ 11.5 140.2

6 $V = lbh \Rightarrow 29 = 5.5 \times 3.5 \times h$

$\qquad\qquad\qquad 29 = 19.25 \times h$

$\therefore h = \dfrac{29}{19.25}$

$\therefore h = 1.5$

7 $F = \dfrac{9C}{5} + 32 \Rightarrow F = 9 \times \dfrac{20}{5} + 32$

$\qquad\qquad\qquad\qquad F = 36 + 32$

$\qquad\qquad\qquad\quad \therefore F = 68°$

8 $T = \frac{1}{4}(17500 - 6250)$

$\quad = \frac{1}{4} \times 11250$

$\quad = 2812.50$

The man pays £2812.50.

9 $C = 1200 + 40 \times 90$
   $= 1200 + 3600$
   $C = £4800$

10 $h = 0.24 \times 1.7 \times 1.7 \times 9.8 \times 80$
    $h = 543.8$

SOLUTIONS TO EXERCISE 5.4

1 $V = \frac{4}{3} \times \pi \times 5^3$
   $V = 523.6$

> **Comment**
> This is easily worked out
> on a simple calculator,
> but if you have a x^y
> button, you could do:
>
> | Calculator sequence | Display |
> |---|---|
> | 4 | 4 |
> | $\times$ | |
> | π | 3.1415927 |
> | $\times$ | 12.566371 |
> | 5 | 5 |
> | x^y | |
> | 3 | 3 |
> | $\div$ | 1570.7963 |
> | 3 | 3 |
> | $=$ | 523.59878 |

2 $20 = u + 2 \times 5 \quad \Rightarrow \quad 20 = u + 10 \quad \Rightarrow \quad u = 10$

3 $\frac{1}{f} = \frac{1}{3} + \frac{1}{2} = \frac{2}{6} + \frac{3}{6} = \frac{5}{6}$
   $f = \frac{6}{5}$

> **Comment**
> In question 3 the answer
> was found by inverting
> both sides, which is
> possible when there is a
> single fraction each side.

4 $A = \frac{1}{2}(7.5 + 11.5) \times 4.5 = \frac{1}{2} \times 18.75 \times 4.5 = 42.2$

5 $45 = 30 \times t \quad \Rightarrow \quad t = \frac{45}{30} = 1.5$ hours

6 $P = \frac{38}{80} \times 18000 = £8550$

7 Volume of A $= \dfrac{15}{3.2} = 4.6875$

   Volume of B $= \dfrac{11}{2.7} = 4.074$

   $\therefore$ A occupies the greater space.

8 $810 = \frac{1}{2} \times 20 \times v^2$
   $810 = 10 \text{ x } v^2$
   $81 = v^2 \quad \Rightarrow \quad 9 = v$

9 $C = 2 + \frac{4}{2} = 2 + 2 = £4$

10 Since p and V multiplied together always gives the same answer, as
    V increases p decreases, and vice versa.

SOLUTIONS TO EXERCISE 5.5

1   Correct

2   Correct

3   $(x + 2)(y + 1) = x \times y + x \times 1 + 2 \times y + 2 \times 1 = xy$
    $+ x + 2y + 2$

4   Correct but can be simplified $\because 3x + 5x = 8x$
    $\therefore$ answer can be written as $x^2 + 8x + 15$

5   $(k + l)\, w = kl + kw$

6   $(p - q)(s + t) = p \times s + p \times t + (-q) \times s + (-q) \times t$
    $\qquad\qquad = ps + pt - qs - qt$

Comment
This is the first time we have met multiplication involving negative
numbers. There is a multiplication rule.
When multiplying or dividing, if the signs are the same the answer is
positive, if the signs are different the answer is negative. This rule is
illustrated by these statements.

1   I have some money $\Rightarrow$ yes
2   I have no money $\Rightarrow$ no
3   I do not have any money $\Rightarrow$ no
4   I do not have no money $\Rightarrow$ yes

---

7   $x(a + x) = xa + xx = xa + x^2$

8   $x(a + c)(p + q) = x(ap + aq + cp + cq)$
    $\qquad\qquad\quad = xap + xaq + xcp + xcq$

More on indices later.

9   Correct but $-7a + 3a = -4a$
    $\therefore$ answer is $a^2 - 4a - 21$

10   Correct

SOLUTIONS TO EXERCISE 5.6

A			B		
	1	$2 \times 3 \times 3$		1	$2 \times 3 \times 7$
	2	$a(x + y)$		2	$7(x - 2y)$
	3	$3p(q + 3r)$		3	$b(4a - 1)$
	4	$x(y^2 + z^2 + 2yz)$		4	$x(x^2 - 2xy + 3y^2)$
	5	$pq(p - q)$		5	$2a(ab + 3b^2 - 2c^2 + 4ac)$
C	1	7×13	D	1	$2 \times 2 \times 3 \times 11$
	2	$p(a + b - c)$		2	$k(x + 2y + 3z)$
	3	$2k(l - 4m)$		3	$5u(2t + v - 3w)$
	4	$abc(c + b + a)$		4	$b(8ac + 6a^2 - 3bc)$
	5	$(a + b)(3 + x)$		5	$2c(3c^2 - 2c + 1)$

SOLUTIONS TO EXERCISE 5.7

A **1** $5x + 1 = 21$
$20 + 1 = 21$
$\therefore 5x = 20$
$5 \times 4 = 20$
$\therefore x = 4$

2 $3a - 5 = 13$
$18 - 5 = 13$
$\therefore 3a = 18$
$3 \times 6 = 18$
$\therefore a = 6$

3 $\frac{1}{2}c + 1 = 7$
$6 + 1 = 7$
$\therefore \frac{1}{2}c = 6$
$\frac{1}{2} \times 12 = 6$
$\therefore c = 12$

4 $2x - 14 = 0$
$14 - 14 = 0$
$\therefore 2x = 14$
$2 \times 7 = 14$
$\therefore x = 7$

5 $5 = 8 - \frac{1}{3}k$
$5 = 8 - 3$
$\therefore \frac{1}{3}k = 3$
$\frac{1}{3} \times 9 = 3$
$\therefore k = 9$

B **1** $t = 12$

2 $a = -1$ $3 - 5a = 8$
$3 + 5 = 8$
$\therefore -5a = 5$
$-5 \times -1 = 5$
$\therefore a = -1$

3 $q = 40\frac{1}{2}$

4 $z = \frac{1}{5}$

5 $x = 2$

SOLUTIONS TO EXERCISE 5.8

1 $3(x + 1) = 12$
$\Rightarrow \ x + 1 = 4 \quad \Rightarrow x = 3$
or $\ \Rightarrow \ 3x + 3 = 12 \quad \Rightarrow 3x = 9 \ \Rightarrow x = 3$

2 $\dfrac{12}{x} + 3 = 7$

$\Rightarrow \quad \dfrac{12}{x} = 4 \quad \Rightarrow \quad x = 3$

3 $7n$

$7n + n = 32 \quad \Rightarrow \quad 8n = 32 \quad \Rightarrow \quad n = 4$

$\therefore$ boy is 4 years old and man is 28 years old.

4 $2(x - 1) = 13 - x$

$\Rightarrow \quad 2x - 2 = 13 - x$

$\Rightarrow \quad 2x + x = 13 + 2$

$\Rightarrow \qquad 3x = 15$

$\therefore \qquad\quad x = 5$

> The only thing to do is remove the brackets.

> The result of adding x and adding 2 to both sides.

5 $7x + 3(7 - 2x) = 23.5$

$\Rightarrow \quad 7x + 21 - 6x = 23.5$

$\Rightarrow \qquad\qquad x = 23.5 - 21$

$\Rightarrow \qquad\qquad x = 2.5$

6 Price of maths books: x and $3x$ $\quad \because$ one is three times the other.

$x + 3x + 3.6 = 10.00$

$\Rightarrow \qquad\qquad 4x = 10.00 - 3.6$

$\Rightarrow \qquad\qquad 4x = 6.4$

$\Rightarrow \qquad\qquad x = \dfrac{6.4}{4} = 1.6$

Books cost £1.60 and £4.80.

7 $\frac{3}{4}x + \frac{1}{6} = \frac{5}{12}$

$\Rightarrow \quad 12 \times \frac{3}{4}x + 12 \times \frac{1}{6} = 12 \times \frac{5}{12}$

$\Rightarrow \qquad 9x + 2 = 5$

$\Rightarrow \qquad\qquad 9x = 3$

$\Rightarrow \qquad\qquad x = \frac{3}{9} = \frac{1}{3}$

> Multiplying by 12 will remove the fractions.

8 The angles of a triangle add up to $180°$.

$\therefore \quad x + 2x + 10 + 3x + 20 = 180$

$\Rightarrow \qquad\qquad 6x + 30 = 180$

$\Rightarrow \qquad\qquad\quad 6x = 150$

$\Rightarrow \qquad\qquad\quad x = \dfrac{150}{6} = 25°$

$\therefore$ angles are $25°$, $60°$ and $95°$.

9 $\dfrac{3}{x + 2} + \dfrac{2}{5} = \dfrac{7}{10}$

$\Rightarrow \qquad \dfrac{3}{x + 2} = \dfrac{7}{10} - \dfrac{2}{5} = \dfrac{7}{10} - \dfrac{4}{10}$

$\Rightarrow \qquad \dfrac{3}{x + 2} = \dfrac{3}{10}$

$\Rightarrow \qquad x + 2 = 10$

$\therefore \qquad\quad x = 8$

10 $3 \times 4.50 + 2x = 21.50$ where x = price of reduced blouse
$\Rightarrow \qquad 2x = 21.50 - 13.50$
$\Rightarrow \qquad 2x = 8.00$
So reduced price of blouse is £4.00.
$\Rightarrow \quad c - \frac{1}{5}c = 400$ where c = original price
$\Rightarrow \qquad c = £5.00$

SOLUTIONS TO EXERCISE 5.9

1 $\left. \begin{array}{l} x + y = 22 \\ \\ x - y = 4 \end{array} \right\}$ add $\Rightarrow$ $2x = 26$ $\Rightarrow$ $x = 13, y = 9$
Solution: $x = 13, y = 9$

2 $\left. \begin{array}{l} x + y = 5 \\ \\ x - y = 11 \end{array} \right\}$ add $\Rightarrow$ $2x = 16$ $\Rightarrow$ $x = 8, y = -3$
Solution: $x = 8, y = -3$

3 $\left. \begin{array}{l} x + 2y = 9 \Rightarrow 2x + 4y = 18 \\ \\ 3x + 4y = 20 \Rightarrow 3x + 4y = 20 \end{array} \right\}$ subtract $\Rightarrow$ $x = 2, y = 3\frac{1}{2}$
Solution: $x = 2, y = 3\frac{1}{2}$

In question 3 we only need to multiply one equation (the first). We multiply by 2 so we have the same number of y in both equations. Then we subtract the bottom equation from the top, because we have '+ 4y' in both.

4 $\left. \begin{array}{l} 3x + 2y = 27.7 \Rightarrow 9x + 6y = 81.9 \\ \\ 4x - 3y = 22.8 \Rightarrow 8x - 6y = 45.6 \end{array} \right\}$ add $\Rightarrow$ $17x = 127.5$
$\Rightarrow$ $x = \dfrac{127.5}{17} = 7.5$

Substituting: $3 \times 7.5 + 2y = 27.3$ $\Rightarrow$ $y = 2.4$
Solution: $x = 7.5, y = 2.4$

5 $\left. \begin{array}{l} 5e + 2m = 98 \quad \Rightarrow 25e + 10m = 490 \\ \\ 12e + 5m = 241 \Rightarrow 24e + 10m = 482 \end{array} \right\}$ subtract $\Rightarrow$ $e = 8$
Substituting: $40 + 2m = 98$ $\Rightarrow$ $m = 29$
Solution: eggs are 8p each, milk is 29p per pint.

6 $5c + 2h = 345$
$4c + 1h = 240$
The question is asking for $3c + 3h$.
Careful inspection of the equations shows that, by subtracting, we can get
$1c + 1h = 105$
$3c + 3h = 315$
So three catches and three handles will cost £3.15.

7    $F = 8B + 12 \Rightarrow F - 8B = 12$
      $F + B = 156 \Rightarrow F + B = 156$ $\Big\}$ subtract $\Rightarrow -9B = -144$
      $\Rightarrow B = \dfrac{-144}{-9} = 16$

Substituting: $F + 16 = 156 \Rightarrow F = 140$
So a fountain pen costs £1.40.

Comment

Although the question asks for the cost of a fountain pen, we found the cost of the ball pen first. This was because of the algebra involved; it was easier that way.

8    $x + y = 27 \Rightarrow 2x + 2y = 54$
      $5x - 2y = 2 \Rightarrow 5x - 2y = 2$ $\Big\}$ add $\Rightarrow 7x = 56 \Rightarrow x = 8$
Substituting: $8 + y = 27 \Rightarrow y = 19$
So the larger number is 19, the smaller number is 8.

9    $8 = 2m + c$
      $-7 = -1m + c$ $\Big\}$ subtract $\Rightarrow 8 - -7 = 2m - -m$
      $\Rightarrow 15 = 3m \Rightarrow m = 5$

Substituting: $8 = 10 + c \Rightarrow c = -2$
Solution: $m = 5, c = -2$

Comment

'...is satisfied by...' means that the values fit the equation.

10   $x = 2y \Rightarrow 2x - 4y = 0$
      $x + x + y = 75 \Rightarrow 2x + y = 75$ $\Big\}$ subtract $\Rightarrow y - -4y = 75 - 0$
      $\Rightarrow 5y = 75$
Substituting: $x = 2 \times 15 \Rightarrow x = 30$
Solution: $x = 30, y = 15$

SOLUTIONS TO EXERCISE 5.10

A   1 $(x + 5)(x + 3) = x^2 + (5 + 3)x + 15 = x^2 + 8x + 15$
      2    $(x + 2)(x + 3) = x^2 + (2 + 3)x + 6 = x^2 + 5x + 6$
      3    $(x + 10)(x + 1) = x^2 + (10 + 1)x + 10 = x^2 + 11x + 10$
      4    $(x + 7)(x + 8) = x^2 + (7 + 8)x + 56 = x^2 + 15x + 56$
      5    $(x + 6)(x - 2) = x^2 + (6 - 2)x + 6 \times -2 = x^2 + 4x - 12$

B   1 $x^2 + 2x - 8$
      2    $x^2 - 4x + 3$
      3    $x^2 + 3x - 10$
      4    $x^2 - 9x + 14$
      5    $x^2 - 25$

C 1 $x^2 - x - 110$
2 $x^2 - 49$
3 $x^2 - x - 6$
4 $x^2 - a^2$
5 $x^2 - 1$

SOLUTIONS TO EXERCISE 5.11

6 No no x^2 term

7 Yes not essential to have term in x and/or constant term

8 Yes

9 No this is a **quartic** (degree 4) but it does have the quadratic pattern; it could be thought of as a quadratic in x^2

10 Yes

SOLUTIONS TO EXERCISE 5.12

A 1 $(x + 1)(x + 6)$
2 $(x + 3)(x + 4)$
3 $(x + 2)(x + 5)$

4 $(x + 1)(x + 24)$
5 $(x + 2)(x + 12)$
6 $(x + 3)(x + 8)$
7 $(x + 4)(x + 6)$

8 $(x - 2)(x - 5)$

9 $(x - 6)(x - 2)$

10 $(x - 3)(x + 3)$

Comment

Notice how an apparently small change to the question produces very different factors.

Comment

And again in these questions.

Comment

A little shock to disturb the routine, but it should make sense. $-2 - 5 = -7$ and $-2 \times -5 = +10$

Comment

Another shock, but still OK. $-6 + 2 = -4$ and $-6 \times +2 = -12$

Remember

The difference of two squares – see page 69.

B   **1** $(x - 1)(x + 6)$ **C** **1** $(x + 8)(x - 2)$

     2 $(x - 3)(x + 4)$ **2** $(x + 1)^2$

     3 $(x + 2)(x - 5)$ **3** $(6 - x)(6 + x)$

     4 $(x - 2)(x - 12)$ **4** $(x + 6)(x - 5)$

     5 $(x - 7)(x + 3)$ **5** $(x + 7)(x - 8)$

     6 $x(x + 5)$ **6** $(x - 7)^2$

     7 $(x + 2)(x - 2)$ **7**   no factors

     8 $(x + 5)(x - 7)$ **8** $(x + 10)^2$

     9 $(x + 7)(x - 7)$ **9** $(x - 9)(x + 9)$

    10 $(x + 3)^2$ **10** $(x - 4)(x + 10)$

SOLUTIONS TO EXERCISE 5.13

A **1** $x^2 + 7x + 6 = 0 \ \Rightarrow \ (x + 1)(x + 6) = 0 \ \Rightarrow \ x = -1, x = -6$

    2 $x^2 + 7x + 12 = 0 \ \Rightarrow \ (x + 3)(x + 4) = 0 \ \Rightarrow \ x = -3, x = -4$

    3 $x^2 + 7x + 10 = 0 \ \Rightarrow \ (x + 2)(x + 5) = 0 \ \Rightarrow \ x = -2, x = -5$

    4 $x^2 + 25x + 24 = 0 \ \Rightarrow \ (x + 1)(x + 24) = 0 \ \Rightarrow \ x = -1, x = -24$

    5 $x^2 + 14x + 24 = 0 \ \Rightarrow \ (x + 2)(x + 12) = 0 \ \Rightarrow \ x = -2, x = -12$

    6 $x^2 + 11x + 24 = 0 \ \Rightarrow \ (x + 3)(x + 8) = 0 \ \Rightarrow \ x = -3, x = -8$

    7 $x^2 + 10x + 24 = 0 \ \Rightarrow \ (x + 4)(x + 6) = 0 \ \Rightarrow \ x = -4, x = -6$

    8 $x^2 - 7x + 10 = 0 \ \Rightarrow \ (x - 2)(x - 5) = 0 \ \Rightarrow \ x = 2, x = 5$

    9 $x^2 - 4x - 12 = 0 \ \Rightarrow \ (x - 6)(x + 2) = 0 \ \Rightarrow \ x = 6, x = -2$

   10 $x^2 - 9 = 0 \ \Rightarrow \ (x - 3)(x + 3) = 0 \ \Rightarrow \ x = 3, x = -3$

$$\text{or } x^2 = 9 \ \Rightarrow \ x = \pm 3$$

B **1** $1, -6$ **C** **1** $-8, 2$

    2 $3, -4$ **2** $-1, -1$

    3 $-2, 5$ **3** ± 6

    4 $2, 12$ **4** $-6, 5$

    5 $7, -3$ **5** $-7, 8$

    6 $0, -5$ **6** $7, 7$

    7 ± 2 **7**   no solutions (explanation in Chapter 6)

    8 $-5, 7$ **8** $-10, -10$

    9 ± 7 **9** ± 9

   10 $-3, -3$ (explanation in Chapter 6)   **10** $-10, 4$

SOLUTIONS TO EXERCISE 5.14

1 Initial table, taking positive values of x:

x	0	1	2	3
$x^3 - 3x^2 + 2x - 1$	-1	-2	-1	5

The change from negative to positive values of the expression shows that the solution must be between $x = 2$ and $x = 3$.

$$\left. \begin{array}{l} x = \quad 2 \quad \Rightarrow \quad -1 \\ \qquad 3 \quad \Rightarrow \quad 5 \end{array} \right\} \text{so try } x = 2.2$$

$$\left. \begin{array}{l} x = \quad 2.2 \quad \Rightarrow \quad -0.472 \\ \qquad 3 \quad \Rightarrow \quad 5 \end{array} \right\} \text{so try } x = 2.4$$

$$\left. \begin{array}{l} x = \quad 2.2 \quad \Rightarrow \quad -0.472 \\ \qquad 2.4 \quad \Rightarrow \quad 0.344 \end{array} \right\} \text{so try } x = 2.3$$

$$\left. \begin{array}{l} x = \quad 2.3 \quad \Rightarrow \quad -0.103 \\ \qquad 2.4 \quad \Rightarrow \quad 0.344 \end{array} \right\} \text{so try } x = 2.33$$

$$\left. \begin{array}{l} x = \quad 2.3 \quad \Rightarrow \quad -0.103 \\ \qquad 2.33 \quad \Rightarrow \quad 0.022637 \end{array} \right\} \text{so try } x = 2.32$$

$$\left. \begin{array}{l} x = \quad 2.32 \quad \Rightarrow \quad -0.020032 \\ \qquad 2.33 \quad \Rightarrow \quad 0.022637 \end{array} \right\} \text{so try } x = 2.325$$

$x = \quad 2.325 \quad \Rightarrow \quad -0.001203 \quad$ which tells us the solution is nearer 2.32 than 2.33.

The solution is 2.32 to 2 d.p.

Algebra	Calculator sequence		Display
	C/CE		0
x	2.2		2.2
	x^y		2.2
	3		3
x^3	=		10.648
	M+	M	10.648
x	2.2	M	2.2
x^2	x^2	M	4.84
	×	M	4.84
	3	M	3
$3x^2$	=	M	14.52
$-3x^2$	+/−	M	−14.52
	M+	M	−14.52
x	2.2	M	2.2

		M	2.2
	2	M	2
$2x$	=	M	4.4
	M+	M	4.4
1	1	M	1
	+/−	M	−1
−1	M+	M	−1
	MR	M	−0.472

2 $x - x^3 + 2 = 0$

			Calculator sequence	**Display**
1	$\Rightarrow$ 2	⎫ so try 1.3	1.3	1.3
2	$\Rightarrow$ −4	⎭	−	1.3
1.3	$\Rightarrow$ 1.103	⎫ so try 1.5	1.3	1.3
2	$\Rightarrow$ −4	⎭	x^y	1.3
1.5	$\Rightarrow$ 0.125	⎫ so try 1.6	3	3
2	$\Rightarrow$ −4	⎭	=	−0.897
1.5	$\Rightarrow$ 0.125	⎫ so try 1.55	+	−0.897
1.6	$\Rightarrow$ −0.496	⎭	2	2
1.5	$\Rightarrow$ 0.125	⎫ so try 1.53	=	1.103
1.55	$\Rightarrow$ −0.173875	⎭		
1.5	$\Rightarrow$ 0.125	⎫ so try 1.52		
1.53	$\Rightarrow$ −0.051577	⎭		
1.52	$\Rightarrow$ 0.008192	⎫ so try 1.525		
1.53	$\Rightarrow$ −0.051577	⎭		

1.525 $\Rightarrow$ −0.0215781 $\Rightarrow$ the solution is nearer to 1.52

The solution is 1.52 correct to 2 d.p.

3 $x^2 + 2x - 2 = 0$

			Calculator sequence	**Display**
−2	$\Rightarrow$ −2	⎫	2.5	2.5
−3	$\Rightarrow$ 1	⎭	x^2	6.25
−2.5	$\Rightarrow$ −0.75	⎫	−	6.25
−3	$\Rightarrow$ 1	⎭	2	2
−2.7	$\Rightarrow$ −0.11	⎫	×	2
−3	$\Rightarrow$ 1	⎭	2.5	2.5
−2.7	$\Rightarrow$ −0.11	⎫	−	1.25
−2.8	$\Rightarrow$ 0.24	⎭	2	2
−2.7	$\Rightarrow$ −0.11	⎫	=	−0.75
−2.75	$\Rightarrow$ 0.0625	⎭		
−2.73	$\Rightarrow$ −0.0071	⎫		
−2.75	$\Rightarrow$ 0.0625	⎭		
−2.73	$\Rightarrow$ −0.0071	⎫		
−2.74	$\Rightarrow$ 0.0276	⎭		

−2.735 $\Rightarrow$ 0.010225

The solution is −2.73 correct to 2 d.p.

4 $5 - x - x^2 = 0$

$$x = 0 \quad 1 \quad 2$$

$$5 - x - x^2 = 5 \quad 3 \quad -1$$

$$\begin{aligned} 1 &\Rightarrow 3 \\ 2 &\Rightarrow -1 \end{aligned} \Bigg\}$$

$$\begin{aligned} 1.7 &\Rightarrow 0.41 \\ 1.8 &\Rightarrow -0.04 \end{aligned} \Bigg\}$$

$$\begin{aligned} 1.78 &\Rightarrow 0.0516 \\ 1.79 &\Rightarrow 0.0059 \end{aligned} \Bigg\}$$

$$\begin{aligned} 1.8 &\Rightarrow -0.04 \\ 1.795 &\Rightarrow -0.017025 \end{aligned} \Bigg\}$$

The solution is 1.79 correct to 2 d.p.

Calculator sequence	Display
5	5
−	5
1.7	1.7
−	3.3
1.7	1.7
x^2	2.89
=	0.41

5 $2x^2 + 9x + 8 = 0$

$$x = -1 \quad -2 \quad -3$$

$$2x^2 + 9x + 8 = \quad 1 \quad -2$$

$$\begin{aligned} -1 &\Rightarrow 1 \\ -2 &\Rightarrow -2 \end{aligned} \Bigg\} \quad \therefore \text{ solution between } -1 \text{ and } -2$$

$$-1.3 \Rightarrow -0.32$$

$$-1.2 \Rightarrow 0.08$$

$$-1.25 \Rightarrow -0.125 \quad \therefore \text{ solution is between } -1.25 \text{ and } -1.2$$

The solution is -1.2 correct to 1 d.p.

Calculator sequence	Display
1.25	1.25
+/−	−1.25
Min (or STO)	−1.25
x^2	1.5625
×	1.5625
2	2
+	3.125
9	9
×	9
MR	−1.25
+	−8.125
8	8
=	−0.125

Remember

This variation using the Min button can be used if the memory is not needed for anything else.
There are fewer keys to press using this method.

SOLUTIONS TO EXERCISE 5.15

1 $x^2 + 2x - 2 = 0$ when compared with
$ax^2 + bx + c = 0$ gives $a = 1$, $b = 2$ and $c = -2$.
The formula is $x = \dfrac{-b \pm \sqrt{(b^2 - 4ac)}}{2a}$

$\Rightarrow \qquad x = \dfrac{-2 \pm \sqrt{(2^2 - 4 \times 1 \times -2)}}{2 \times 1}$

$\Rightarrow \qquad x = \dfrac{-2 \pm \sqrt{(4 + 8)}}{2} = \dfrac{-2 \pm \sqrt{12}}{2}$

$\Rightarrow \qquad x = 0.732$ or $x = -2.732$

Calculator sequence	Display	
12	12	
$\sqrt{\ }$	3.4641016	
Min	3.4641016	
−	3.4641016	
2	2	
=	1.4641016	This [=] is important.
÷	1.4641016	
2	2	
=	0.7320508	First solution
MR	3.4641016	
+/−	−3.4641016	
−	−3.4641016	
2	2	
=	−5.4641016	This [=] is important.
÷	−5.4641016	
2	2	
=	−2.7320508	Second solution

A note on the ± sign
This symbol is read as *plus or minus* and it is an abbreviation.
Instead of
$A + B$ or $A - B$
we write $A \pm B$
This should be clear if the solution to question 1 is followed through.

2 $2x^2 + 9x + 8 = 0 \Rightarrow a = 2$, $b = 9$, $c = 8$

$x = \dfrac{-9 \pm \sqrt{(9^2 - 4 \times 2 \times 8)}}{2 \times 2}$

$= \dfrac{-9 \pm \sqrt{(81 - 64)}}{4}$

$= \dfrac{-9 \pm \sqrt{17}}{4}$

$\Rightarrow \quad x = -1.22$ or $x = -3.28$

3 $x^2 + 7x + 6 = 0 \Rightarrow a = 1, b = 7, c = 6$

$$x = \frac{-7 \pm \sqrt{25}}{2 \times 1}$$

$$x = \frac{-7 \pm 5}{2}$$

$x = -1$ or $x = -6$

> This example verifies that the formula can always be used even if you cannot find the factors. However, you may be asked to use a particular method, factorising, formula or iteration and then, of course, you have to use the method asked for.

SOLUTIONS TO EXERCISE 5.16

1 $a = 1, b = 5, c = -3 \Rightarrow x = 0.54$ or $x = -5.54$

2 $a = 2, b = -3, c = -3 \Rightarrow x = 4.37$ or $x = -0.69$

3 $a = 1, b = -3, c = 1 \quad \because x^2 + 1 = 3x \Rightarrow x^2 - 3x + 1 = 0$
$\Rightarrow x = 2.62$ or $x = 0.38$

4 $2x^2 = 5x + 2 \Rightarrow 2x^2 - 5x - 2 = 0 \Rightarrow a = 2, b = -5, c = -2$
$\Rightarrow x = 2.85$ or $x = -0.35$

5 $\frac{1}{2}x^2 + 2\frac{1}{2}x - 3\frac{1}{2} = 0 \Rightarrow x^2 + 5x - 7 = 0 \Rightarrow a = 1, b = 5,$
$c = -7 \Rightarrow x = 1.14$ or $x = -6.14$

6 $a = 2.3, b = 4.7, c = -1.8 \Rightarrow x = 0.33$ or $x = -2.37$

7 $x + 3 - 3x^2 = 0 \Rightarrow -3x^2 + x + 3 = 0 \Rightarrow a = -3, b = 1, c = 3$
$\Rightarrow x = -0.85$ or $x = 1.18$

8 $x^4 - 6x^2 + 2 = 0 \Rightarrow (x^2)^2 - 6(x^2) + 2 = 0$

> i.e. quadratic pattern

$$a = 1, b = -6, c = 2 \Rightarrow x^2 = \frac{6 \pm \sqrt{36 - 8}}{2}$$

> We are solving for x^2.

$\Rightarrow \quad x^2 = 5.65 \qquad$ or $x^2 = 0.55$
$\qquad x = \pm \sqrt{5.65} \qquad$ or $x^2 = \pm \sqrt{0.55}$
$\qquad x = 2.38$ or $-2.38 \quad$ or $x = 0.74$ or -0.74

SOLUTIONS TO EXERCISE 5.17

1 $2x + 5 > 13$
$\therefore 2x > 13 - 5 = 8$
$\therefore x > \frac{8}{2} = 4$
$\therefore x > 4$
i.e. x can have any value greater than 4.

2 $n \leqslant 56$

3 $W \geqslant 8$ and $W \leqslant 8 + 15 = 23$
$\Rightarrow \quad 8 \leqslant W \leqslant 23$

4 x has values 5, 6, 7, ... 21, 22 ...

$\dfrac{1}{x}$ has values $\frac{1}{5}, \frac{1}{6}, \frac{1}{7}, \dots \frac{1}{21}, \frac{1}{22} \dots$

i.e. $\frac{1}{4} < \frac{1}{5}$

Also, since x is never negative

so $\dfrac{1}{x}$ is never negative $\Rightarrow \dfrac{1}{x} > 0$

Finally, we have $0 < \dfrac{1}{x} < \frac{1}{5}$

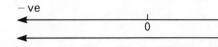

5 $11 - x > 2$

$11 - 2 > x$

i.e. $x < 9$

6 $2(3 - x) < 7$

$3 - x < \frac{7}{2} = 3.5$

$3 - 3.5 < x$

$-0.5 < x$

7 (a) $24 - 2\% < p < 24 + 2\%$

(b) 2% of $24 = \frac{2}{100} \times 24 = 0.48$

$\Rightarrow$ $23.52 < p < 24.48$

8 Wood is available in any width from three inches to twenty-four inches inclusive.

9 $-3 \leqslant (x + 1) \leqslant 7$

$\Rightarrow$ $-3 - 1 \leqslant x \leqslant 7 - 1$

$\Rightarrow$ $-4 \leqslant x \leqslant 6$

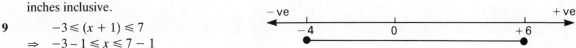

10 $-6 \leqslant 2(x - 1) < 5$

$-3 \leqslant x - 1 < \frac{5}{2}$

$-3 + 1 \leqslant x < \frac{5}{2} + 1$

$-2 \leqslant x < 3.5$

INVESTIGATION RESULT

When multiplying both sides of an inequality by a negative number the inequality sign must be reversed; with a positive number it stays the same.

SOLUTIONS TO EXERCISE 5.18

1 {vowels} = {a, e, i, o, u}

2 {20th century monarchs} = {Victoria, Edward VII, George V, Edward VIII, George VI, Elizabeth II}

3 {30 < prime numbers < 50} = {31, 37, 41, 43, 47}

4 $A \cap B$ = {1991, 2002}

5 $n(P) = 5$

6   A Venn diagram is essential for this type of question.

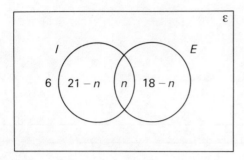

ε is the set of 40 students : $n(ε) = 40$
Let n be the number who read both.
Then there are $21 - n$ in the *Independent* only set and
$18 - n$ in the *Express* only set.
An equation which can be formed is
$$6 + (21 - n) + n + (18 - n) = 40$$
$$45 - n = 40$$
$$n = 5$$
i.e. 5 students read both the *Independent* and the *Express*.

7

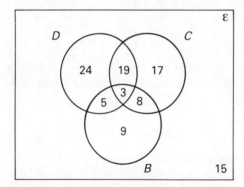

Whenever possible these questions are done by starting at the middle and working outwards.
Number of people in D, C and $B = 3$.
Put 3 in the area common to all three.
Now number of people with a dog and a cat is 22.
Since we already have accounted for 3, we put 19 in the 'dog and cat but no budgie' space.
Similarly the 5 and the 8 are inserted.
Now 51 people have a dog but we already have $19 + 3 + 5$ in the dog set.
So 24 goes in the 'dog only' space.

Comments

The figure 22 for dog and cat is independent of whether they keep a budgie or not. If it had meant dog and cat only then the word only would have been used.

Similarly the 17 goes in 'cat only' and the 9 goes in the 'budgie only' space.

Number of people with at least one animal is

$24 + 19 + 17 + 5 + 3 + 8 + 9 = 85$

So 15 do not keep any animals.

8 **(a)** $n(D \cap C \cap B) = 3$ Those who keep a dog, a cat and a budgie.

    (b) $n(D \cap C \cap B') = 19$ Those with a dog and a cat but not a budgie.

    (c) $n(D \cup C \cup B) = 85$ Those who keep at least one of a dog, a cat and a budgie.

    (d) $n(D \cup C \cup B)' = 15$ Those who keep none of a dog a cat and a budgie.

    (e) $n(C \cup B) = 19 + 17 + 3 + 8 + 5 + 9 = 61$

                              Those who keep at least a cat or a budgie.

    (f) $n(B \cap D' \cap C') = 9$ Those who keep a budgie but neither cat nor dog.

9 **(a)** $n(B \cap C) = 3 + 8 = 11$

    (b) $n(C \cap D' \cap B') = 17$

    (c) $n(B) = 5 + 3 + 8 + 9 = 25$

    (d) $n(D \cup B) = 24 + 19 + 5 + 3 + 8 + 9$

10 Let x take both.

$35 - x + x + 21 - x = 50 \quad \Rightarrow \quad x = 6$

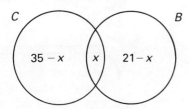

11 Let n be the number in $(M \cap P \cap C)$.

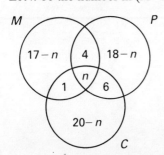

Put 4, 1 and 6 in the correct spaces.

        $22 - (1 + n + 4) = 17 - n$ in maths only

        $28 - (4 + n + 6) = 18 - n$ in physics only

and $27 - (1 + n + 6) = 20 - n$ in chemistry only

Totalling gives the equation

$(17 - n) + 1 + n + 4 + (18 - n) + 6 + (20 - n) = 36$

$$66 - 2n = 36$$

$$n = 15$$

i.e. 15 take all three and $17 - 15 = 2$ do maths only.

SOLUTIONS TO EXERCISE 5.19

1 $\dfrac{x^3 \times x^7}{x^6} = x^{3+7-6} = x^4$

2 $2x^2 \times 5x^5 = (2 \times 5)x^{2+5} = 10x^7$

3 $\dfrac{2^3 \times 3^2}{6^2} = \dfrac{8 \times 9}{36} = 2$

4 $36^{\frac{1}{2}} \times 27^{\frac{1}{3}} = \sqrt{36} \times \sqrt[3]{27} = 6 \times 3 = 18$

5 $x^2 \times y^5 = x^2 y^5$

6 $2^6 \times 4^{-2} = 64 \times \dfrac{1}{16} = 4$

    or $2^6 \times \dfrac{1}{4^2} = 2^6 \times \dfrac{1}{(2^2)^2} = 2^6 \times \dfrac{1}{2^4} = 2^2 = 4$

7 $81^{\frac{1}{2}} \times 3^{-2} = \sqrt{81} \times \dfrac{1}{3^2} = 9 \times \dfrac{1}{9} = 1$

8 $(5^7 \times 3^5)^0 = 1$

9 $3x^3 \times 2y^2 \times 2x^{-2} \times y = (3 \times 2 \times 2) \times x^{3-2} \times y^{2+1} = 12xy^3$

10 $27^{-\frac{2}{3}} \times 6^2 = \dfrac{1}{27^{\frac{2}{3}}} \times 36 = \dfrac{1}{\sqrt[3]{27^2}} \times 36 = \dfrac{1}{9} \times 36 = 4$

> Question 4 is a trick question highlighting a popular mistake. Nothing can be done in this case and answers like xy^7 and xy^{10} are rubbish. The bases must be the same before rules of indices apply.

> $5^7 \times 3^5$ is a bit of a red herring in question 8: anything to the power 0 is 1.

> When working out $27^{\frac{2}{3}}$ you have a choice of ways, one of which is better than the other.
> $27^{\frac{2}{3}} = \sqrt[3]{27^2} = \sqrt[3]{729} = 9$
> or
> $27^{\frac{2}{3}} = \sqrt[3]{27^2} = 3^2 = 9$
> the preferred method

6 Functions and graphs

The title of this chapter may make no sense to you, but that will all be different by the time you have worked through it. The content involves drawing diagrams of what the algebra is about. Illustrations of things we are talking about almost always simplify matters, and often they are essential.

For this chapter you will need a good supply of graph paper. By the end of the chapter you will be able to:

- draw **conversion graphs**
- use **Cartesian coordinates**
- draw algebraic **straight-line graphs**
- draw **curved graphs**

and go on to:

- learn the significance of the **gradient** and **area under the graph**
- work out the **gradient of a graph**
- use the **trapezium rule** to find the area under a graph

finishing up with:

- **composite functions**, forming fg(x) from f(x) and g(x).

★Introduction

In the last chapter we studied – at length – expressions such as $2x + 3$ and $x^2 - 3x + 2$. The mathematical name used for this sort of expression is **function**, and we say they are **functions of x**. Generally a function of anything is a purpose for which it exists: the function of a door is to keep out the cold and intruders, the function of a school is to educate its pupils, and the function of $2x + 3$ is to convert one number into another. A function such as $2x + 3$ can be considered as a machine: put one number in and out comes another. If we put 3 into the function $2x + 3$ we get 9 out; if we put in 5 out comes 13. It's a bit like a sausage machine; in goes the traditional secret recipe and out comes a delicious banger. In both cases, if we change the **input** (what goes in), the **output** is also different.

It is not very difficult to draw diagrams which illustrate or link together the input and the output. In mathematics, these diagrams are called **graphs**. In this chapter we shall look at different functions, and their graphs.

★Practical graphs

We shall start by looking at straightforward or practical graphs. Later ones are more theoretical, but we needn't worry about them yet.

The graph below shows the link between temperatures in Celsius (°C) and Fahrenheit (°F). The equation which links them is
$F = \frac{9}{5}C + 32$

If we want to convert a temperature of 20°C into Fahrenheit we substitute 20 for C in the equation.
$F = \frac{9}{5} \times 20 + 32 = 68$

If we put $C = 0$ we get $F = 32$.
On the graph they are the points A and B respectively.

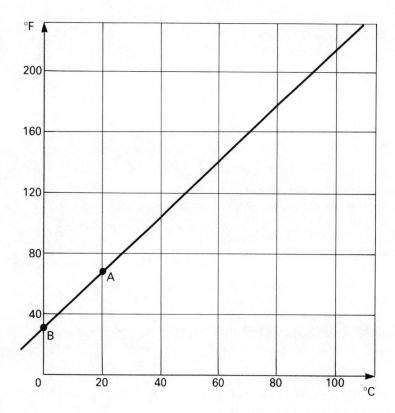

A graph of this type has one advantage, since it is much quicker to use than the formula. A disadvantage is that it is not always as accurate. From the graph a temperature of 76°C is converted to 168°F. Using the formula, a value of 168.8°F is obtained.

Remember

Formula is another word for equation.

Definitions

Before going any further, there are some terms which we need to understand.

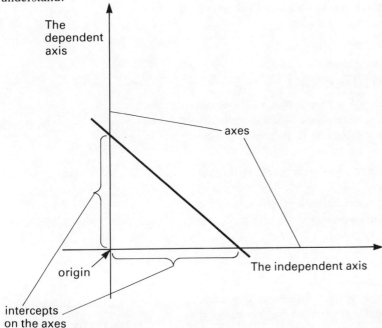

The lines up and across the page are the **axes**.

The horizontal axis is the **independent** axis.

The vertical axis is the **dependent** axis.

The point where the axes meet is the **origin**.

The places where the graph cuts the axes are the **intercepts**.

The axes are rather like **number lines**.

The **scale** remains the same along an axis; the size of the units along an axis does not vary.

The scales do not have to be the same on both axes.

The independent variable is the one which doesn't depend on anything. It's often called x.

The dependent variable is the one which *depends* on the independent variable. It is what comes out when a value of the independent variable is put in. It is often called y.

In the case of $F = \frac{9}{5}C + 32$ C is the independent variable because we put in values for C to get out values for F; F is the dependent variable because its value is determined by what is put in for C.

The formula can be rearranged to give

$C = \frac{5}{9}(F - 32)$

and now the roles are reversed because the value of C depends on what we put in for F. Now F is the independent variable and C is the dependent variable.

> **Remember**
>
> A graph which converts one value to another, as here, is called a **conversion graph**.

EXERCISE 6.1

Draw conversion graphs for questions 1 – 4.

1   Up to 20 litres, to gallons and pints (1 litre = 1.8 pints, 1 gallon = 8 pints)

2   Up to 60 mph to kph (5 miles = 8 km)

3   Test marks out of 160 into percentage marks

4   Up to £40 to Deutschmarks (DM) (£1 = 2.7 DM)

5   A salesman is paid a basic wage of £75 per week plus 0.01% of the value of each car he sells. The most he can hope to sell in a week is to the value of £125 000. Draw a graph to show the range of wage he could hope to earn.

6   A man earns £4.50 per hour for up to 35 hours worked. After that he earns overtime and his hourly rate is £6.80. The maximum allowed amount of overtime is 20 hours. Draw a graph relating the wage earned to the number of hours worked.

Algebraic functions

We shall now go on to think about drawing graphs of algebraic functions. Some people find it difficult to believe that algebra can be drawn, but it can. We shall concentrate on producing graphs from algebraic functions but it must be remembered that the reverse process also operates. Often, in science and engineering, the results of an experiment are plotted, a graph is drawn and then the formula or function connecting the results is deduced.

> This is a very important aspect of mathematics – its use as a tool for development in science and other areas.

The graphs we shall draw are known as **Cartesian graphs**, after the creator of the technique, René Descartes (1596 – 1650).

> **Investigation**
> Find out about Descartes. You should find him very interesting.

Cartesian coordinates

By using two lines, known as **axes**, at right angles to each other, and numbering them as in the diagram opposite, we can identify or define any point, using just two numbers. Those two numbers, taken together, cannot possibly refer to any other point. Every possible point has its own unique pair of numbers, rather like every person having a unique thumbprint.

> **Remember**
>
> The *first* number in the pair is always measured *along* the horizontal axis or the *x*-axis and is called the *x*-coordinate of the point. The *second* number is measured *up* the vertical or *y*-axis and is called the *y*-coordinate.

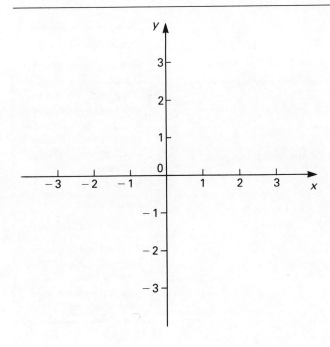

The system is very simple but even here carelessness leads to mistakes.

In this diagram, is A the point (1, 3) or is it (3, 1)?

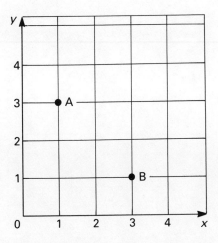

In the diagram, A is the point (1, 3). The point (3, 1) is B.

Comment

This system compares with latitude and longitude, and grid references.

★Straight-line graphs

It goes without saying that straight-line graphs, often called **linear graphs**, are the easiest to draw. You need just two plotted points and a ruler.

★EXERCISE 6.2

Decide whether the following equations are linear or not, and if not give reasons.

1   $2y + 3x = 6$

2   $y = 4x - 1$

3   $xy = 4$

4   $y^2 = 8x$

5   $\dfrac{1}{y} = x + 2$

6   $2(y - 1) = 3x$

7   $y = 5$

8   $\dfrac{x}{3} + \dfrac{y}{2} + \dfrac{1}{6} = 0$

9   $\sqrt{x} = \sqrt{y} + 1$

10   $x^2 + y^2 = 1$

> **Remember**
>
> How can we tell if an equation has a straight-line graph? The answer is, it must be of **degree 1**. Degree 1 means that the highest power of x or y which appears in the equation is 1.
> So x^2, y^3, $x^{\frac{1}{2}}$, x^{-2} and $\dfrac{1}{y^5}$ are not allowed.
> Nor is $\dfrac{1}{x}$ because that is the same as x^{-1}.
> Nor is xy, because this is a product of the two variables and is equivalent to degree 2.

★Drawing the graph

Now that we have decided that the equation in question 1 is linear, we can draw its graph.
We need two points.

When $x = 0$ $\Rightarrow$ $2y + 3 \times 0 = 6$
         $\Rightarrow$ $2y = 6$
         $\Rightarrow$ $y = 3$
When $y = 0$ $\Rightarrow$ $2 \times 0 + 3x = 6$
         $\Rightarrow$ $3x = 6$
         $\Rightarrow$ $x = 2$

∴ we have two points: $x = 0, y = 3$ $\Rightarrow$ $(0, 3)$
                $x = 2, y = 0$ $\Rightarrow$ $(2, 0)$

Let's find a third point.
When $x = 1$ $\Rightarrow$ $2y + 3 = 6$
         $\Rightarrow$ $2y = 3$
         $\Rightarrow$ $y = \frac{3}{2}$

Why do we need a third point? Think about it.

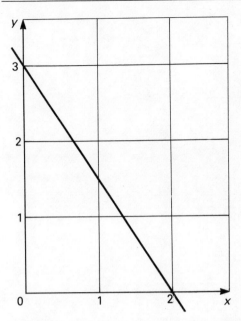

If we look at the point $(1, \frac{3}{2})$ we see that it is on the line, which is just as well, because it should be. It has been worked out using the same equation as for the other two points. The third point is a check. If it is not on the line, there is something wrong.

EXAMPLE

Draw the graph of $2y = 3x + 2$.
Now we need to think carefully. Does this mean draw all the graph? We can't do that, because it will go on for ever, both ways. The question should give us more information.
Let's try again.

EXAMPLE

Draw the graph of $2y = 3x + 2$ for values of x from -3 to $+3$.

Solution

$2y = 3x + 2$
When $x = -3 \Rightarrow 2y = -9 + 2 = -7$
$\qquad\qquad \Rightarrow y = -\frac{7}{2}$
$\qquad\qquad \Rightarrow$ point $(-3, -\frac{7}{2})$
When $x = 3 \Rightarrow 2y = 9 + 2 = 11$
$\qquad\qquad \Rightarrow y = \frac{11}{2}$
$\qquad\qquad \Rightarrow$ point $(3, \frac{11}{2})$

Check point, $x = 0 \Rightarrow 2y = 2 \Rightarrow y = 1 \Rightarrow$ point $(0, 1)$

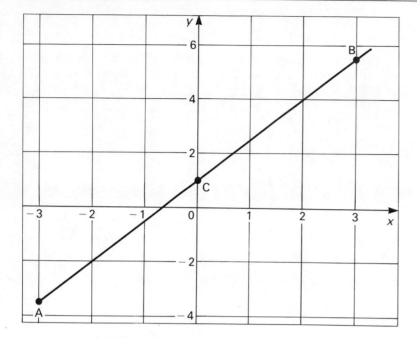

Notes

1   Points A and B are chosen as far apart as conveniently possible; this leads to greater accuracy.

2   Point C(0, 1) is on the line; it is the check point.

3   Units do not have to be the same size on both axes. In this case, 1 square represents 1 unit on the x-axis but 1 square represents 2 units on the y-axis.

> When referring to the axes, it is common to call the x-axis Ox and the y-axis Oy.

★EXERCISE 6.3

Draw the following graphs.

1 $y = 2x - 1$ for values of x from 0 to 6, using 2 cm = 1 unit on Ox, 2 cm = 2 units on Oy.

2 $3y + 2x + 3 = 0$ for values of x from -4 to $+2$, using 2 cm = 1 unit on each axis.

3 $5y - 2x = 5$ for values of x from -4 to $+2$, using 2 cm = 1 unit on each axis.

4 $2y + 3x = 6$ for values of x from -2 to $+4$, using 2 cm = 1 unit on the x-axis, 1 cm = 1 unit on the y-axis.

5 $x = 3$ and $y = 2$ on the same diagram, for values of x from 0 to 4 and values of y from 0 to 3.

★Curved graphs

Graphs which are not straight lines are often referred to as **curves**. We shall now look at some of these.

Let us first draw the graph of $y = x^2 + 5x - 2$.

We cannot draw the graph until we have a range of values for x, and a set of points. We shall take values of x from -4 to $+3$.

We can work out the y-values in two ways. The first is by calculator. This method is recommended, especially for those who are confident using a calculator. Those who are not should have a real try.

When $x = -4$

	Calculator sequence	**Display**
$2x^2$	4	4
	+/−	−4
	×	−4
	4	4
	+/−	−4
	×	16
	2	2
	=	32
	M+	32
$5x$	4	4
	+/−	−4
	×	−4
	5	5
	=	−20
	M+	−20
-2	2	2
	+/−	−2
	M+	−2
	MR	10

Totalling $2x^2$, $5x$ and -2 in the memory

First point is $(-4, 10)$.

We can use the same routine for all the other values of x to produce this table.

x	−4	−3	−2	−1	0	1	2	3
y	10	1	−4	−5	−2	5	16	31

The second method is to draw up a more detailed table and fill it in, using the calculator if desired.

x	-4	-3	-2	-1	0	1	2	3
$2x^2$	32	18	8	2	0	2	8	18
$5x$	-20	-15	-10	-5	0	5	10	15
-2	-2	-2	-2	-2	-2	-2	-2	-2
y	10	1	-4	-5	-2	5	16	31

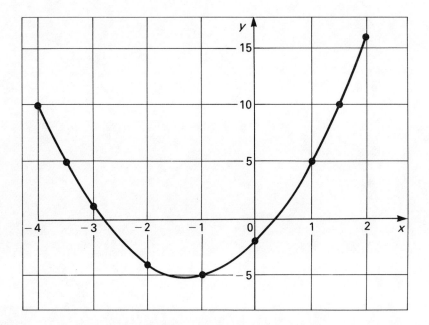

Notes

1   The curve is smooth and continuous, and achieving the skill to draw such curves needs practice. Most people find it easier to turn the paper round and draw *inside* the curve.

2   To help with the accuracy, extra points were worked out at (-3.5, 5) and (1.5, 10). These provided help between what were otherwise quite widely spaced points.

3   The length of the axes and the scale need to be worked out from the table of values.

★**EXERCISE 6.4**

1 Draw the graph of $y = \dfrac{2}{x}$ from $x = 0.5$ to $x = 6$, using 2 cm = 1 unit on each axis.

2 Draw the graph of $y = x^3 - 6x^2 + 9x + 3$ from $x = 0$ to $x = 5$, using 2 cm = 1 unit on the x-axis, 1 cm = 1 unit on the y-axis.

3 On the same axes, with values of x from -2 to 2, draw the graphs of
(a) $y = x^2$ (b) $y = x^2 + 2$ (c) $y = x^2 - 1$.
What would the y-intercept be on the graph of $y = x^2 + k$?

4 On the same axes, with values of x from -2 to 2, draw the graphs of
(a) $y = x^2$ (b) $y = 2x^2$ (c) $y = -x^2$
using 2 cm = 1 unit on Ox, 1 cm = 1 unit on Oy.

5 On the same axes, for values of x from -4 to 5, draw the graphs of
(a) $y = x^2$ (b) $y = (x - 2)^2$ (c) $y = (x + 3)^2$
using 2 cm = 1 unit on Ox, 1 cm = 1 unit on Oy.

6 Study the solutions to questions 3, 4 and 5 and describe the effects you notice in each case. Try to use the words 'stretch', 'translation' and 'reflection' in your answer.

7 On the same axes, for values of x from -2 to 4, draw the graphs of
(a) $y = x^2 - 2x - 1$ (b) $y = x$.
Write down the coordinates of the points where the graphs intersect.

8 You must have tried question 7 and worked through it before you can do this question.
Draw the graphs of $y = (x - 2)^2$ and $2y = x + 8$ for values of x from -1 to 5.
Hence solve the simultaneous equations $y = x^2 - 4x + 4$ and $2y = x + 8$.

9 Solve the simultaneous equations $2y + x = 5$ and $2y = x + 1$ graphically.

10 By drawing the graphs of $y = x^2$ and $y + x = 6$ for values of x from -3 to 3 solve the equation $x^2 + x - 6 = 0$.

11 Solve the equation $x^2 - x - 2 = 0$ graphically.

12 On the same axes, draw the graphs of
(a) $y = x$ (b) $x = 3$ (c) $y = 2$
using 2 cm = 1 unit on each axis. Shade the area for which $0 \leqslant y \leqslant 2$, $x \leqslant 3$ and $y < x$.

13 On the same diagram, draw the graphs of the relations $2y = x + 2$ and $4y + 3x = 6$ for values of x from -2 to 3. Shade the area for which $4y > 6 - 3x$, $2y < x + 2$ and $y > 0$. Define, using inequalities, the area enclosed by the two graphs and the x-axis.

14   Draw the graphs of $y = x$ and $y = 2x$ on the same axes, for values of x from 0 to 8, using 1 cm = 1 unit on each axis. Now draw a third graph which, with $y = x$ as the axis of symmetry, is symmetrical with $y = 2x$.
Find the equation of this last graph. Complete these tables of values.

$y = 2x$ your last graph

x	1	2	3	4	5
$2x$					

x	2	4	6	8	10

State any conclusions you can make.

15   Draw the graph of $y = x^3 + 3x^2 - x - 3$ for values of x from -4 to 2, using 2 cm = 1 unit on Ox, 2 cm = 5 units on Oy.

16   Draw the graph of $y = \dfrac{x^2}{2} - 1$ for values of x from 0 to 3, using 2 cm = 1 unit on each axis. Mark your x-axis from -1 to 3 but draw the graph only for values indicated. On the same diagram, draw the graph of the inverse of $\dfrac{x^2}{2} - 1$.

Find the algebraic form of the inverse function.

> A function and its inverse are symmetrical about the line $y = x$ which is the axis of symmetry.

> Setting the last question here is unfair, but think about it before you look at the answer.

★Gradients and areas

There are two other important features of graphs which we have to look at, and these are the **gradient** and the **area under the graph.**

Consider two cyclists, Sean Kelly and your mathematics teacher. They set off at the same time to ride from Rochdale to Blackpool, a distance of 50 miles. The graphs of their journeys are shown, assuming accurately their average speeds.

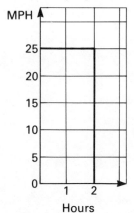

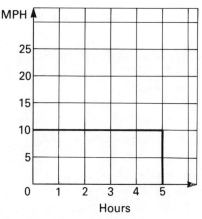

There are no prizes for guessing which is Sean Kelly's.
What do you notice about the areas under the two graphs?

They are both the same.
What does the area represent?
Sean Kelly: area = 25 × 2 = 50
Maths teacher: area = 10 × 5 = 50

In each case, this is
equal to the distance
travelled.

Now look at their graphs just as they set off; the first ten seconds in fact.

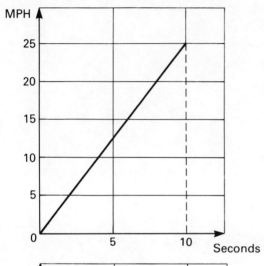

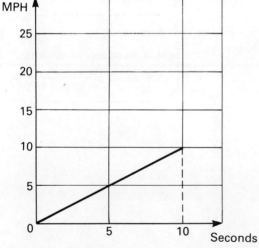

The appearance of the graphs tells its own story. The first is much steeper
and reflects the fact that Sean Kelly accelerates much faster than the
maths teacher.

Here we have established that the slope of the graph and the area do
have some significance. We can now look at them more carefully.

★Gradient

The definition of the gradient is quite simple, in mathematical terms.

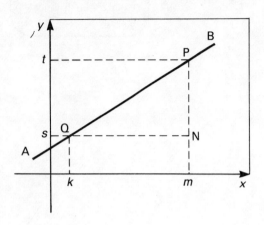

Remember

The gradient of a line is the same as the slope of the line.

The gradient of line AB in the diagram is $\dfrac{PN}{QN}$.

If the coordinates are as shown in the diagram, then $PN = t - s$
and $QN = m - k$

So the gradient of the line is $\dfrac{t - s}{m - k}$.

This may also be written as $\dfrac{s - t}{k - m}$

but not $\dfrac{s - t}{m - k}$ or $\dfrac{t - s}{k - m}$.

Look for the pattern in these and you will remember which are correct. It may be easier to remember

$$\text{gradient} = \frac{y_P - y_Q}{x_P - x_Q}$$

Remember

Mathematically, we can write
$$\text{gradient} = \frac{\text{change in } y\text{-values}}{\text{change in } x\text{-values}}$$

What about the gradient of the line CD?

$$\text{Slope CD} = \frac{y_C - y_D}{x_C - x_D} = \frac{5 - 1}{1 - 6} = \frac{4}{-5} = \frac{-4}{5}$$

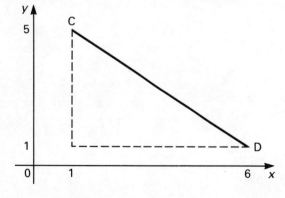

★Negative and positive gradients

A positive gradient is conventionally one which slopes *up* from left to right. A negative gradient slopes *down* from left to right.

Positive gradient ⇒ increasing function ⇒ the value of the function increases as x increases

y increases as x increases

Negative gradient ⇒ decreasing function ⇒ the value of the function decreases as x increases

y decreases as x increases

We have looked at gradients of straight lines. How could we find the gradient of a curve? A straight line keeps the same gradient all the way along its length, but a curve has a slope that is always changing. In the case of a curve, we can only find the gradient of or at a point on the curve.

The **tangent** is the line which touches the curve in just one place, and is parallel to the curve.

To find the gradient of a curve, we have to do it practically. We first draw the curve, then add the tangent, find the coordinates of two points on the tangent then find the gradient.

> **Remember**
>
> By the slope of or at a point on the curve we mean the slope of the tangent to the curve at that point.

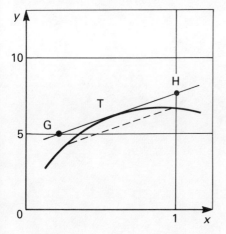

Consider the curve in this diagram.
Suppose we want the slope at the point T, where $x = \frac{1}{2}$.

One way to find an accurate tangent is to place a ruler along the curve near T, as indicated by the dotted line in the diagram, so that the shape between the curve and the ruler looks symmetrical about T. If we slide the ruler gently, keeping it parallel to its original position, towards the curve until it touches it at T, we can draw a straight line which will touch the curve only once at T. This will be the tangent.

Now we need to find two points, such as G and H in the diagram, to find the gradient.

G is (0.2, 5) and H is (1, 7.8).

$$\text{The slope or gradient} = \frac{y_H - y_G}{x_H - x_G} = \frac{7.8 - 5}{1 - 0.2} = \frac{2.8}{0.8} = 3.5$$

We have found that the slope or gradient of the curve at the point T (0.5, 6) is 3.5.

It is worth mentioning here that, although we do not do much work on gradients in this book, the gradient of a function is very important and a lot of work is done on it in future studies in mathematics.

★★Finding the area under a curve – the trapezium rule

Remember

A trapezium (plural trapezia) is a four-sided plane shape with one pair of opposite sides parallel but unequal.

We shall now look at one way of finding the area under a curve.
The method is to divide the area under the curve into many trapezia and then find the total of all their areas. This gives an approximation to the actual area, but it is a very good approximation.

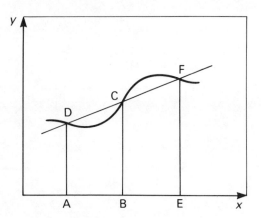

The diagram represents part of a curve and ABCD and BEFC are trapezia of equal width, AB = BE. The area of trapezium ABCD is clearly larger than the area under the curve ABCD, and similarly the area of trapezium BEFC is less than the curve BEFC, but when the areas of the trapezia are added together the result will be approximately the same as area AEFD under the curve. The narrower we make the trapezia, the more accurate will be the approximation.

We shall now consider another example. Look at the curve drawn in question 2 of **Exercise 6.4**.

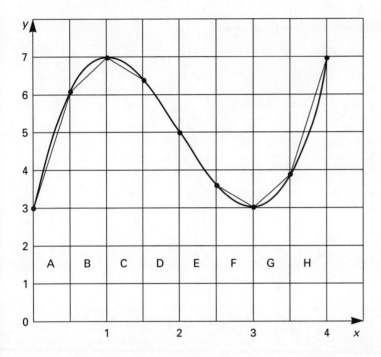

Each trapezium is 0.5 units wide.

The area of trapezium A $= \frac{1}{2}(3 + 6.1) \times \frac{1}{2}$
The area of trapezium B $= \frac{1}{2}(6.1 + 7) \times \frac{1}{2}$
The area of trapezium C $= \frac{1}{2}(7 + 6.4) \times \frac{1}{2}$
The area of trapezium D $= \frac{1}{2}(6.4 + 5) \times \frac{1}{2}$
The area of trapezium E $= \frac{1}{2}(5 + 3.6) \times \frac{1}{2}$
The area of trapezium F $= \frac{1}{2}(3.6 + 3) \times \frac{1}{2}$
The area of trapezium G $= \frac{1}{2}(3 + 3.9) \times \frac{1}{2}$
The area of trapezium H $= \frac{1}{2}(3.9 + 7) \times \frac{1}{2}$

$\Rightarrow$ the total area $= \frac{1}{2}(3 + 6.1) \times \frac{1}{2} + \frac{1}{2}(6.1 + 7) \times \frac{1}{2} + \frac{1}{2}(7 + 6.4) \times \frac{1}{2}$
$\qquad + \frac{1}{2}(6.4 + 5) \times \frac{1}{2} + \frac{1}{2}(5 + 3.6) \times \frac{1}{2} + \frac{1}{2}(3.6 + 3) \times \frac{1}{2}$
$\qquad + \frac{1}{2}(3 + 3.9) \times \frac{1}{2} + \frac{1}{2}(3.9 + 7) \times \frac{1}{2}$
$\qquad = \frac{1}{2} \times \frac{1}{2}\{3 + 2(6.1 + 7 + 6.4 + 5 + 3.6 + 3 + 3.9) + 7\}$ (1)
$\qquad = 20$ square units

Finding the area by a more sophisticated method, outside the GCSE

> **Remember**
>
> The area of a trapezium is $\frac{1}{2}(a + b)h$ where a and b are the lengths of the parallel sides and h is the distance between them.

course, also gives the result of 20 square units. The trapezium rule does not always give such accuracy, but this example shows that it is a very good method.

Let's look back over the last example, paying particular attention to the line marked (1).

If we put it into words, it would be something like this.

$A = \frac{1}{2} \times \frac{1}{2}\{3 + 7 + 2(6.1 + 7 + 6.4 + 5 + 3.6 + 3 + 3.9)\}$

Area is half the width times the sum of the first and last y-values and twice the sum of all the other y-values.

★★EXERCISE 6.5

1   The diagram represents the cross-section of a canal tunnel, all dimensions are given in metres.

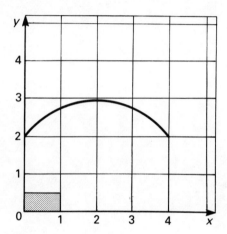

The x-axis represents the water level. The tow-path is shown shaded and its surface is $\frac{1}{2}$ m above the water.

The equation of the roof is given by $y = 3 - \dfrac{(x-2)^2}{4}$ where the y-axis is shown.

Using graph paper and taking 2 cm to represent 1m on each axis:
(a) draw accurately $y = x^2$ and then transform it to draw the roof section
(b) complete the diagram of the cross-section
(c) find the slope of the roof at the point where $x = 3$
(d) find the area of the air space between the roof and the water, using the trapezium rule with $\frac{1}{2}$m widths.

2   By drawing the curve and the necessary tangents find the slope of $y = x^2$ at the points where $x = -2, -1, 0, 1, 2$.
Additionally, find the slope where $x = -0.5$ and 0.5.
It will help if you draw a large graph.

Comment

This question is really an investigation!

On a second graph plot your slope values against corresponding values of x.

Can you draw any conclusions?

3   Find the area between $y = x^2 + 3x + 4$, the x-axis, the line $x = 1$ and the line $x = 3$ by using the trapezium rule with strips $\frac{1}{4}$ unit wide. You do not need to draw the graph.

★★Composite functions

We have spent some time working on functions. Now there is one last bit of work concerning them. We are going to look at composite functions which are the compositions of two or more functions.

Consider $f(x) = 2x + 1$.

What has been done to x to make the function?

- $\times 2$
- $+ 1$

So two things have been done and $2x + 1$ is a composition of the two functions:

- multiply by 2   mathematically $g(x) = 2x$
- add 1   mathematically $h(x) = x + 1$

Our function is $hg(x)$ which is the function h of the function g.

$\begin{aligned} hg(x) &= h(2x) &&\text{carrying out the function g which is} &&\times 2 \\ &= 2x + 1 &&\text{carrying out the function h which is} &&+ 1 \end{aligned}$

How about $gh(x)$?

$\begin{aligned} gh(x) &= g(x + 1) &&\text{carrying out the function h which is} &&+ 1 \\ &= 2(x + 1) &&\text{carrying out the function g which is} &&\times 2 \end{aligned}$

> $f(x)$ may look odd but it is just another way of writing the equation.

★★EXERCISE 6.6

1   $f(x) = x^2$ $h(x) = x + 1$ $g(x) = 3x$
    Find
    (a) $fh(x)$ (b) $fg(x)$ (c) $gh(x)$ (d) $hg(x)$ (e) $gf(x)$
    (f) $fgh(x)$ (g) $fhg(x)$ (h) $ghf(x)$ (i) $ffg(x)$ (j) $hhh(x)$.

2   A composite function pq is defined by $pq(x) = (x - 2)^3$.
    Find $p(x)$ and $q(x)$.

3   Find the three functions of which $\dfrac{(x + 2)^3}{5}$ is a composition.

    Express the function in the form $pqr(x)$.

4   $f(x) = 2x$ and $gf(x) = 2x + 3$.
    Find $g(x)$.

5   Can you find a function, $f(x)$, for which $ff(x) = x$?

Solutions to exercises

SOLUTIONS TO EXERCISE 6.1

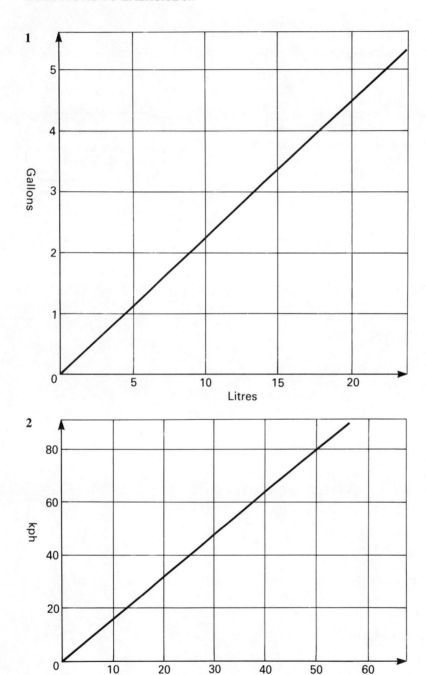

Comment

The gallons scale was chosen to make the conversion to gallons and pints easier: there are eight pints in one gallon.

3

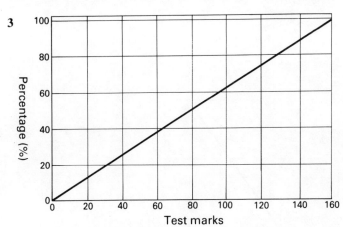

4

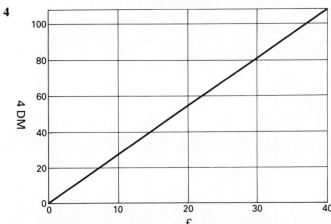

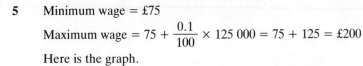

5 Minimum wage = £75

Maximum wage = $75 + \dfrac{0.1}{100} \times 125\,000 = 75 + 125 = £200$

Here is the graph.

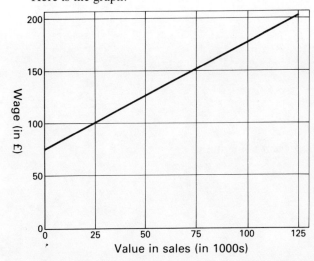

6   35 hours at £4.50 = £157.50
This coincides with point A on the graph.
20 hours at £6.80 = £136
This is section AB of the graph.

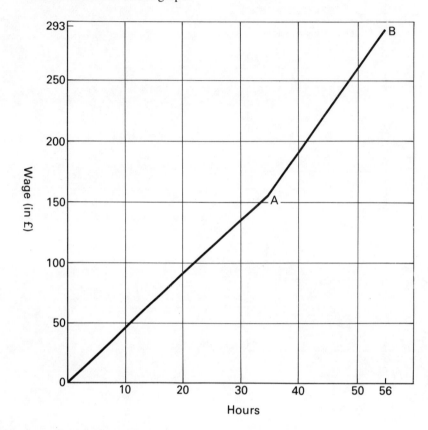

SOLUTIONS TO EXERCISE 6.2

1   Yes

2   Yes

3   No xy is degree 2

4   No y^2 is degree 2

5   No $\dfrac{1}{y} = y^{-1}$ i.e. degree^{-1}

6   Yes

7   Yes. You may think this equation does not represent a line but it does: think about it.

8   Yes

9   No $\sqrt{x} = x^{\frac{1}{2}}$, $\sqrt{y} = y^{\frac{1}{2}}$ i.e. degree $\frac{1}{2}$

10   No   degree 2

SOLUTIONS TO EXERCISE 6.3

All the graphs are half-size, or is it quarter size? A fair question – answer later.

1    $\left.\begin{array}{l} x = 0, y = -1 \\ x = 6, y = 11 \end{array}\right\}$ two points are $(0, -1)$ and $(6, 11)$.

     $x = 2, y = 3$ the check point.

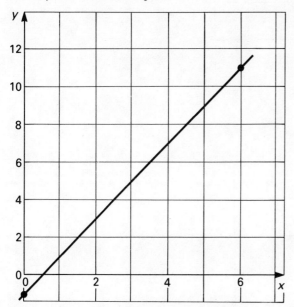

2    $x = -4 \;\Rightarrow\; 3y - 8 + 3 = 0 \;\Rightarrow\; y = \frac{5}{3}$

     $x = 2 \;\Rightarrow\; 3y + 4 + 3 = 0 \;\Rightarrow\; y = -\frac{7}{3}$

     So the points to plot are $(-4, \frac{5}{3})$ and $(2, -\frac{7}{3})$.

     Check point: $x = 0 \;\Rightarrow\; 3y + 3 = 0$

     $\therefore (0, -1)$

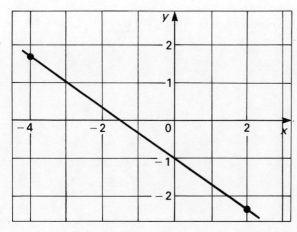

3 $x = -4 \Rightarrow 5y + 8 = 5 \Rightarrow y = -\frac{3}{5}$
  $x = 2 \Rightarrow 5y - 4 = 5 \Rightarrow y = \frac{9}{5}$
  Check point: $x = 0 \Rightarrow 5y = 5 \Rightarrow y = 1$

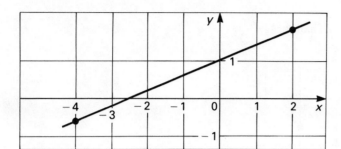

4 $x = -2 \Rightarrow 2y - 6 = 6 \Rightarrow y = 6$
  $x = 4 \Rightarrow 2y + 12 = 6 \Rightarrow y = -3$
  Check point: $x = 0 \Rightarrow y = 3$

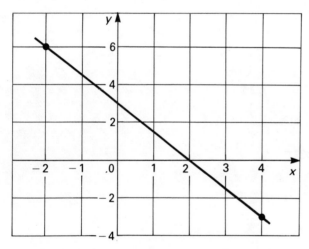

5   Many people think this question does not make sense, but it does.
  The graph of $x = 3$ is the line joining all the points where $x = 3$.
  And similarly for $y = 2$.

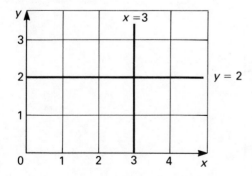

SOLUTIONS TO EXERCISE 6.4

1   Table of values

x	0.5	1	2	3	4	5	6
y	4	2	1	-7	-5	-4	-3

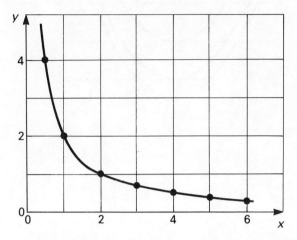

2   Table of values

x	0	1	2	3	4	5
y	3	7	5	3	7	23

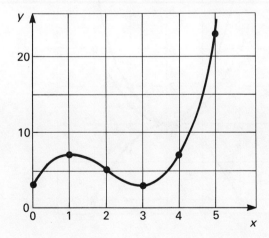

3   Table of values

x	-2	-1	0	1	2
x^2	4	1	0	1	4
$x^2 + 2$	6	3	2	3	6
$x^2 - 1$	3	0	-1	0	3

y intercept $= k$

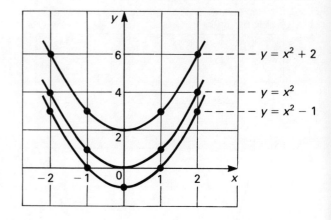

4   Table of values

x	-2	-1	0	1	2
x^2	4	1	0	1	4
$2x^2$	8	2	0	2	8
$-x^2$	-4	-1	0	-1	-4

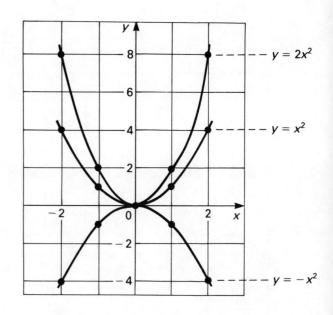

5   Table of values

x	x^2	$(x-2)^2$	$(x+3)^2$
-4	$-$	$-$	1
-3	9	$-$	0
-2	4	$-$	1
-1	1	9	4
0	0	4	9
1	1	1	$-$
2	4	0	$-$
3	9	1	$-$
4	$-$	4	$-$
5	$-$	9	$-$

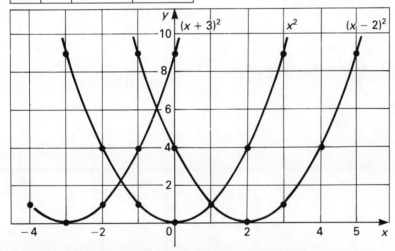

6   In question 3 the effect of altering the constant from 0 to $+2$ and to -1 was to move the curve two units up and one unit down from the starting position. Such a movement, where the curve keeps the same size and shape but slides across the paper is called a **translation.**

In question 4 the effect of multiplying by 2 was to stretch the curve upwards : this is sometimes called a **scaling.**

Multiplying by -1 did not stretch or alter the shape but it did cause a **reflection** in the x-axis.

How about multiplying by, say, -3? This results in **stretching** by a factor of 3 and **reflecting** in the x-axis.

Question 5 is similar to question 3 except that the translations are to the left and the right.

7   Table of values

x	-2	-1	0	1	2	3	4
$x^2 - 2x - 1$	7	2	-1	-2	-1	2	7

The line and curve intersect at $(-0.3, -0.3)$ and $(3.3, 3.3)$.
At these two points the x values, -0.3 and 3.3, give the same value
for y when substituted in $y = x$ or $y = x^2 - 2x - 1$. These
values satisfy both equations $y = x$ and $y = x^2 - 2x - 1$ at the
same time, i.e. simultaneously.

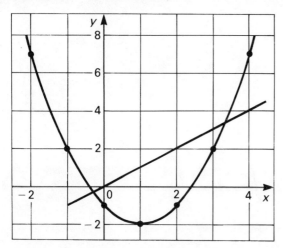

8   Table of values

x	$(x - 2)^2$	$\dfrac{(x + 8)}{2}$
-1	9	$-$
0	4	4
1	1	$-$
2	0	5
3	1	$-$
4	4	6
5	9	

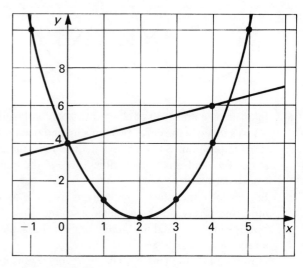

$y = x^2 - 4x + 4 = (x - 2)^2$

∴ both equations are shown on the graph we have drawn and the
solutions are where the graphs intersect.
∴ solutions are $(0, 4)$ and $(4.5, 6.2)$.

9 $2y + x = 5 \Rightarrow x = 0, y = 2\frac{1}{2}$ and $x = 3, y = 1$
$2y = x + 1 \Rightarrow x = 0, y = \frac{1}{2}$ and $x = 3, y = 4$
The solution is where the lines cross.
$x = 2, y = 1\frac{1}{2}$

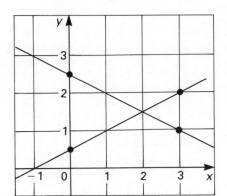

Comment

The question gave no guide on which values of x to use. This is normal in questions of this type and you have to be prepared to draw a rough diagram first to find out where the lines are and to get an approximate idea of where they cross.

10   Firstly you have to find a link between the graphs you are asked to draw and the equation you have to solve. This is done by inspection.
$x^2 + x - 6 = 0$
$\Rightarrow x^2 = 6 - x \Rightarrow$ finding where $y = x^2$ and $y = 6 - x$ meet.
$\Rightarrow$ the equation is solved for $x = -3$ and $x = 2$.

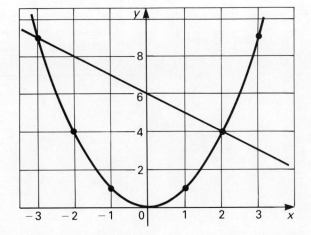

11   This is similar to question 10.

$x^2 - x - 2 = 0$

$\Rightarrow \quad x^2 = x + 2$

$\therefore$ draw $y = x^2$ and $y = x + 2$

The solutions are $x = -1$ and $x = 2$.

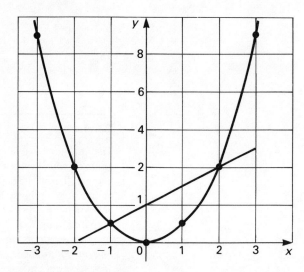

12 $0 \leqslant y \leqslant 2$ means the values of y above the x-axis and below $y = 2$ and including both lines.

$x \leqslant 3$ means the values of x to the left of $x = 3$ and including $x = 3$.

$y < x$ means the area below the line $y = x$ but not including the line.

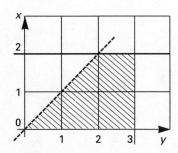

Comment

Note how we show whether or not a line is included : if the line is included it is solid and if it is not it is dotted.

13 It sometimes seems difficult to decide which side of a line to shade.
We have drawn $4y + 3x = 6$ and we have to shade $4y > 6 - 3x$.
It helps to transform both these into
$y = \frac{6}{4} - \frac{3}{4}x$ the equation of the line, and
$y > \frac{6}{4} - \frac{3}{4}x$ the area to be shaded.
The $>$ then means the area above the line, as in the diagram.

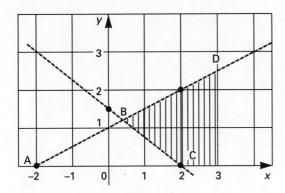

The area enclosed is DBC.
Considering AB: the equation is $2y = x + 2 \Rightarrow y = \frac{x}{2} + \frac{2}{2}$
The area is below the line $\therefore y < \frac{x}{2} + \frac{2}{2} \Rightarrow 2y < x + 2$

Then the area is defined as the area in which
$2y < x = 2,\qquad 4y < 6 - 3x \qquad$ and $\qquad y > 0.$

14 The equation is $y = \frac{1}{2}x$.
The tables are:

x	1	2	3	4	5
$y = 2x$	2	4	6	8	10

and

x	2	4	6	8	10
$y = \frac{1}{2}x$	1	2	3	4	5

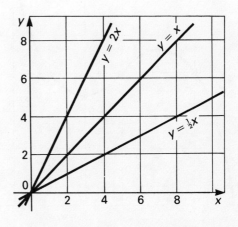

Conclusion: The x and y values have been interchanged i.e. what was x on one graph is y on the other and vice versa. When this happens the two functions are the **inverses** of each other. So $y = 2x$ is the inverse function of $y = \frac{1}{2}x$ and $y = \frac{1}{2}x$ is the inverse function of $y = 2x$.

$y = 2x$ is the function which converts 3 into 6 and $y = \frac{1}{2}x$ is the function which converts 6 back into 3 again.

A function and its inverse are always reflections of each other in the line $y = x$.

Investigation

Your calculator is full of functions and their inverses. Experiment, incuding chains, even if you do not yet understand the functions.

---

15   Table of values

x	-4	-3.5	-3	-2	-1	0	1	1.5	2
y	-15	-5.6	0	3	0	-3	0	5.6	15

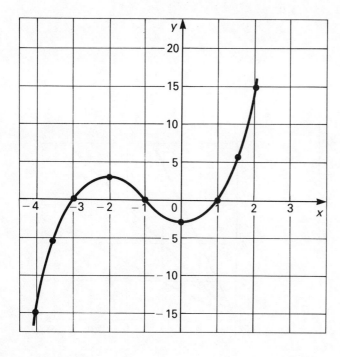

16 The symmetry will appear only when the units are the same size on each axis, as in this question.

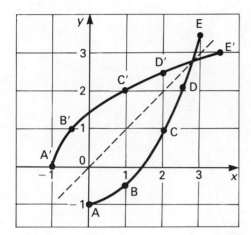

A', B', C', D' and E' are reflections of A, B, C, D and E respectively in the line $y = x$.

Remember that the inverse function is the one which reverses everything. Firstly we look at our function and see how it is made up.

Comment

Compare this with transformation of formulae in Chapter 5, page 63.

$\dfrac{x^2}{2} - 1$ is formed by:

1 squaring $\Rightarrow x^2$

2 dividing by 2 $\Rightarrow \dfrac{x^2}{2}$

3 subtracting 1 $\Rightarrow \dfrac{x^2}{2} - 1$

The inverse function is formed by doing the inverse (opposite) of each of the above and in reverse order,

$\Rightarrow$ add 1 $\qquad\qquad \Rightarrow x + 1$

multiply by 2 $\qquad \Rightarrow 2(x + 1)$

find the square root $\Rightarrow \sqrt{2(x + 1)}$

The original function could have been written as $f(x) = \dfrac{x^2}{2} - 1$

and then the inverse is written $\qquad\qquad f^{-1}(x) = \sqrt{2(x + 1)}$

SOLUTIONS TO EXERCISE 6.5

1 **(a)** Points marked ● and numbered 1 are points on $y = x^2$.
Points marked ● and numbered 2 are points on $y = (x - 2)^2$.

Points marked ● and numbered 3 are points on $y = \dfrac{(x - 2)^2}{4}$

Points marked ● and numbered 4 are points on $y = \dfrac{-(x - 2)^2}{4}$

Points marked ● and numbered 5 are points on $y = 3 - \dfrac{(x - 2)^2}{4}$

(b)

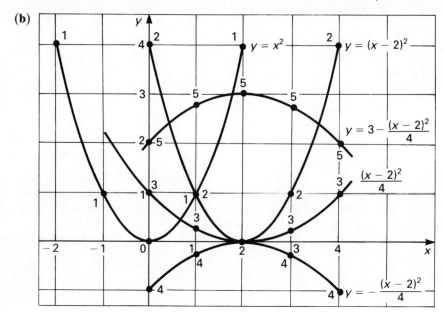

(c)

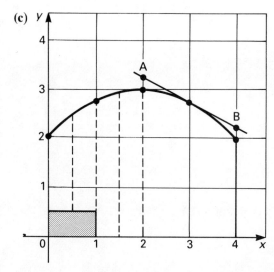

$$\text{Slope of AB} = \frac{y_A - y_B}{x_A - y_B}$$

$$= \frac{3.25 - 2.25}{2 - 4}$$

$$= \frac{1}{-2} = -0.5.$$

(d) $\because$ symmetry area required $= 2 \times$ area between $\quad x = 0 \quad$ and $\quad x = 2$.

$A = 2 \times \frac{1}{2} \times \frac{1}{2} \times \{2 + 3 + 2\,(2.4 + 2.75 + 2.9)\} - \frac{1}{2} \times 1$

$\quad = 10.05 \text{ m}^2$

> This is the tow-path (shaded).

2 The exact values of the slopes are:

x	slope
-2	-4
-1	-2
-0.5	-1
0	0
0.5	1
1	2
2	4

When these results are drawn on graph paper a straight line is formed.

3 $y = x^2 + 3x + 4$

x	1	1.25	1.5	1.75	2	2.25	2.5	2.75	3
y	8	9.3	10.8	12.3	14	15.8	17.8	19.8	22

$A = \frac{1}{2} \times \frac{1}{4} \times \{8 + 22 + 2\,(9.3 + 10.8 + 12.3 + 14 + 15.8 + 17.8 + 19.8)\}$

$\quad = 28.7 \text{ square units}$

The accurate answer is $28\frac{2}{3}$ square units.

SOLUTIONS TO EXERCISE 6.6

1 **(a)** $\text{fh}(x) = \text{f}(x + 1) = (x + 1)^2$

(b) $\text{fg}(x) = \text{f}(3x) = 9x^2$

(c) $\text{gh}(x) = \text{g}(x + 1) = 3(x + 1)$

(d) $\text{hg}(x) = \text{h}(3x) = 3x + 1$

(e) $\text{gf}(x) = \text{g}(x^2) = 3x^2$

(f) $\text{fgh}(x) = \text{fg}(x + 1) = \text{f}(3(x + 1)) = 9(x + 1)^2$

(g) $\text{fhg}(x) = \text{fh}(3x) = \text{f}(3x + 1) = (3x + 1)^2$

(h) $\text{ghf}(x) = \text{gh}(x^2) = \text{g}(x^2 + 1) = 3(x^2 + 1)$

(i) $\text{ffg}(x) = \text{ff}(3x) = \text{f}(9x^2) = 81x^4$

(j) $\text{hhh}(x) = \text{hh}(x + 1) = \text{h}(x + 2) = x + 3$

2 $\text{pq}(x) = (x - 2)^3 \ \Rightarrow \ \text{p}(\text{q}(x)) = (x - 2)^3 \quad \therefore \ \text{p}(x) = x^3$

$\Rightarrow \ \text{q}(x) = x - 2$

3 The functions are $\quad x + 2 = \text{r}(x), \quad x^3 = \text{q}(x), \quad \dfrac{x}{5} = \text{p}(x)$

$\text{pqr}(x) = \dfrac{(x + 2)^3}{5}$

4 $\text{g}(2x) = 2x + 3 \ \Rightarrow \ \text{g}(x) = x + 3$

5 $\text{f}(x) = \dfrac{1}{x}$

7 Mensuration

After Chapters 5 and 6 we all deserve a little respite and this chapter should be a lot easier than what has gone before. Once again there is an assessment exercise with answers to start with and this should be used in the usual way.

In this concise unit you will learn:

- names of **shapes**
- the difference between **area** and **volume**
- formulae for **calculating areas**
- formulae for **calculating volumes**

and finally there are some investigations.

Mensuration assessment test

1   Find the area of a rectangle 12 cm long and 7 cm wide.

2   Find the surface area of a cube of edge 3 inches.

3   A cylindrical can has diameter 6.5 cm and height 11 cm. Find its surface area including the ends, and its volume.

4   A pyramid has height 6 feet and a square base of side 3.5 feet. Find its volume.

5   Find the volume of the shape shown.

6   A sphere has radius of 13 cm.
    Find **(a)** its surface area **(b)** its volume.

7   The area of a circle is 78.5 cm².
    Find **(a)** its radius **(b)** its circumference.

ANSWERS TO MENSURATION ASSESSMENT TEST

1   84 cm²

2   54 sq in

3   291.0 cm², 365 cm³

4   24.5 cu ft

5   382.5 cm³

6   **(a)** 2123.7 cm² **(b)** 9202.7 cm³

7   **(a)** 5 cm   **(b)** 31.4 cm

Area, volume and length

There are two quantities with which we are concerned very often in everyday life, and the study of these takes up most of this chapter. They are **area** and **volume**; and in the process we are bound to deal with **length**. **Length** involves measurements in *one* dimension; examples of units of length are inches (in), yards (yd), centimetres (cm) and metres (m).

Area is the *size* of a surface and it involves measurements in *two* dimensions; examples of units of area are square inches (sq in), square yards (sq yd), square centimetres (cm²) and square metres (m²).

Volume is the name given to the *amount of space* inside a shape and it involves measurements in *three* dimensions; units used might be cubic inches (cu in), cubic yards (cu yd), cubic centimetres (cm³), cubic metres (m³).

Many of the shapes we have to deal with in the GCSE course fall into a particular category; recognising this can be helpful, particularly when finding volumes. The category is **prisms**.

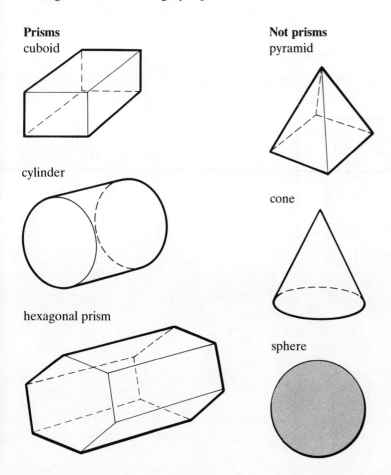

Prisms
cuboid

cylinder

hexagonal prism

Not prisms
pyramid

cone

sphere

Can you see what condition is necessary for a solid shape to be a prism? The answer is that, in at least one direction, all the edges must be **parallel** to each other; or in other words, the shape and size of the cross-section is always the same.

Now we can work out a simple area and a simple volume to help establish which is which.

ABCD is a rectangle which measures 4 ft long by 3 ft wide.

The squares are each of edge 1 ft.

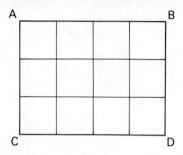

The area of each square is $1 \times 1 = 1$ sq ft and the area of ABCD is 12 sq ft ($4 \times 3 = 12$ sq ft).

Now look at this one.

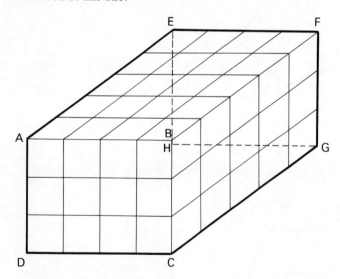

ABCDEFGH is a rectangular block, a **cuboid**, which measures 4 ft × 3 ft × 5 ft. It is shown divided up into blocks each measuring 1 ft × 1 ft × 1 ft. Each of these small blocks has a volume of 1 cu ft. If you study the diagram you should be able to see that there are 60 blocks, $4 \times 3 \times 5$, altogether i.e. the volume of the cuboid is 60 cu ft.

Calculating areas and volumes

The secret of working out areas and volumes is simply a matter of knowing the correct formula and being able to substitute in it.
Firstly we shall look at areas.

Rectangle $\quad\quad A = lb \quad\quad\quad$ Area = length times breadth.

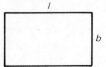

Triangle $\quad\quad\quad A = \frac{1}{2}bh \quad\quad\quad$ Area = half base times perpendicular height.

★Parallelogram $\quad A = bh \quad\quad\quad$ Area = base times perpendicular height.

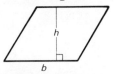

> **Remember**
>
> π is a Greek letter, said 'pi', and used to represent the ratio of the circumference of a circle to its radius. It is a constant irrational number.

★Circle $\quad\quad\quad A = \pi r^2 \quad\quad\quad$ Area = π times radius squared.

★Sector of circle $\quad A = \dfrac{n}{360}\pi r^2 \quad$ Area = $\dfrac{\text{sector angle}}{360}$ times π times radius squared

★★Trapezium $\quad A = \frac{1}{2}(a + b)h \quad$ Area = half sum of parallel side times perpendicular distance between them.

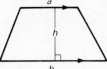

★★Sphere $\quad\quad A = 4\pi r^2 \quad\quad$ Area = four π times the radius squared.

Note

The sphere is mentioned here because, although it is a three dimensional shape its area cannot be derived from anything else; in contrast, a cube has 6 square faces, so the area can easily be found.

And now for volumes!

Cuboid $\qquad V = lbh \quad$ Volume = length times breadth times height.

In this case we have a triangular prism.
The cylinder (above) is also a prism.

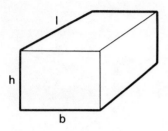

★Cylinder $\qquad V = \pi r^2 l \quad$ Volume = π times radius squared times length.

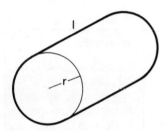

★★Sphere $\qquad V = \frac{4}{3}\pi r^3 \quad$ Volume = four thirds times π times radius cubed.

★★Prism $\qquad V = Al \quad$ Volume = area of cross section times length.

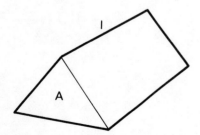

★★**Pyramid** $V = \frac{1}{3}Ah$ Volume = one third times area of base times height.

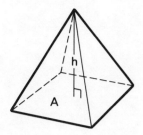

> Shapes like these, which come to a point, all have the same formula:
> $\frac{1}{3}$ times area of base times perpendicular height.
> This is true whether or not the shapes are symmetrical.

★★**Tetrahedron** $V = \frac{1}{3}Ah$ Volume = one third times area of base times height.

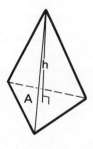

★★**Cone** $V = \frac{1}{3}Ah$ Volume = one third times area of base times height.

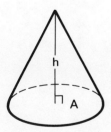

The areas and volumes which we shall have to find will be of the shapes listed or simple combinations of them.

EXERCISE 7.1

1   Find the area of a triangle of base 5 cm and height 7 cm.

★★ 2   The triangle in question 1 forms the base of a tetrahedron of height 12 cm. Find its volume.

3   An ordinary house brick measures 21 cm by 10 cm by 7 cm.
Find   (a) its volume   (b) the area of its surface.

4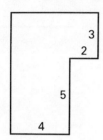

Find the perimeter and the area of the shape shown. All dimensions are in inches.

★★ 5   The shape in question 4 is the cross-section of a solid iron bar 3 feet long. Find the volume of the bar in cubic feet.
Find also the area of the surface of the bar, excluding the ends.

> Watch the units.

★ 6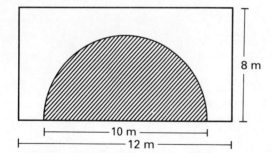

The diagram is symmetrical and it represents a semi-circular lawn (shaded) in a rectangular garden. Find the area of the flower beds (unshaded).

★ 7   The water tank in a house measures 1 m by 0.8 m by 0.6 m high. Water pours into the tank at a constant rate of 0.08 m³ per minute. If the tank is empty to start with, how deep will the water be after 4 minutes?

> The tank is a cuboid.

8 The water tank in question 7 has to be coated with rust proofing material, inside and out. The tank does not have a lid. What is the area to be coated and what would it cost at £3 per m²?

★★ **9**

The diagram shows a cross-section of a wooden diabolo which is cut from a cylinder, shown dotted.
(a) Find the volume of the original cylinder.
(b) Find the volume of the diabolo.
(c) Find the fraction of the original wood which is used.

> A diabolo is like two cones joined at the points.

★★ **10**

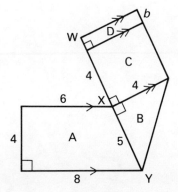

Whilst doodling during a boring Heads of Department meeting, the Head of Mathematics produced the diagram shown. All the lengths are in centimetres.
(a) Find the areas of the shapes A, B and C.
(b) Find the dimensions of area D so that WXY divides the area of the total shape equally.

Investigations

The subject of areas and volumes provides scope for many investigations.

1   On a standard A4 sheet of graph paper, find how many squares you can draw subject to the following conditions.
(**a**) All sides must be in cm units – no fractions of a centimetre.
(**b**) There must not be two squares the same size.
(**c**) The squares must not overlap.

2   Find the maximum area which can be enclosed by a piece of string 60 cm long in both the following cases.
(**a**) The shape must be a quadrilateral (four straight sides).
(**b**) It can take any shape.
You will find a piece of graph paper useful.

3   By cutting squares from the corners of a piece of A4 paper and then folding, you can make an open box (without a lid). The box is to hold salt.
Find the size of the squares that need to be cut out so that the amount of salt that can be stored is a maximum.

4   The shape which is cut out of a flat sheet and then folded to make a container or a three-dimensional shape is called a **net**.
The net of a tetrahedron looks like this.

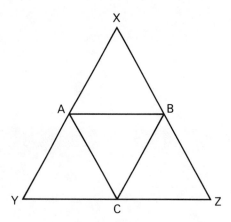

Folds would be made along AB, BC and CD to bring X, Y and Z together and so make a tetrahedron.
If you like practical projects use your library to research more complicated nets and make up some shapes.

Solutions to exercises

SOLUTIONS TO EXERCISE 7.1

1 $A = \frac{1}{2}bh = \frac{1}{2} \times 5 \times 7 = 17.5$ cm²

2 $V = \frac{1}{3}Ah = \frac{1}{3} \times 17.5 \times 12 = 70$ cm³

3 **(a)** $V = 21 \times 10 \times 7 = 1470$ cm³

  (b) $A = \quad 2 \times 21 \times 10 \quad + 2 \times 21 \times 7 \quad + \quad 2 \times 10 \times 7$
  $\qquad\qquad$ top and bottom $\qquad$ both sides $\qquad$ both ends

  $\qquad = 854$ cm²

4 Perimeter (distance round the edges) $= 4 + 5 + 2 + 3 + 6 + 8 = 28$ in

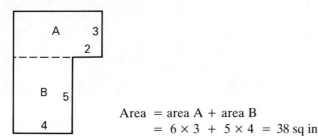

Area = area A + area B
$\qquad = 6 \times 3 + 5 \times 4 = 38$ sq in

5 The bar is a prism and $V = \dfrac{38}{144} \times 3 = 0.79$ cu ft.

> This 144 changes the 38 sq in to sq ft.

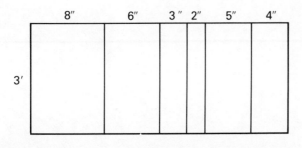

The surface is one large rectangle folded along the lines drawn.

$A = \dfrac{28}{12} \times 3 = 7$ sq ft

> When using feet and inches, it is common to use ′ for feet and ″ for inches.

6 $A = 8 \times 12 - \frac{1}{2} \times \pi \times 5^2$
  $= 56.7$ m²

7 Water flows at 0.08 m³/min
  ∴ after 4 minutes there are $4 \times 0.08 = 0.32$ m³ of water in the tank.
  If h is the height of the water then the volume $= 1 \times 0.8 \times h = 0.8h$

  ∴ $0.8h = 0.32 \quad \Rightarrow \quad h = \dfrac{0.32}{0.8} = 0.4$ m

> If you look at these two solutions and follow them through carefully you should appreciate the warning about units.

8 Area = $(1 \times 0.8$ + $2 \times 1 \times 0.6$ + $2 \times 0.8 \times 0.6) \times$ 2
            bottom   two sides   two ends   inside and out
         = 4.96 m²
   Cost = $3 \times 4.96 = £14.88$

9 (a) Volume of cylinder $= \pi \times (\frac{7}{2})^2 \times 12 = 461.8$ cm³

   (b) Volume of diabolo $= 2 \times \frac{1}{3} \times \pi \times (\frac{7}{2})^2 \times 6 = 153.9$ cm³

   (c) Fraction used $= \dfrac{2 \times \frac{1}{3} \times \pi \times (\frac{7}{2})^2 \times 6}{\pi \times (\frac{7}{2})^2 \times 12}$

        $= \frac{1}{3}$

10 (a) Area A $= \frac{1}{2} \times (6 + 8) \times 4 = 28$ cm²
       Area B $= \frac{1}{2} \times 5 \times 4 = 10$ cm²
       Area C $= 4 \times 4 = 16$ cm²

   (b) A $= 28$ cm²
       B + C $= 10 + 16 = 26$ cm²
       $\therefore$ D $= 2$ cm²
       Length of D is 4 cm $\Rightarrow$ $4 \times b = 2$ $\Rightarrow$ $b = \frac{1}{2}$ cm
       $\therefore$ dimensions of D are $l = 4$ cm, $b = \frac{1}{2}$ cm.

8 The right-angled triangle – Pythagoras and trigonometry

In this chapter you will be looking at right-angled triangles, from two points of view. This should mean that you find out everything you need to know about such triangles.

By the end of the chapter you will be able to solve any problems concerning angles and sides and you will be able to apply the techniques to realistic problems. In the process you will become familiar with:

- the **theorem of Pythagoras**
- **Pythagorean triangles**
- **trigonometry**: **sine**, **cosine** and **tangent**
- **using trigonometry** to find a **side**
- **using trigonometry** to find an **angle**
- angles of **elevation** and **depression**
- **bearings**.

> A theorem is a proved result which can be quoted and used.
> A right angle = 90°.

Introduction

The right-angled triangle is a very common shape. It is one which appears often in theoretical problems and in everyday practical situations. Many other problems concerning shape can be simplified by reducing them to problems about right-angled triangles.

In this chapter we shall look at two aspects of the right-angled triangle:

- Pythagoras' theorem: a geometrical result concerning areas and the lengths of the sides of the triangle
- trigonometry: arithmetical ratios involving the sides and the angles of the triangle.

★Pythagoras' theorem

This is a theorem which is used in geometry and, like many simple rules, it is very useful. It is concerned with, and applies only to right-angled triangles. Using it we can:

- calculate the third side of a right-angled triangle if any two are known
- test for a right angle
- solve many problems relating to everyday situations.

> **Remember**
> **Pythagoras**
>
> Pythagoras was a Greek who lived between 595 and 495 BC. He was the founder of the subject of geometry. He also:
> - founded a religious school
> - discovered the musical octave
> - attached interpretions to numbers
> - founded numerology.
>
> He was the first to prove this theorem, although it was used 1000 years previously by the Babylonians. There now exist over 350 proofs of the theorem.

★The right-angled triangle

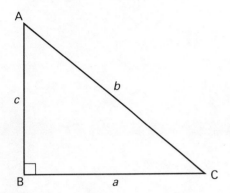

Capital letters are used to identify the vertices or corners, and angles where possible.

Small letters are used for lengths of sides: note that the side of length *a* is opposite to angle A etc.

The side opposite the right angle is called the **hypotenuse** (may also be spelt hypoteneuse).

The right angle is denoted by a special symbol which looks like a small square.

Generally, angles are usually marked like this,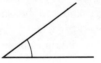

but right angles are marked like this.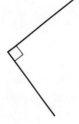

Before going on, see if you can answer these questions.

1 What is an acute-angled triangle?

2 What is an obtuse-angled triangle?

Pythagoras' theorem is actually a theorem about areas, although this aspect is usually forgotten when it is being used.

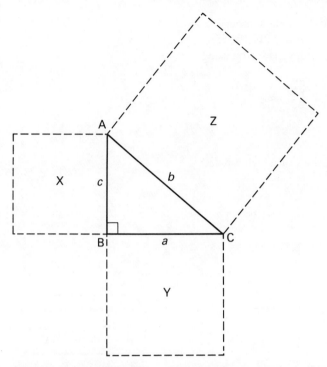

The theorem states that the total area of the two small squares is equal to the area of the big one.

i.e. area X + area Y = area Z

but area X = AB^2, area Y = BC^2 and area Z = AC^2.

$AB^2 + BC^2 = AC^2$

or, in small letters,

$c^2 + a^2 = b^2$

Eureka! We now have an algebraic equation and if we know any two of a, b and c we can work out the third.

★EXAMPLE

In the right-angled triangle ABC, right-angled at B, find b if $c = 4$ cm and $a = 6$ cm.

Solution

$b^2 = a^2 + c^2$ Pythagoras

Substituting, $b^2 = 6^2 + 4^2$

         $b^2 = 36 + 16 = 52$

         $b = \sqrt{52}$ Taking the square root of both sides.

         $b = 7.2$ cm

Remember

By writing 'Pythagoras' here we are showing that we know why $b^2 = a^2 + c^2$; it is good style.

One decimal place is usually sufficiently accurate, unless otherwise specified; it would be unneccessarily precise to write $b = 7.211\ 102\ 551$. After the line $b^2 = 6^2 + 4^2$ you could go straight to the answer by using your calculator. The sequence is:

Calculator sequence:	6	x^2	$+$	4	x^2	$=$	$\sqrt{}$
Display:	6	36	36	4	16	52	7.211102551

★EXAMPLE

Find the hypotenuse given that the two shorter sides of a right-angled triangle are 13.7 in and 19.4 in.

Solution

$h^2 = 13.7^2 + 19.4^2$ Pythagoras

$h = 23.7$ in   by calculator

The converse of the theorem is also useful.

If, in a triangle, $a^2 = b^2 + c^2$ then the triangle has a right angle at A.

> **Converse:** Opposite; simply, this means if $A = B$ then $B = A$.

★EXAMPLE

A triangle has sides of 7.5 cm, 10 cm and 12.5 cm.
Is it right-angled?

Solution

It is right-angled if $7.5^2 + 10^2 = 12.5^2$

$7.5^2 + 10^2 = 56.25 + 100$

$\qquad\qquad = 156.25$

$\qquad 12.5^2 = 156.25$

$\Rightarrow$ the triangle is right-angled.

★EXERCISE 8.1

In each of the following questions, find the length of the third side given that all the triangles are right-angled as indicated.

1   AB = 7.2 cm, BC = 5.9 cm, $B = 90°$

2   AB = 7.2 cm, BC = 5.9 cm, $C = 90°$

3      $p = 3$ in, $q = 4$ in, $R = 90°$

4      $x = 5$ cm, $y = 12$ cm, $Z = 90°$

5      $a = 35$ yd, $b = 51$ yd, $C = 90°$

★EXERCISE 8.2

In each of the following questions determine whether or not the triangle
is right-angled.

1    $x = 3.1$ cm, $y = 4.9$ cm, $z =$ 5.8 cm

2    $a = 80$ mm, $b = 150$ mm, $c = 170$ mm

3   KL = 13.2 yd, JK = 14.8 yd, TL = 8.7 yd

4    $p = 4''$, $q = 5''$, $r = 6''$

5   AB = 2.5 m, BC = 6.5 m, AC = 6.0 m

★Investigation

Try to find a rule for telling whether a triangle is acute-angled,
right-angled or obtuse-angled when you know the lengths of the sides.
Draw several triangles and observe the results when you apply the
right-angle test.

Remember

acute-angled triangle –
all angles less than 90°
obtuse-angled triangle –
one angle greater than
90°

★Two special triangles – Pythagorean triangles

Generally, right-angled triangles do not have integers for the lengths of
all three sides: if two of the sides have lengths which are integers the third
one will probably not. However, there are exceptions and we shall now
look at two of these. An investigation of this follows.)

You have already met the triangles in questions 3 and 4 of **Exercise 8.1**.
The most commonly used is the one in question 3 but they are:

An integer is a whole
number.

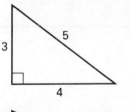

known as the five, twelve, thirteen triangle,
written 5, 12, 13 △

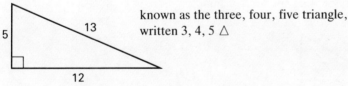

known as the three, four, five triangle,
written 3, 4, 5 △

If the lengths of the sides are halved, or trebled, or multiplied by any
number, the triangle is reduced or enlarged but it retains the same shape
– and its right angle.

An example of this was question 5 in **Exercise 8.2**. In this case the sides
were $5 \times \frac{1}{2}$ (2.5), $12 \times \frac{1}{2}$ (6.0) and $13 \times \frac{1}{2}$ (6.5).

You need to know these triangles and be able to spot them when they
appear in problems.

★EXAMPLE

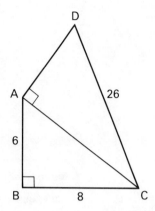

In the quadrilateral ABCD the angles and lengths are as marked.
Find the length of AD.

Solution

AC = 10 cm   ∵ △ABC is a 3, 4, 5 △
AD = 24 cm   ∵ △ADC is a 5, 12, 13 △
In each case the lengths have been doubled.

★EXERCISE 8.3

1   A rectangle has length $9\frac{1}{2}$ ft and width 6 ft. Find the length of its
     diagonal.

2   In general practice, when a ladder leans against a wall the distance
     up the wall the ladder reaches should be three times the distance
     the foot of the ladder is from the wall (for safety reasons). Find
     how far up a wall a 26 foot ladder should reach.

3   The light from a lamp is effective up to a distance of 16 ft.
     If it is suspended $7\frac{1}{2}$ ft above a level floor, find the area of floor
     which is effectively lit.

 4

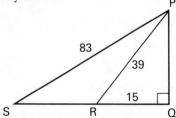

In the diagram, PR = 39, RQ = 15 and PS = 83.
Find the length of SR.

5   Find the side of a rhombus with diagonals of 12 cm and 8 cm.

6 A room has the shape of a pentagon (five straight sides) and it is thought that the angle at one corner is 90°. Describe how, using only a tape measure, this can be checked.

★★ **7** A rectangular box has base measurements 9 in by 12 in and it is 8 in high. Find the length of the longest stick which can be placed in the box.

8 Two cyclists set off from the same point at the same moment. One goes south at 10 mph and the other goes west at 12 mph.
How far apart are they after **(a)** 1 hour **(b)** 3 hours?

9 The pendulum on a clock is 18 inches long and it swings 3 inches horizontally either side of the vertical. How far, vertically, does the tip of the pendulum rise?

10 The difference in height above sea level between the hotel at Wasdale Head and the summit of Kirk Fell is 752 m. On the 1:25 000 map the distance between these points is 7.7 cm. What is the length of the actual walk from the hotel to the summit?

★Investigation

Triangles like the 3, 4, 5 and the 5, 12, 13 produce sets of three numbers which are called Pythagorean numbers or Pythagorean triples.
There is an infinite number of these triples.
Try **(a)** to find some more triples **(b)** to find a rule for forming triples.

3	4	5	produce the square numbers	9	16	25
5	12	13	produce the square numbers	25	144	169
7	24	25	produce the square numbers	49	576	625

Find a pattern between the numbers in these two columns and this one.

This is the first time we have met this one.

Continue by considering odd numbers in the first column.
Then consider even numbers in the first column starting with

8	15	17	produce the square numbers	64	225	289
10	24	26	produce the square numbers	100	576	676
12	35	37	produce the square numbers	144	1225	1369

This is a 5, 12, 13

★Trigonometry

So far we have concentrated on sides of the right-angled triangle. Now we shall have a look at the angles as well.

Let's begin with some practical work.

Draw any triangle, any size, but it must have a right-angle.

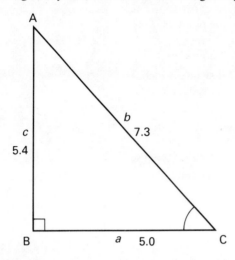

Measure a, b and c.

Work out
$$\frac{c}{b} = \frac{5.4}{7.3} = 0.74$$
$$\frac{a}{b} = \frac{5.0}{7.3} = 0.68$$
$$\frac{c}{a} = \frac{5.4}{5} = 1.08$$

In our example

Measure angle C. $C = 47.5°$

Using your calculator, enter: 47.5 sin   the display should show   0.74
                              47.5 cos   the display should show   0.68
                              47.5 tan   the display should show   1.09

Make sure it is in degree mode, not Rad or Grad.

Now repeat the whole exercise with a different triangle, and then do it a third time after which you should be able to form some conclusions.

Again, these triangles must be right-angled.

The conclusion can be summed up as

$$\sin C = \frac{c}{b}, \cos C = \frac{a}{b}, \tan C = \frac{c}{a}$$

These are known as the **trigonometric ratios**.

We call them trig ratios, for short.

Now to explain one or two points.

● sin is the abbreviation for sine

- cos is the abbreviation for cosine
- tan is the abbreviation for tangent
- trig is the common abbreviation for trigonometry, which is the branch of mathematics we are now considering.

Sine, cosine and tangent do not have any units, they are just numbers. Each is defined as one length divided by another.

Each of the equations involves one angle and two sides of the triangle and one of our biggest problems will be in deciding which one to use. The longest side in a right-angled triangle is the hypotenuse.

> **Remember**
>
> If you consider the difference between 6 cm/3 cm and 6 cm/3 you will be able to see why there are no units. Ratios do not have units.

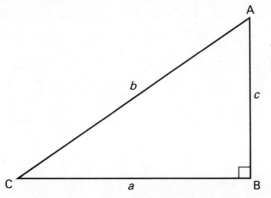

This side is opposite C and it is adjacent to A.

This side is opposite (across the triangle from) A and it is adjacent (next to) C.

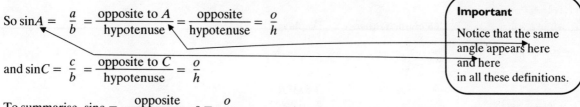

So $\sin A = \dfrac{a}{b} = \dfrac{\text{opposite to } A}{\text{hypotenuse}} = \dfrac{\text{opposite}}{\text{hypotenuse}} = \dfrac{o}{h}$

and $\sin C = \dfrac{c}{b} = \dfrac{\text{opposite to } C}{\text{hypotenuse}} = \dfrac{o}{h}$

> **Important**
>
> Notice that the same angle appears here and here in all these definitions.

To summarise, $\text{sine} = \dfrac{\text{opposite}}{\text{hypotenuse}} \quad s = \dfrac{o}{h}$

Now $\cos A = \dfrac{c}{b} = \dfrac{\text{adjacent to } A}{\text{hypotenuse}} = \dfrac{\text{adjacent}}{\text{hypotenuse}} = \dfrac{a}{h}$

and $\cos C = \dfrac{a}{b} = \dfrac{\text{adjacent to } C}{\text{hypotenuse}} = \dfrac{a}{h}$

To summarise, $\text{cosine} = \dfrac{\text{adjacent}}{\text{hypotenuse}} \quad c = \dfrac{a}{h}$

Finally, $\tan A = \dfrac{a}{c} = \dfrac{\text{opposite to } A}{\text{adjacent to } A} = \dfrac{\text{opposite}}{\text{adjacent}} = \dfrac{o}{a}$

and $\tan C = \dfrac{c}{a} = \dfrac{\text{opposite to } C}{\text{adjacent to } C} = \dfrac{\text{opposite}}{\text{adjacent}} = \dfrac{o}{a}$

To summarise, tangent $= \dfrac{\text{opposite}}{\text{adjacent}}$ $t = \dfrac{o}{a}$

A mnemonic –
something to help you
remember.

All this then reduces to

$$s = \frac{o}{h} \qquad c = \frac{a}{h} \qquad t = \frac{o}{a}$$

All this then reduces to

$$s = \frac{o}{h} \qquad c = \frac{a}{h} \qquad t = \frac{o}{a}$$

which is well remembered by many as | sohcahtoa. |

Now how do we use it?

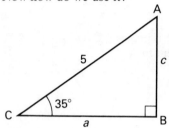

To find c:

Look at the triangle: we know $h = 5$ and $C = 35°$.
How does c lie in relation to C? It is opposite.
So we want something which connects angle, opposite and hypotenuse.
Scan through sohcahtoa to see where o and h are together.
Here! ⌐

$\therefore$ we use soh.

$\sin C = \dfrac{c}{h}$

$\sin 35° = \dfrac{c}{5}$

$\quad c = 5\sin 35°$

$\quad\ = 2.9$

Calculator sequence	Display
5	5
×	5
35	35
sin	0.5735764
=	2.8678822

To find a:
We have a choice of methods: Pythagoras or trigonometry.
We will use trigonometry.
Assess the problem: C is known ($35°$), h is known (5).
a is wanted and this is adjacent to C.
Now look for a and h $\Rightarrow$ cah

$$\Rightarrow \quad \cos C = \frac{a}{h}$$

$$\cos 35° = \frac{a}{5}$$

$$a = 5\cos 35° = 4.1$$

★EXAMPLE

Find A.

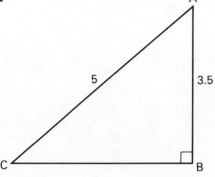

Solution

Assess the problem: $c = 3.5$ which is adjacent to A, $b = 5$ which is the hypotenuse.

We need a and h $\Rightarrow$ cah

$$\Rightarrow \quad \cos A = \frac{3.5}{5}$$
$$= 0.7$$
$$A = 45.6°$$

Calculator sequence	Display
3.5	3.5
÷	3.5
5	5
=	0.7
INV	0.7
cos	45.572996

> **Remember**
>
> $\sin^{-1}$, $\cos^{-1}$ and $\tan^{-1}$ are the inverse functions and you use these to turn a ratio, in this case $\frac{3.5}{5}$, into an angle.
>
> They are sometimes called arcsin, arccos and arctan.

★EXERCISE 8.4

1 Find x.

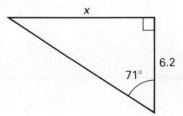

2 Find y.

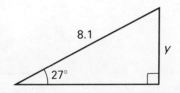

3 Find a.

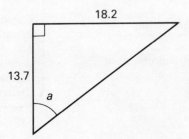

4 Find q.

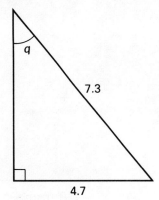

7.3

4.7

5 Find z.

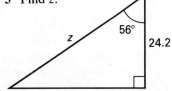

z 56° 24.2

★Angles

Angles are used to measure direction, vertically and horizontally.

★Vertically

Consider a man standing on a cliff.

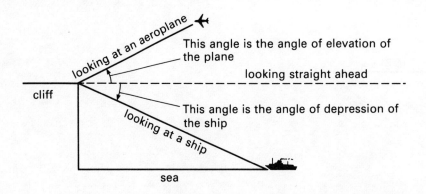

looking at an aeroplane

This angle is the angle of elevation of the plane

looking straight ahead

cliff

This angle is the angle of depression of the ship

looking at a ship

sea

Remember

Elevation is measured upwards from the horizontal and depression is measured downward from the horizontal.

★Horizontally

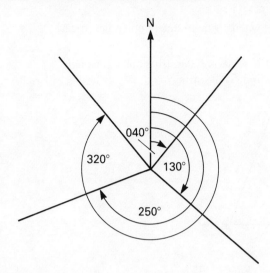

The diagram shows how directions are measured clockwise from the north line. These directions are called **bearings** and they can have any value up to 360°. In this system, if the bearing is less then 100° it starts with a zero, hence 040° as in the diagram. This is the system of **three figure bearings.**

★EXERCISE 8.5

1   From a cliff top 250 feet high, a ship is sighted at an angle of depression of 12.5°. How far away from the foot of the cliff is it?

2

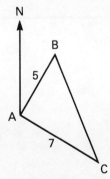

A, B and C are three points on level ground.
B is 5 km from A on a bearing of 030°.
C is 7 km from A on a bearing of 120°.

(**a**) Find how far C is from B.

(**b**) Find the bearing of C from B.

3   Find the angle of slope, with the horizontal, of a path which climbs 3 ft vertically for each 11 ft measured along its surface.

4 Find the elevation of the sun when a 9 metre telephone pole casts a shadow 14 metres long.

5 A kite is flying at a height of 75 yards and the string makes an angle of 37° with the ground. How long is the string?

6

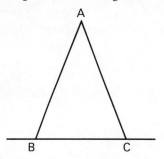

BAC represents a step ladder, opened up.
BA = AC = 6 ft
BC = 3.5 ft
Find the angle the ladder makes with the ground.

★★ **7**

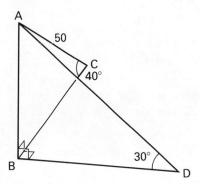

AB is a vertical mast and B, C and D are on level ground.
AC and AD are two of the stays supporting the mast.
AC is 50 ft long.
Find the lengths of AB and AD.

★★ **8** **(a)** Find the length of the diagonal of a cuboid which measures 6 cm × 3 cm × 2 cm.

(b) Find the angle this diagonal makes with the shortest edge.

9 One pylon is 15 km away from a man on a bearing of 040° and a second pylon is 11 km away on a bearing of 125°. Which one is further eastwards and by how much?

Solutions to exercises

SOLUTIONS TO EXERCISE 8.1

1

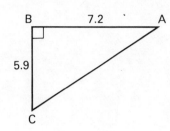

$AC^2 = 7.2^2 + 5.9^2$
$\quad\ = 51.84 + 34.81$
$\quad\ = 86.65$
$AC\ = 9.31$ cm

2

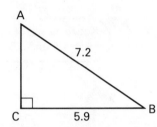

$7.2^2 = AC^2 + 5.9^2$
$\Rightarrow\ \ AC^2 = 7.2^2 - 5.9^2$
$\quad\quad\quad\ = 51.84 - 34.81$
$\quad\quad\quad\ = 17.03$
$AC = 4.1$ cm

3

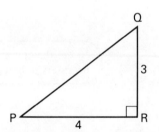

$r^2 = 3^2 + 4^2$
$\Rightarrow\ \ r = 5$ in

4 $z^2 = 5^2 + 12^2 \ \Rightarrow\ z = 13$ cm
5 $c^2 = 35^2 + 51^2 \ \Rightarrow\ c = 61.9$ yd

SOLUTIONS TO EXERCISE 8.2

1 $3.1^2 + 4.9^2 = 33.62 = 5.8^2$ (to 1 d. p.)   right-angled at Z.
2 $80^2 + 150^2 = 28\ 900 = 170^2$ right-angled at C.
3 $13.2^2 + 8.7^2 = 249.93 \neq 14.8^2$ not right-angled.
4 $4^2 + 5^2 = 41 \neq 6^2$ not right-angled.
5 $2.5^2 + 6.0^2 = 42.25 = 6.5^2$ right-angled at A.

> **Remember**
>
> $\neq$ means *does not equal.*

SOLUTION TO INVESTIGATION

The conclusion is, if a is the longest side in $\triangle ABC$, then
if $a^2 > b^2 + c^2$ the triangle is obtuse-angled and
if $a^2 < b^2 + c^2$ the triangle is acute-angled.

SOLUTIONS TO EXERCISE 8.3

1

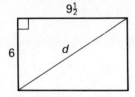

$$d^2 = 9\tfrac{1}{2}^2 + 6^2 \qquad \text{Pythagoras}$$
$$\Rightarrow \quad d = 11.2 \text{ ft}$$

2

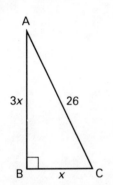

AC is the ladder, AB is the wall.
The dimensions are as shown.

$$9x^2 + x^2 = 26^2 \qquad \text{Pythagoras}$$
$$\Rightarrow \quad 10x^2 = 26^2$$
$$\Rightarrow \quad x = 8.2 \text{ ft.}$$
$$\therefore \text{ height up the wall is } 3 \times 8.2 = 24.6 \text{ ft.}$$

> Notice the use of x and $3x$ for BC and AB.

3

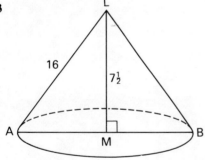

> Notice that it is not necessary to find AM.

The lamp L will cast a circle of light
with diameter AB, midpoint M.
$$AM^2 = 16^2 - 7\tfrac{1}{2}^2 \quad \Rightarrow \quad AM^2 = 199.75$$

Area of light $= \pi \times AM^2 = 627.5$ sq ft.

Calculator sequence: | 16 | x^2 | $-$ | 7.5 | x^2 | $=$ | $\times$ | π | $=$
Display: 16   256   256   7.5   56.25   199.75   199.75   3.141...   627.5...

4   PQ = 36 $\triangle$PQR is a 5, 12, 13, $\triangle$ RQ = 5 × 3 and PR = 13 × 3
PQ = 12 × 3
$SQ^2 = 83^2 - 36^2 \Rightarrow SQ = 74.8$
SR = SQ − RQ = 74.8 − 15 = 59.8

5

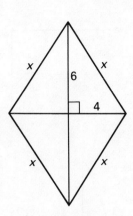

$x^2 = 6^2 + 4^2 \quad \Rightarrow \quad x = 7.2$ cm

> **Remember**
>
> A rhombus is a diamond; the diagonals bisect each other at right angles.

6 Suppose the angle at A is thought to be a right angle. You could measure AB, AE and BE, then test as in the similar questions of **Exercise 8.2**.

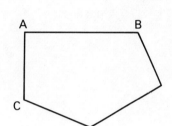

7 The problem is, to find EC.

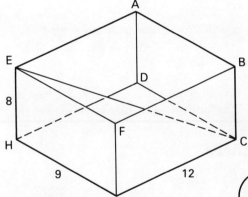

> This is the reasoning necessary before you actually start to work out the answer.

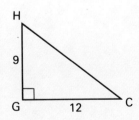

EC is in △EHC in which, initially, we know only EH.

∴ look at HC.

HC is in triangle HGC in which we know HG and GC.
So it is possible to find HC and solve the problem.
$HC^2 = 15^2$ △HGC is a 3, 4, 5 △.
Then $EC^2 = 8^2 + 15^2 = 17^2$
⇒   EC = 17   the third of the special triangles, the 8, 15, 17 △.
So the longest stick which will fit inside the box is 17 in.

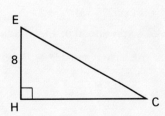

8

The diagram shows the distances after 1 hour.
$WS^2 = 12^2 + 10^2 \Rightarrow WS = 15.6$ miles
After three hours the distances are trebled
and then they are $3 \times 15.6 = 46.8$ miles apart.

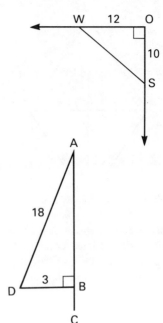

9

AD is the pendulum which starts from position AC.
Amount of rise is BC and BC = AC – AB
$AB^2 + 3^2 = 18^2 \Rightarrow AB = 17.7$ in
∴ the rise BC = $18 - 17.7 = 0.3$ in

10

For HG: 7.7 cm on map = $7.7 \times 25\,000$ cm on on ground
$\qquad\qquad\qquad = 7.7 \times 250$ m
Then $SH^2 = 752^2 + (7.7 \times 250)^2$
$\Rightarrow \quad SH = 2066.7$ m
SH = 2067 m and GH = 1925 m
i.e. $2067 - 1925 = 142$ m further to walk than the map shows.

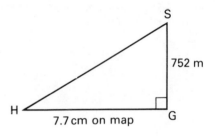

SOLUTIONS TO EXERCISE 8.4

1 x is opposite to 71°, 6.2 is adjacent.

$\Rightarrow$ we have o and $a \Rightarrow \tan71° = \dfrac{x}{6.2}$

$x = 6.2\tan71° = 18$

2 y is opposite to 27°, 8.1 is the hypotenuse.

$\Rightarrow$ we have o and $h \Rightarrow \sin27° = \dfrac{y}{8.1}$

$y = 8.1\sin27° = 3.7$

3   18.2 is opposite to p, 13.7 is adjacent to p.

$\Rightarrow$ we have o and $a \Rightarrow \tan p = \dfrac{18.2}{13.7}$

$p = \tan^{-1}\dfrac{18.2}{13.7} = 53°$

4   4.7 is opposite to q, 7.3 is the hypotenuse.

$\Rightarrow$ we have o and h $\Rightarrow$ $\sin q = \dfrac{4.7}{7.3}$

$q = \sin^{-1}\dfrac{4.7}{7.3} = 40°$

5 z is the hypotenuse, 24.2 is adjacent to 56°.

$\Rightarrow$ we have a and h $\Rightarrow$ $\cos 56° = \dfrac{24.2}{z}$

$\Rightarrow$ $z = \dfrac{24.2}{\cos 56°} = 43.3$

SOLUTIONS TO EXERCISE 8.5

1

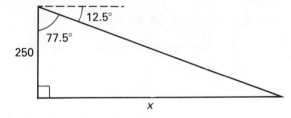

Angle of depression is 12.5°.
So the angle in the triangle is 77.5°.

$\Rightarrow$ $\tan 77.5° = \dfrac{x}{250}$

$\therefore x = 250 \tan 77.5° = 1127.7$ ft $= 375.9$ yards

2

Required to find: BC and θ (bearing of C from B)
Known angles are as shown $\therefore$ B$\hat{A}$C $= 90°$
$\therefore$ we can use Pythagoras and/or trigonometry in this triangle.
$BC^2 = 5^2 + 7^2$ Pythagoras
$\Rightarrow$ BC $= 8.6$ km
At B there is an angle of 150° as shown $\parallel$ lines

In $\triangle$ABC $\tan B = \dfrac{7}{5}$

$\therefore B = \tan^{-1}\dfrac{7}{5} = 65.5°$

$\therefore \theta = 360° - (150° + 54.5°) = 155.5°$
So the bearing of C from B is 155.5°.

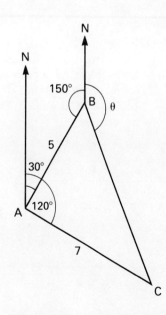

3

$$\sin x = \frac{3}{11}$$

$$x = \sin^{-1}\frac{3}{11} = 15.8°$$

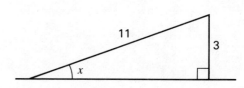

4

e = angle of elevation of the sun
9 is opposite e, 14 is adjacent to e.

$$\Rightarrow \quad \tan e = \frac{9}{14} = 15.8°$$

$$e = \tan^{-1}\frac{9}{14} = 32.7°$$

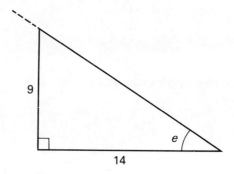

5

l is the hypotenuse, 75 is opposite to 37°.

$$\sin 37° = \frac{75}{l}$$

$$\therefore l = \frac{75}{\sin 37°} = 124.6 \text{ yd}$$

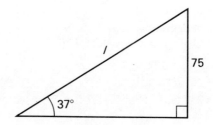

6

Before we can use trigonometry we need a right-angled triangle.
Since BA = AC a perpendicular line from A to the middle of BC
forms a right angle at D.
In $\triangle$DAC C is wanted, DC = 1.75 is adjacent to C, AC = 6 is the
hypotenuse.

$$\Rightarrow \quad \cos C = \frac{1.75}{6}$$

$$\therefore \qquad C = \cos^{-1}\frac{1.75}{6} = 73°$$

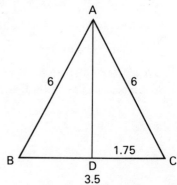

7   In three-dimensional problems such as this, we find that it breaks down into a problem about separate right-angled triangles.
In $\triangle$ABD only the angles are known; we need to know at least one side before we can work out anything.
AB is also in $\triangle$ABC.
In $\triangle$ABC we know the angles and one side so that is where we start work.

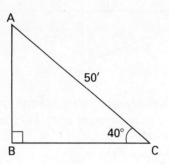

AB is opposite 40°, AD is the hypotenuse.

$\Rightarrow$ $\sin40° = \dfrac{AB}{50}$

$\Rightarrow$ AB = 32.1 ft

Now to $\triangle$ABD.

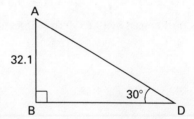

$\sin30° = \dfrac{32.1}{AD}$ $\Rightarrow$ AD = $\dfrac{32.1}{\sin30°}$ = 64.2 ft

$\tan30° = \dfrac{32.1}{AD}$ $\Rightarrow$ AD = $\dfrac{32.1}{\tan30°}$ = 55.6 ft

8   For simplicity, only part of the cuboid has been drawn.
$AC^2 = AF^2 + FC^2 = 6^2 + 3^2 = 45$
$BC^2 = AC^2 + AB^2 = 45 + 22 = 49$
$\therefore$ BC = 7
The angle required is ABC (or BCD).
Since AB = 2, AC = $\sqrt{45}$, BC = 7, all the lengths are known so any ratio can be used.
$\cos ABC = \frac{2}{7}$ $\Rightarrow$ ABC = 73.4°

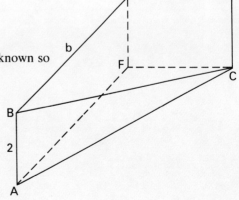

9

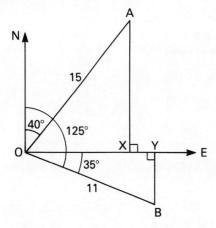

Eastwards is indicated by direction OE (090°).
The distance of A eastwards of O is OX and
the distance of B eastwards of O is OY.

In $\triangle OXA$ $\cos 50° = \dfrac{OX}{15}$ $\Rightarrow$ OX = 9.6 km

In $\triangle OYB$ $\cos 35° = \dfrac{OY}{11}$ $\Rightarrow$ OY = 9.0 km

$\therefore$ A is further east by (9.6 − 9.0) = 0.6 km.

It does not matter that,
now we have worked it
out, the distance is not
true: X and Y should
have been interchanged.

9 Vectors and matrices

This chapter is a small introduction to two more large areas of mathematics and it is a particularly interesting chapter for most people. The ideas in it may seem strange at first but persevere and you will be rewarded with some absorbing problems which could lead you on to some good quality coursework. The chapter covers:

- the definition of **vector** (and **scalar**) quantities
- **storage matrices**
- **multiplication** and **addition** of **matrices**
- **inverse matrices**
- **route matrices**
- **transformation geometry** by matrix.

★Vectors

We have all at some time played Snakes and Ladders and we remember the good bit where we landed at the foot of a ladder and then went up it. In the world of mathematics (and science and engineering and technology) that ladder is called a **vector**, a displacement which takes us from precisely one point to exactly another. By contrast, if we think about a queen in the middle of a chess board, we recall that her move is not predetermined; provided there is nothing in the way she can move anywhere and in any direction. In mathematics we say that her potential move is a **scalar**.

Consider this diagram. The vector displacement takes us from the point (1, 1) to the point (5, 3) i.e. 4 units in the x direction and 2 units in the y direction.

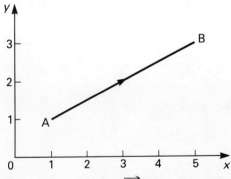

We call this the **vector $\overrightarrow{AB}$.** This arrow indicates the direction from A to B.

We can also write it as $\begin{pmatrix} 4 \\ 2 \end{pmatrix}$ which tells us its size.

The top figure is the distance moved in the x direction and the bottom figure is the distance moved in the y direction.

In this diagram we can see how easy it is to add vectors.

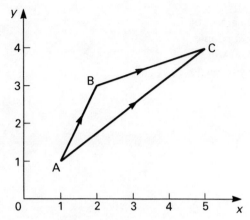

To get from A to C we can go either via B or directly.

i.e. $\overrightarrow{AB} + \overrightarrow{BC} = \overrightarrow{AC}$

$$\begin{pmatrix} 1 \\ 2 \end{pmatrix} + \begin{pmatrix} 3 \\ 1 \end{pmatrix} = \begin{pmatrix} 4 \\ 3 \end{pmatrix}$$

Using the standard notation for triangles, the length of AB is represented by c and this leads to another way of writing vectors.

Notation

$\overrightarrow{AB} = \mathbf{c}$, and this $\mathbf{c}$ appears differently in print from the way it does in handwriting. In print $\mathbf{c}$, in handwriting $\underline{c}$.

Vectors may be multiplied by a number.

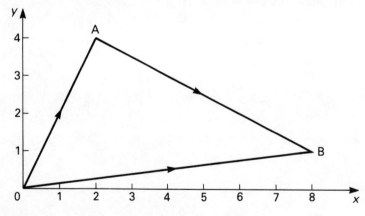

e.g. $\overrightarrow{OA} = 2\begin{pmatrix} 1 \\ 2 \end{pmatrix}$, $\overrightarrow{AB} = 3\begin{pmatrix} 2 \\ -1 \end{pmatrix}$

and we have

$$2\begin{pmatrix} 1 \\ 2 \end{pmatrix} + 3\begin{pmatrix} 2 \\ -1 \end{pmatrix} = \begin{pmatrix} 2 \\ 4 \end{pmatrix} + \begin{pmatrix} 6 \\ -3 \end{pmatrix} = \begin{pmatrix} 8 \\ 1 \end{pmatrix} = \overrightarrow{OB}$$

★EXERCISE 9.1

1   Given that $\mathbf{a} = \begin{pmatrix} 3 \\ 4 \end{pmatrix}$, $\mathbf{b} = \begin{pmatrix} 2 \\ -1 \end{pmatrix}$, $\mathbf{c} = \begin{pmatrix} -2 \\ 3 \end{pmatrix}$

find the single vector which would replace

(a) $\mathbf{a} + 2\mathbf{b} + \mathbf{c}$ and show your result on a diagram

(b) $\mathbf{b} - \mathbf{a}$ and show your result on a diagram.

2   ABC is a triangle in which M and N
are the midpoints of AB and AC respectively.
$\overrightarrow{AM} = \mathbf{a}$, $\overrightarrow{AN} = \mathbf{b}$.

Find, in terms of $\mathbf{a}$ and $\mathbf{b}$,
(a) $\overrightarrow{AB}$ (b) $\overrightarrow{AC}$ (c) $\overrightarrow{MN}$ (d) $\overrightarrow{BC}$.

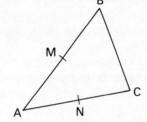

3   Given that $\mathbf{p} = \begin{pmatrix} 1 \\ 3 \end{pmatrix}$, $\mathbf{q} = \begin{pmatrix} -2 \\ -1 \end{pmatrix}$ and $\mathbf{r} = \begin{pmatrix} 3 \\ -1 \end{pmatrix}$ find

(a) the single vector which would replace $\mathbf{p} + \mathbf{q} + \mathbf{r}$

(b) the vector $\mathbf{s}$ which when added to $\mathbf{p} + \mathbf{q} + \mathbf{r}$ would produce a
net result of zero.

4   If $\begin{pmatrix} 1 \\ d \end{pmatrix} + \begin{pmatrix} 3 \\ 4 \end{pmatrix} + \begin{pmatrix} c \\ 1 \end{pmatrix} = \begin{pmatrix} 8 \\ 2 \end{pmatrix}$, find c and d.

5   You are given that $\mathbf{a} = \begin{pmatrix} 1 \\ 2 \end{pmatrix}$, $\mathbf{b} = \begin{pmatrix} 4 \\ -1 \end{pmatrix}$, $\mathbf{c} = \begin{pmatrix} 3 \\ 5 \end{pmatrix}$, $\mathbf{d} = \begin{pmatrix} -4 \\ -2 \end{pmatrix}$ and $\mathbf{e} = \begin{pmatrix} -2 \\ -3 \end{pmatrix}$.

Draw diagrams to show
(a) $\mathbf{a} + \mathbf{b} + \mathbf{c} + \mathbf{d} + \mathbf{e}$ (b) $\mathbf{b} - \mathbf{e} + \mathbf{d}$ (c) $2\mathbf{a} + \frac{1}{2}\mathbf{b} - \mathbf{c}$
and state the resultant vector in each case.

★★ 6

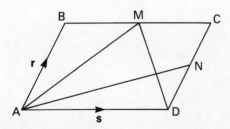

ABCD is a parallelogram in which M and N are midpoints and
$\overrightarrow{AB} = \mathbf{r}$ and $\overrightarrow{AD} = \mathbf{s}$.
Express (a) $\overrightarrow{AM}$ (b) $\overrightarrow{AN}$ (c) $\overrightarrow{MD}$ in terms of $\mathbf{r}$ and $\mathbf{s}$.

★★Matrices

A survey of 100 people produced the following result about their voting intentions.

	Conservative	Labour
Men	27	21
Women	23	29

A chart drawn up like this is called a **matrix**. In particular, charts like these are called **storage matrices** because they store information. They have an everyday use, because they are convenient, and examples are service records in garages, stock in warehouses, ticket sales at theatres and so on.

We use matrices in mathematics in many ways and they form a large section within the subject. In our course we consider only one or two areas where they are used but firstly we need to establish some basic rules.

> The plural of matrix is matrices.

- A matrix can have any number of rows or columns. The example above has two rows, Men and Women, and two columns, Conservative and Labour.
- If matrices are of the same type they can be added or subtracted.

★★EXAMPLE

A survey of the people in two classes, to find out how many were right-handed and how many were left-handed, was recorded like this.

Class 1	RH	LH		Class 2	RH	LH		Total	RH	LH
Boys	12	2	+	Boys	11	4	⇒	Boys	23	6
Girls	10	5		Girls	12	1		Girls	22	6

Matrices can also be multiplied in certain circumstances.

★★EXAMPLE

A school has two rugby teams: the over 16 and the under 16. Both teams enter a tournament in which a win earns 2 points, a draw earns 1 point and a loss no points. Their fortunes are summed up as follows.

$$
\begin{array}{c} >16 \\ <16 \end{array}
\begin{pmatrix} 4 & 1 & 0 \\ 2 & 0 & 3 \end{pmatrix}
\times
\begin{pmatrix} 2 \\ 1 \\ 0 \end{pmatrix}
=
\begin{pmatrix} 4 \times 2 + 1 \times 1 + 0 \times 0 \\ 2 \times 2 + 0 \times 1 + 3 \times 0 \end{pmatrix}
=
\begin{pmatrix} 9 \\ 4 \end{pmatrix}
$$

(columns labelled W D L)

This last example highlights a seemingly strange rule for multiplying. It is best described as *the rows of the first matrix going down the columns of the second matrix.*

$$>16 \quad \overset{\text{W D L}}{\begin{pmatrix} 4 & 1 & 0 \end{pmatrix}} \times \begin{pmatrix} 2 \\ 1 \\ 0 \end{pmatrix} \Rightarrow \begin{pmatrix} 2 \times 4 \\ 1 \times 1 \\ 0 \times 0 \end{pmatrix} \Rightarrow \begin{pmatrix} 8 + 1 + 0 \end{pmatrix} = \begin{pmatrix} 9 \end{pmatrix}$$

row of 1st matrix

Remember this rule as we consider the next exercise.

★★EXERCISE 9.2

1 $A = \begin{pmatrix} 2 & 1 \\ 3 & 4 \end{pmatrix}$ $B = \begin{pmatrix} 3 & 5 \\ 1 & 2 \end{pmatrix}$

Find **(a)** $A + B$ **(b)** AB.

2 Using the matrices in question 1, decide whether the following are true or false.
(a) $A + B = B + A$ **(b)** $AB = BA$

3 $A = \begin{pmatrix} 2 & 1 \\ 3 & 4 \end{pmatrix}$ $B = (3\,2\,4)$ $C = \begin{pmatrix} 2 & 0 & 1 \\ -1 & 3 & 2 \end{pmatrix}$ $D = \begin{pmatrix} 4 & -2 \\ 1 & 1 \\ 2 & -1 \end{pmatrix}$ $E = \begin{pmatrix} 3 & 2 \\ -1 & 5 \end{pmatrix}$ $F = \begin{pmatrix} 2 \\ 3 \\ 1 \end{pmatrix}$

Work these out if they are at all possible.
(a) AE **(b)** BD **(c)** CD **(d)** AD **(e)** BF
(f) EA **(g)** DB **(h)** DC **(i)** DA **(j)** FB
(k) compare **(a)** and **(f)** **(l)** compare **(b)** and **(g)** **(m)** compare **(c)** and **(h)**
(n) compare **(d)** and **(i)** **(o)** compare **(e)** and **(j)**.

4 From the results of question 3, which pair produced the same order of matrix for an answer? The order of a matrix is written as (number of rows × number of columns.)
Matrix **A** is (2 × 2), **B** is (1 × 3), **F** is (3 × 1).

5 Evaluate **(a)** $\begin{pmatrix} 5 & 3 \\ 1 & 4 \end{pmatrix}\begin{pmatrix} 4 & -3 \\ -1 & 5 \end{pmatrix}$ **(b)** $\begin{pmatrix} 2 & 1 \\ -3 & 4 \end{pmatrix}\begin{pmatrix} 4 & -1 \\ 3 & 2 \end{pmatrix}$
Then work out **(c)** $\begin{pmatrix} a & b \\ c & d \end{pmatrix}\begin{pmatrix} d & -b \\ -c & a \end{pmatrix}$

6 Find the inverses of the following matrices.
(a) $\begin{pmatrix} 7 & 5 \\ 4 & 3 \end{pmatrix}$ **(b)** $\begin{pmatrix} 8 & 5 \\ 3 & 2 \end{pmatrix}$ **(c)** $\begin{pmatrix} 7 & 9 \\ 3 & 4 \end{pmatrix}$ **(d)** $\begin{pmatrix} 7 & 2 \\ 9 & 3 \end{pmatrix}$
(e) $\begin{pmatrix} 4 & 5 \\ 1 & 2 \end{pmatrix}$ **(f)** $\begin{pmatrix} 9 & 8 \\ -2 & 2 \end{pmatrix}$

7 Does $AA^{-1} = A^{-1}A$? Let $A = \begin{pmatrix} p & q \\ r & s \end{pmatrix}$ and find out.

> **Remember**
>
> If the inverse matrix of **A** is **P** then
> $$PA = \begin{pmatrix} 1 & 0 \\ 0 & 1 \end{pmatrix}$$

★★Route matrices

Let us now return to storage type matrices and, in particular, to route matrices. We find we have some interesting problems.

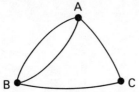

Imagine that A, B and C are three places and the roads linking them are shown. We can draw up a matrix listing the numbers of routes.

$$\begin{array}{c} \\ \\ \text{From} \\ \\ \end{array} \begin{array}{c} \\ \text{A} \\ \text{B} \\ \text{C} \end{array} \begin{array}{c} \text{To} \\ \text{A B C} \\ \left(\begin{array}{ccc} 0 & 2 & 1 \\ 2 & 0 & 1 \\ 1 & 1 & 0 \end{array}\right) \end{array}$$

When working through this you may have wondered, say, as you worked out 'routes from B to A' whether you should include B to C to A, as well as the two direct routes from B to A. Well, the answer is 'No,' because here we are drawing up a one-stage matrix and the question should have specified that.

Can you work out what a two-stage matrix means? Try it. For this example you should find it to be

$$\begin{array}{c} \\ \\ \text{From} \\ \\ \end{array} \begin{array}{c} \\ \text{A} \\ \text{B} \\ \text{C} \end{array} \begin{array}{c} \text{To} \\ \text{A B C} \\ \left(\begin{array}{ccc} 5 & 1 & 2 \\ 1 & 5 & 2 \\ 2 & 2 & 2 \end{array}\right) \end{array}$$

Now if we call the one-stage matrix **A**, can we find the product **A** × **A**?

> One-stage means from A to B in one step.

Investigation

Draw up the three-stage matrix and see if it has any connection with **A**. This type of work is from an area of mathematics called **topology**, which may be loosely defined as the study of shapes, areas, surfaces, edges etc., generally in three dimensions. Topology is a large and complicated subject but, like most others, it does have easy beginnings and it is worth visiting your library and doing a little research. Once again, you could easily find yourself with some interesting coursework material. You could start by looking up

- the Mobius strip
- Euler's equation for faces, edges and vertices
- the four-colour problem (this is harder).

Let's take a final look at this present problem. Possibly the entry 5 for A to A may puzzle you.

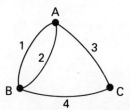

The possibilities are:

A → B via route 1 and back to A on route 1
A → B via route 2 and back to A on route 2
A → B via route 1 and back to A on route 2
A → B via route 2 and back to A on route 1
A → C via route 3 and back to A on route 3

★★EXERCISE 9.3

1   Draw up a route matrix for this network (a one-stage matrix).

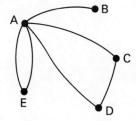

2   Draw up one-stage and two-stage matrices for the following network.

3   In the following network the arrows indicate that direction only e.g. A → B ⇒ A to B only, B to A impossible.
     Draw up one-stage and two-stage matrices and check whether or not the rule (one-stage) × (one-stage) = (two-stage) still applies.

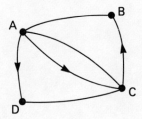

4   Make up one-stage and two-stage matrices for this network.

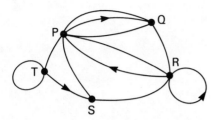

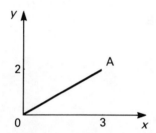

A   a loop, which has two routes ∴ either way

B   a loop, which has one route ∴ only one way

Also, find the three-stage matrix.

Transformation matrices

Our last look at matrices is in the area where we use them to carry out geometrical transformations.

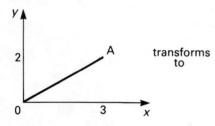

The point A has coordinates (3, 2) and the vector $\overrightarrow{OA}$ is written $\begin{pmatrix} 3 \\ 2 \end{pmatrix}$.

We now consider what certain matrices do to this vector.
The idea now is that you complete the following table.
Some have already been worked out.

e.g. if the matrix $\begin{pmatrix} 1 & 0 \\ 0 & -1 \end{pmatrix}$ operates on the vector $\begin{pmatrix} 3 \\ 2 \end{pmatrix}$

we have $\begin{pmatrix} 1 & 0 \\ 0 & -1 \end{pmatrix}\begin{pmatrix} 3 \\ 2 \end{pmatrix} = \begin{pmatrix} 3 \\ -2 \end{pmatrix}$

i.e.

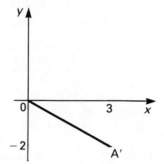

transforms to

and this can be summed up as a **reflection in the *x*-axis.**

Remember to operate on the vector $\begin{pmatrix} 3 \\ 2 \end{pmatrix}$ in every case. The answers are in the answer section.

Reflection matrices	$\begin{pmatrix} 1 & 0 \\ 0 & -1 \end{pmatrix}$	Reflection in *x*-axis
	$\begin{pmatrix} -1 & 0 \\ 0 & 1 \end{pmatrix}$	
	$\begin{pmatrix} 0 & 1 \\ 1 & 0 \end{pmatrix}$	
	$\begin{pmatrix} 0 & -1 \\ -1 & 0 \end{pmatrix}$	
Rotation matrices	$\begin{pmatrix} 0 & 1 \\ -1 & 0 \end{pmatrix}$	
	$\begin{pmatrix} 0 & -1 \\ 1 & 0 \end{pmatrix}$	
	$\begin{pmatrix} -1 & 0 \\ 0 & -1 \end{pmatrix}$	
Shear matrices	$\begin{pmatrix} 1 & 0 \\ 1 & 1 \end{pmatrix}$	
	$\begin{pmatrix} 1 & 1 \\ 0 & 1 \end{pmatrix}$	

Now the triangle with vertices at A (2, 1), B (1, 4) and C (4, 3) is the triangle formed by joining the extremities of the vectors

$\overrightarrow{OA} = \begin{pmatrix} 2 \\ 1 \end{pmatrix}$, $\overrightarrow{OB} = \begin{pmatrix} 1 \\ 4 \end{pmatrix}$ and $\overrightarrow{OC} = \begin{pmatrix} 4 \\ 3 \end{pmatrix}$. If the matrix $\begin{pmatrix} 1 & 0 \\ 0 & -1 \end{pmatrix}$ operates on each of these vectors we get OA', OB' and OC' and the triangle ABC has been reflected in the x-axis to get A'B'C'.

> This area of mathematics, in which we are altering positions and shapes by using matrices, is known as **transformation geometry.**

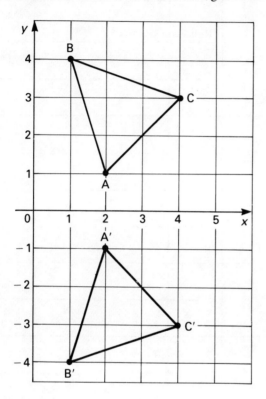

★★**EXERCISE 9.4**

1   The rectangle A(1, 1) B(1, 4) C(5, 4) D(5, 1) is transformed, using the matrix $\begin{pmatrix} 0 & 1 \\ -1 & 0 \end{pmatrix}$, into A'B'C'D'.

Find the coordinates of A', B', C' and D' and show the transformation in a diagram.

Describe the result if, instead, the matrix $\begin{pmatrix} 0 & 2 \\ -2 & 0 \end{pmatrix}$ had been used.

2   A square has the points with coordinates (0, 0), (0, 2), (2, 2), and (2, 0) for its vertices. It is transformed under the matrix $\begin{pmatrix} 1 & 1 \\ 0 & 1 \end{pmatrix}$.

What shape is formed and how does its area compare with the original square?

3 A triangle ABC has coordinates A (0, 2), B (2, 0) and C (0, −3). Find the new positions, if any, of A, B and C under the transformation $\begin{pmatrix} -1 & 0 \\ 0 & 1 \end{pmatrix}$.

What is the name of the shape obtained by combining the original and its image?

4

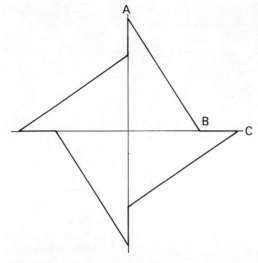

This shape was achieved by various transformations of ABC. Describe these, and the matrices used, to obtain the various images which were joined to obtain the shape.

5 Describe the transformations necessary, with matrices, to form the square CDEF from the line AB.

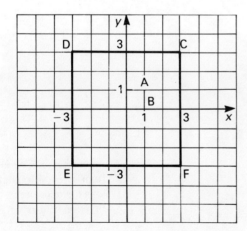

Solutions to exercises

SOLUTIONS TO EXERCISE 9.1

1 **(a)**

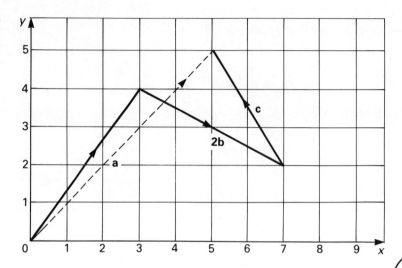

$$\mathbf{a} + 2\mathbf{b} + \mathbf{c} = \begin{pmatrix} 3 \\ 4 \end{pmatrix} + \begin{pmatrix} 4 \\ -2 \end{pmatrix} + \begin{pmatrix} -2 \\ 3 \end{pmatrix} = \begin{pmatrix} 5 \\ 5 \end{pmatrix} = 5\begin{pmatrix} 1 \\ 1 \end{pmatrix}$$

> This form is the answer because a single vector is asked for, and it is shown as a dashed line.

(b)

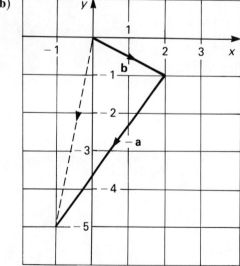

$$\mathbf{b} - \mathbf{a} = \begin{pmatrix} 2 \\ -1 \end{pmatrix} - \begin{pmatrix} 3 \\ 4 \end{pmatrix} = \begin{pmatrix} -1 \\ -5 \end{pmatrix}$$

> To draw −**a** you simply go in the opposite direction from +**a**.

2

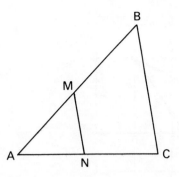

(a) $\overrightarrow{AB} = 2\overrightarrow{AM} = 2\mathbf{a}$

(b) $\overrightarrow{AC} = 2\overrightarrow{AN} = 2\mathbf{b}$

(c) $\overrightarrow{MN} = \overrightarrow{MA} + \overrightarrow{AN} = -\overrightarrow{AM} + \overrightarrow{AN} = -\mathbf{a} + \mathbf{b} = \mathbf{b} - \mathbf{a}$

(d) $\overrightarrow{BC} = \overrightarrow{BA} + \overrightarrow{AC} = -2\mathbf{a} + 2\mathbf{b} = 2(\mathbf{b} - \mathbf{a})$

> The answers to parts (**c**) and (**d**) show that MN is parallel to BC and equal in length to half of BC. This is known as the **midpoint theorem**.

3   (a) $\mathbf{p} + \mathbf{q} + \mathbf{r} = \begin{pmatrix} 1 \\ 3 \end{pmatrix} + \begin{pmatrix} -2 \\ -1 \end{pmatrix} + \begin{pmatrix} -3 \\ 1 \end{pmatrix} = \begin{pmatrix} 2 \\ 1 \end{pmatrix}$

   (b) $\mathbf{s}$ has to give a result of zero when added to $\begin{pmatrix} 2 \\ 1 \end{pmatrix}$ $\Rightarrow$ $\mathbf{s} = \begin{pmatrix} -2 \\ -1 \end{pmatrix}$

4 $1 + 3 + c = 8 \Rightarrow c = 4$
and $d + 4 + 1 = 2 \Rightarrow d = -3$

5   (a)

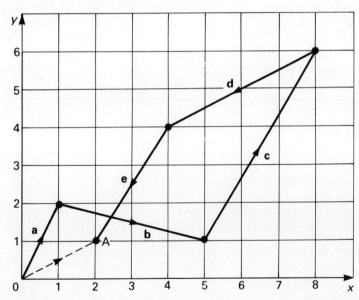

Resultant vector is $\overrightarrow{OA} = \begin{pmatrix} 2 \\ 1 \end{pmatrix}$

(b)

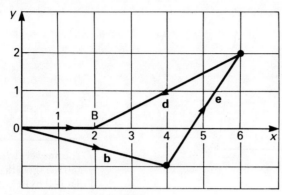

Resultant vector is $\overrightarrow{OB} = \begin{pmatrix} 2 \\ 0 \end{pmatrix}$

(c)

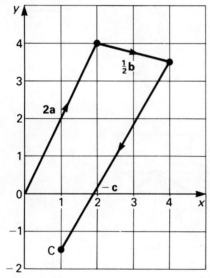

Resultant is $\overrightarrow{OC} = \begin{pmatrix} 1 \\ -\frac{3}{2} \end{pmatrix}$

6 **(a)** $\overrightarrow{AM} = \overrightarrow{AB} + \overrightarrow{BM}$
$\qquad\quad = \overrightarrow{AB} + \frac{1}{2}\overrightarrow{BC}$
$\qquad\quad = \mathbf{r} + \frac{1}{2}\mathbf{s}$

$\quad$ **(b)** $\overrightarrow{AN} = \overrightarrow{AD} + \overrightarrow{DN}$
$\qquad\quad = \overrightarrow{AD} + \frac{1}{2}\overrightarrow{DC}$
$\qquad\quad = \mathbf{s} + \frac{1}{2}\mathbf{r}$

$\quad$ **(c)** $\overrightarrow{MD} = \overrightarrow{MA} + \overrightarrow{AD}$
$\qquad\quad = -\overrightarrow{AM} + \overrightarrow{AD}$
$\qquad\quad = -\mathbf{r} - \frac{1}{2}\mathbf{s} + \mathbf{s}$
$\qquad\quad = \frac{1}{2}\mathbf{s} - \mathbf{r}$

SOLUTIONS TO EXERCISE 9.2

1   (a) $A + B = \begin{pmatrix} 2+3 & 1+5 \\ 3+1 & 4+2 \end{pmatrix} = \begin{pmatrix} 5 & 6 \\ 4 & 6 \end{pmatrix}$

You will notice that already we are using theoretical matrices: the rows and columns are not specifically labelled.

   (b) $AB = \begin{pmatrix} 3 \times 2 & 5 \times 2 \\ 1 \times 1 & 2 \times 1 \\ \\ 3 \times 3 & 5 \times 3 \\ 1 \times 4 & 2 \times 4 \end{pmatrix} = \begin{pmatrix} 7 & 12 \\ \\ 13 & 23 \end{pmatrix}$

2   (a) True: $A + B = B + A$

   (b) $BA = \begin{pmatrix} 2 \times 3 & 1 \times 3 \\ 3 \times 5 & 4 \times 5 \\ \\ 2 \times 1 & 1 \times 1 \\ 3 \times 2 & 4 \times 2 \end{pmatrix} = \begin{pmatrix} 21 & 23 \\ \\ 8 & 9 \end{pmatrix}$

   $\Rightarrow \qquad AB \neq BA$

3   (a) $AE = \begin{pmatrix} 2 & 1 \\ 3 & 4 \end{pmatrix} \times \begin{pmatrix} 3 & 2 \\ -1 & 5 \end{pmatrix} = \begin{pmatrix} 5 & 9 \\ 5 & 26 \end{pmatrix}$

   (b) $BD = (3\ 2\ 4) \times \begin{pmatrix} 4 & -2 \\ 1 & 1 \\ 2 & -1 \end{pmatrix}$

$= (3 \times 4 + 2 \times 1 + 4 \times 2 \quad 3 \times -2 + 2 \times 1 + 4 \times -1)$
$= (22\ -8)$

   (c) $CD = \begin{pmatrix} 2 & 0 & 1 \\ -1 & 3 & 2 \end{pmatrix} \times \begin{pmatrix} 4 & -2 \\ 1 & 1 \\ 2 & -1 \end{pmatrix}$

$= \begin{pmatrix} 2 \times 4 + 0 \times 1 + 1 \times 2 & -1 \times -2 + 3 \times 1 + 2 \times -1 \\ -1 \times 4 + 3 \times 1 + 2 \times 2 & 2 \times \ 2 + 0 \times 1 + 1 \times -1 \end{pmatrix}$

$= \begin{pmatrix} 10 & -5 \\ 3 & 3 \end{pmatrix}$

   (d) $AD = \begin{pmatrix} 2 & 1 \\ 3 & 4 \end{pmatrix} \times \begin{pmatrix} 4 & -2 \\ 1 & 1 \\ 2 & -1 \end{pmatrix}$ is impossible

(e) BF $= (3\ 2\ 4) \times \begin{pmatrix} 2 \\ 3 \\ 1 \end{pmatrix} = (3 \times 2 + 2 \times 3 + 4 \times 1) = (16)$

(f) EA $= \begin{pmatrix} 3 & 2 \\ -1 & 5 \end{pmatrix} \times \begin{pmatrix} 2 & 1 \\ 3 & 4 \end{pmatrix} = \begin{pmatrix} 12 & 11 \\ 13 & 19 \end{pmatrix}$

(g) DB $= \begin{pmatrix} 4 & -2 \\ 1 & 1 \\ 2 & -1 \end{pmatrix} \times (3\ 2\ 4)$ is impossible

(h) DC $= \begin{pmatrix} 4 & -2 \\ 1 & 1 \\ 2 & -1 \end{pmatrix} \times \begin{pmatrix} 2 & 0 & 1 \\ -1 & 3 & 2 \end{pmatrix}$

$= \begin{pmatrix} 10 & -6 & 0 \\ 1 & 3 & 3 \\ 5 & -3 & 0 \end{pmatrix}$

(i) DA $= \begin{pmatrix} 4 & -2 \\ 1 & 1 \\ 2 & -1 \end{pmatrix} \times \begin{pmatrix} 2 & 1 \\ 3 & 4 \end{pmatrix}$

$= \begin{pmatrix} 2 & -4 \\ 5 & 5 \\ 1 & -2 \end{pmatrix}$

(j) FB $= \begin{pmatrix} 2 \\ 3 \\ 1 \end{pmatrix} \times (3\ 2\ 4)$

$= \begin{pmatrix} 6 & 4 & 8 \\ 9 & 6 & 12 \\ 3 & 2 & 4 \end{pmatrix}$

4 (a) and (f). In both cases the result is a 2×2 matrix. This is a square matrix and it is of the same order as **A** and **E**.

5 (a) $\begin{pmatrix} 5 & 3 \\ 1 & 4 \end{pmatrix} \begin{pmatrix} 4 & -3 \\ -1 & 5 \end{pmatrix} = \begin{pmatrix} 17 & 0 \\ 0 & 17 \end{pmatrix} = 17 \begin{pmatrix} 1 & 0 \\ 0 & 1 \end{pmatrix}$

(b) $\begin{pmatrix} 2 & 1 \\ -3 & 4 \end{pmatrix} \begin{pmatrix} 4 & -1 \\ 3 & 2 \end{pmatrix} = \begin{pmatrix} 11 & 0 \\ 0 & 11 \end{pmatrix} = 11 \begin{pmatrix} 1 & 0 \\ 0 & 1 \end{pmatrix}$

(c) $\begin{pmatrix} a & b \\ c & d \end{pmatrix} \begin{pmatrix} d & -b \\ -c & a \end{pmatrix} = \begin{pmatrix} ad - bc & 0 \\ 0 & ad - bc \end{pmatrix}$

$= (ad - bc) \begin{pmatrix} 1 & 0 \\ 0 & 1 \end{pmatrix}$

Now there is obviously some pattern about these questions and results.

Firstly all the answers contain $\begin{pmatrix} 1 & 0 \\ 0 & 1 \end{pmatrix}$

which is called the **identity matrix** and is usually represented by **I**.

Consider the product $\begin{pmatrix} 1 & 0 \\ 0 & 1 \end{pmatrix}\begin{pmatrix} p & q \\ r & s \end{pmatrix} = \begin{pmatrix} p & q \\ r & s \end{pmatrix}$

which gives the same effect as multiplying by 1 ordinarily. Now multiplying by 3, say, and dividing by 3 at the same time is equivalent to multiplying by 1 because the multiplying by three and dividing by three cancel each other out: they are the **inverses** of each other. Similarly two matrices which multiply to give the identity matrix are the inverses of each other. If the first is called **A** the inverse is $\mathbf{A}^{-1}$.

Looking back to **5(c)**, the inverse of $\begin{pmatrix} a & b \\ c & d \end{pmatrix}$ is $\begin{pmatrix} d & -b \\ -c & a \end{pmatrix} \div (ad - bc)$

The diagonals of a matrix are important: (\\) this is the leading diagonal.

Hence to form the inverse

1 change the terms of the leading diagonal

2 change the signs of the other diagonal

3 divide by (product of leading diagonal – product of other diagonal).

6 (a) $\begin{pmatrix} 3 & -5 \\ -4 & 7 \end{pmatrix}$ (b) $\begin{pmatrix} 2 & -5 \\ -3 & 8 \end{pmatrix}$ (c) $\begin{pmatrix} 4 & -9 \\ -3 & 7 \end{pmatrix}$

(d) $\frac{1}{3}\begin{pmatrix} 3 & -2 \\ -9 & 7 \end{pmatrix}$ (e) $\frac{1}{3}\begin{pmatrix} 2 & -5 \\ 1 & 4 \end{pmatrix}$ (f) $\frac{1}{34}\begin{pmatrix} 2 & -8 \\ 2 & 9 \end{pmatrix}$

7 $\mathbf{AA}^{-1} = \begin{pmatrix} p & q \\ r & s \end{pmatrix}\begin{pmatrix} s & -q \\ -r & p \end{pmatrix} = \begin{pmatrix} ps - qr & 0 \\ 0 & ps - qr \end{pmatrix}$

and $\mathbf{A}^{-1}\mathbf{A} = \begin{pmatrix} s & -q \\ -r & p \end{pmatrix}\begin{pmatrix} p & q \\ r & s \end{pmatrix} = \begin{pmatrix} ps - qr & 0 \\ 0 & ps - qr \end{pmatrix}$

$\Rightarrow \quad \mathbf{AA}^{-1} = \mathbf{A}^{-1}\mathbf{A}$

Compare this result with question **2(b)**.

SOLUTIONS TO EXERCISE 9.3

1

		To				
		A	B	C	D	E
	A	0	1	1	1	2
	B	1	0	0	0	0
From	C	1	0	0	1	0
	D	1	0	1	0	0
	E	2	0	0	0	0

2 **One-stage**

			To		
		P	Q	R	S
	P	0	2	1	1
	Q	2	0	1	0
From	R	1	1	0	1
	S	1	0	1	0

Two-stage

			To		
		P	Q	R	S
	P	6	1	3	1
	Q	1	5	2	3
From	R	3	2	3	1
	S	1	3	1	2

3 **One-stage**

			To		
		A	B	C	D
	A	0	1	2	1
	B	1	0	0	0
From	C	1	1	0	1
	D	0	0	1	0

Two-stage

			To		
		A	B	C	D
	A	3	2	1	2
	B	0	1	2	1
From	C	1	1	3	1
	D	1	1	0	1

Yes.

4 **One-stage**

				To		
		P	Q	R	S	T
	P	0	3	1	1	1
	Q	2	0	1	0	0
From	R	2	1	1	1	0
	S	1	0	1	0	0
	T	1	0	0	1	2

Two-stage

				To		
		P	Q	R	S	T
	P	10	1	5	2	2
	Q	2	7	3	3	2
From	R	5	7	5	3	2
	S	2	4	2	2	1
	T	3	3	2	3	5

Three-stage

				To		
		P	Q	R	S	T
	P	16	35	18	17	14
	Q	25	9	15	7	6
From	R	19	20	20	12	9
	S	15	8	10	5	4
	T	18	11	11	10	13

Reflection matrices	$\begin{pmatrix} 1 & 0 \\ 0 & -1 \end{pmatrix}$			Reflection in x-axis
	$\begin{pmatrix} -1 & 0 \\ 0 & 1 \end{pmatrix}$			Reflection in y-axis
	$\begin{pmatrix} 0 & 1 \\ 1 & 0 \end{pmatrix}$			Reflection in $y = x$
	$\begin{pmatrix} 0 & -1 \\ -1 & 0 \end{pmatrix}$			Reflection in $y = -x$
Rotation matrices	$\begin{pmatrix} 0 & 1 \\ -1 & 0 \end{pmatrix}$			Rotation 90° clockwise about O
	$\begin{pmatrix} 0 & -1 \\ 1 & 0 \end{pmatrix}$			Rotation 90° anticlockwise about O
	$\begin{pmatrix} -1 & 0 \\ 0 & -1 \end{pmatrix}$			Rotation 180°
Shear matrices	$\begin{pmatrix} 1 & 0 \\ 1 & 1 \end{pmatrix}$			Shear or stretch parallel to x-axis
	$\begin{pmatrix} 1 & 1 \\ 0 & 1 \end{pmatrix}$			Shear or stretch parallel to y-axis

SOLUTIONS TO EXERCISE 9.4

This confirms the result in the table i.e. 90° rotation clockwise.

1 $\begin{pmatrix} 0 & 1 \\ -1 & 0 \end{pmatrix}\begin{pmatrix} 1 \\ 1 \end{pmatrix} = \begin{pmatrix} 1 \\ -1 \end{pmatrix}$ i.e. A' is $(1, -1)$

$\begin{pmatrix} 0 & 1 \\ -1 & 0 \end{pmatrix}\begin{pmatrix} 1 \\ 4 \end{pmatrix} = \begin{pmatrix} 4 \\ 1 \end{pmatrix}$ i.e. B' is $(4, -1)$

$\begin{pmatrix} 0 & 1 \\ -1 & 0 \end{pmatrix}\begin{pmatrix} 5 \\ 4 \end{pmatrix} = \begin{pmatrix} 4 \\ -5 \end{pmatrix}$ i.e. C' is $(4, -5)$

$\begin{pmatrix} 0 & 1 \\ -1 & 0 \end{pmatrix}\begin{pmatrix} 5 \\ 1 \end{pmatrix} = \begin{pmatrix} 1 \\ -5 \end{pmatrix}$ i.e. D' is $(1, -5)$

Using $\begin{pmatrix} 0 & 2 \\ -2 & 0 \end{pmatrix}$ $\Rightarrow$ A''$(2, -2)$, B''$(8, -2)$, C''$(8, -10)$, D''$(2, -10)$

i.e. clockwise rotation of 90°, doubling the size of the rectangle and moving the vertices twice as far from the origin.

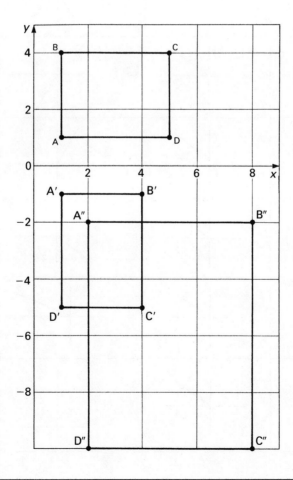

2 $\begin{pmatrix} 1 & 1 \\ 0 & 1 \end{pmatrix}\begin{pmatrix} 0 \\ 2 \end{pmatrix} = \begin{pmatrix} 2 \\ 2 \end{pmatrix}$ $\Rightarrow$ $(0, 2) \rightarrow (2, 2)$

$\begin{pmatrix} 1 & 1 \\ 0 & 1 \end{pmatrix}\begin{pmatrix} 2 \\ 2 \end{pmatrix} = \begin{pmatrix} 4 \\ 2 \end{pmatrix}$ $\Rightarrow$ $(2, 2) \rightarrow (4, 2)$

$\begin{pmatrix} 1 & 1 \\ 0 & 1 \end{pmatrix}\begin{pmatrix} 2 \\ 0 \end{pmatrix} = \begin{pmatrix} 2 \\ 0 \end{pmatrix}$ $\Rightarrow$ $\begin{array}{l} (2, 0) \rightarrow (2, 0) \text{ and} \\ (0, 0) \rightarrow (0, 0) \end{array}$

$\therefore$ square OABD becomes parallelogram OBCD.

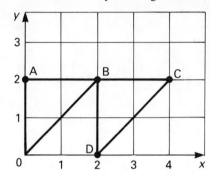

The area of the parallelogram is the same as the area of the square.

3 $\begin{pmatrix} -1 & 0 \\ 0 & 1 \end{pmatrix}\begin{pmatrix} 0 \\ 2 \end{pmatrix} = \begin{pmatrix} 0 \\ 2 \end{pmatrix}$ $\Rightarrow$ $(0, 2) \rightarrow (0, 2)$

$\begin{pmatrix} -1 & 0 \\ 0 & 1 \end{pmatrix}\begin{pmatrix} 2 \\ 0 \end{pmatrix} = \begin{pmatrix} -2 \\ 0 \end{pmatrix}$ $\Rightarrow$ $(2, 0) \rightarrow (-2, 0)$

$\begin{pmatrix} -1 & 0 \\ 0 & 1 \end{pmatrix}\begin{pmatrix} 0 \\ -3 \end{pmatrix} = \begin{pmatrix} 0 \\ -3 \end{pmatrix}$ $\Rightarrow$ $(0, -3) \rightarrow (0, -3)$

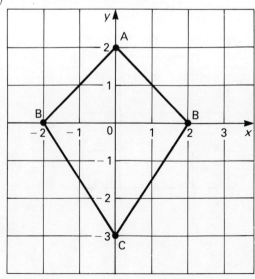

This shape is often called a kite although – officially – that is not a mathematical term.

4

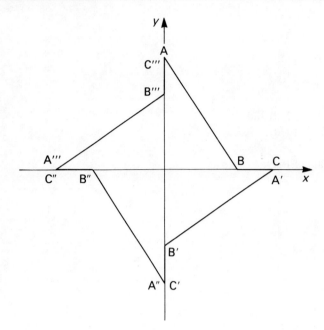

The matrix $\begin{pmatrix} 0 & 1 \\ -1 & 0 \end{pmatrix}$ causes clockwise rotation through 90° to obtain A'B'C'.

The matrix $\begin{pmatrix} 0 & -1 \\ 1 & 0 \end{pmatrix}$ causes anticlockwise rotation through 90° to obtain A'''B'''C'''.

The matrix $\begin{pmatrix} -1 & 0 \\ 0 & -1 \end{pmatrix}$ causes rotation through 180° to obtain A''B''C''.

5 $\begin{pmatrix} 3 & 0 \\ 0 & 3 \end{pmatrix}$ on AB $\rightarrow$ A'B'

(i)

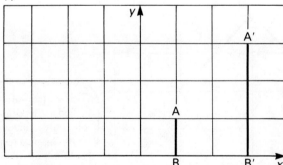

$\begin{pmatrix} 0 & -1 \\ 1 & 0 \end{pmatrix}$ on A'B' $\rightarrow$ A''B''

(ii)

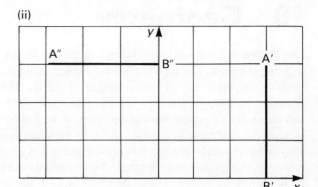

$\begin{pmatrix} -1 & 0 \\ 0 & 1 \end{pmatrix}$ on A'B' and A''B'' $\rightarrow$ PDCQ

(iii)

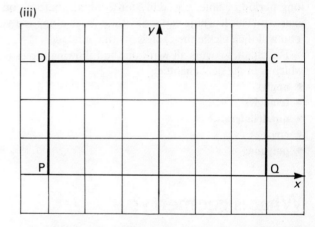

Finally $\begin{pmatrix} 1 & 0 \\ 0 & -1 \end{pmatrix}$ on PDCQ $\rightarrow$ EDCF

(iv)

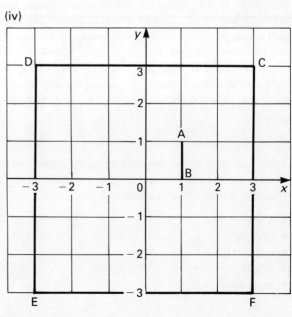

10 Geometry

This chapter is a little different in that all the results you have to know, and there are many, are presented in sections at the beginning of the chapter and there is one long exercise to finish. This reflects what geometry problems are about: you have to know all the relevant facts and then you try to apply them as necessary to diagrams. You are usually looking for relationships between lines or between angles or between lines and angles and often the relationship is equality i.e. you are looking for things being equal to each other. You cannot do the problems if you do not know the theory and the best way to learn this is by a 'little and often'. You should aim to learn only one or two items at a time over a long period of time, e.g. daily for a month, before you plan to do the exercise. This learning can easily take place alongside your other work. You will then tackle the exercise with confidence.

The chapter covers all work on the following topics (except similarity which is in the next chapter):

- **angles**
- **triangles**
- **quadrilaterals**
- **circles**
- **polygons**.

What is geometry?

Geometry is the oldest of the sections which form the subject of mathematics. It was studied in detail and with much depth 2000–4000 years ago, probably earlier, and many of the results are used in the geometry we study for GCSE. Euclid, who was a Greek who lived in about 330–275 BC, collected together much of the work known at that time and he wrote 13 books, known as the *Elements*. It is because of this work that the geometry we study is known as **Euclidean geometry**.

There are many terms and definitions associated with geometry and you need to know these if you are to be successful. They are summarised in this next section under the headings of:

- angles
- triangles
- quadrilaterals
- circles
- polygons.

> **Comment**
>
> There is a rich source of investigative material in studying the work of the Greek mathematicians, or geometers as they were known. You will soon be interested in geometry, number and mechanics but you will have to make good use of your library.

Angles

Angles are defined as the difference in direction between two lines and are measured

- in degrees, °, e.g. 360°

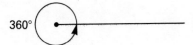

- in turns.

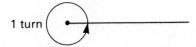

Most angles are **acute**, **obtuse** or **reflex**.

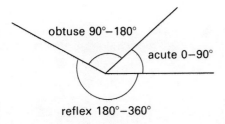

Special cases

The two most common special cases are

- 90° (a **right angle**) and

- 180° (a **straight angle**).

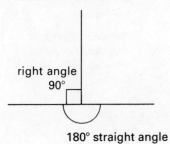

Parallel lines and 0°

Lines which run in the same direction, always the same distance apart, are parallel lines. The angle between them is 0°.

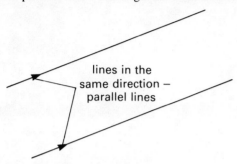

lines in the
same direction –
parallel lines

Perpendicular lines, 90°

Lines which are perpendicular to each other form four right angles.

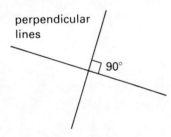

perpendicular
lines

90°

★Vertically opposite angles

When two non-parallel lines cross, they form four angles.
The opposite angles are equal, and are called **vertically opposite angles**.

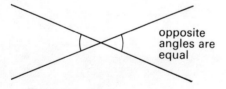

opposite
angles are
equal

★Adjacent angles

Two angles which come together on a straight line add to 180°, they are **supplementary**.

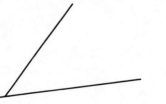

> **Remember**
>
> Supplementary here means *add to 180°*.

★Alternate and corresponding angles

These are formed when a line crosses two parallel lines as shown.

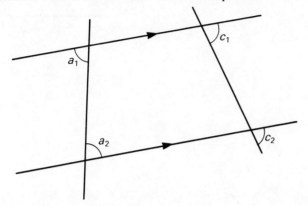

Then a_1 and a_2 are alternate angles and $a_1 = a_2$
$\quad$ c_1 and c_2 are corresponding angles and $c_1 = c_2$.

★Triangles

Triangles are flat or plane shapes with three sides and three angles.

Scalene triangles have all sides different and all angles different.

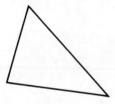

Isosceles triangles have two sides equal and two angles equal.

> Isosceles comes from the Greek: *iso* equal and *celes* legs, so means equal legs.

Equilateral triangles have all three sides equal and all three angles equal.

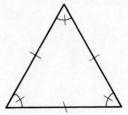

> Equilateral comes from the Latin: *equi* equal and *latus* side.

Right-angled triangles have one angle of 90°, the longest side is the **hypotenuse** and is opposite the right angle.

You have met these before!

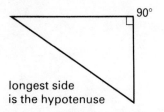

90°

longest side
is the hypotenuse

★Angles of triangles

For any triangle, the interior angles add up to 180°.

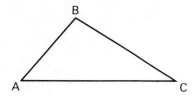

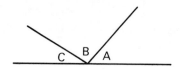

★Quadrilaterals

Quadrilaterals are plane shapes with four sides.
A **trapezium** has one pair of parallel sides.

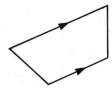

A **parallelogram** has two pairs of parallel sides.
It also has
- opposite angles equal
- opposite sides equal
- diagonals which bisect each other.

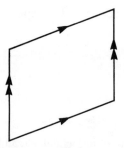

A **rectangle** is a parallelogram with all its angles equal to 90°.

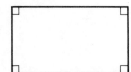

A **rhombus** is a parallelogram with all its sides equal.

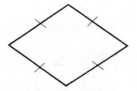

A **square** is a rhombus with all it angles equal,
or a rectangle with all its sides equal.

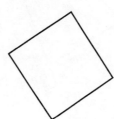

A **kite** is none of the above, but has
two pairs of adjacent sides equal.

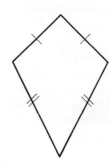

★The angles of quadrilaterals

The interior angles of any quadrilateral add up to 360°.
The quadrilaterals can be represented in a Venn diagram.

Q = {quadrilaterals}

T = {trapezia} $T \subset Q$

P = {parallelograms} $P \subset T$

H = {rhombuses} $H \subset P$

E = {rectangles} $E \subset P$

S = {squares} $S = H \cap E$

K = {kites} $K \subset Q$

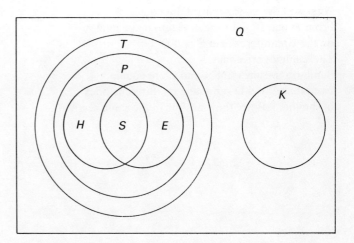

Circles

The basic parts of a circle are shown in this diagram.

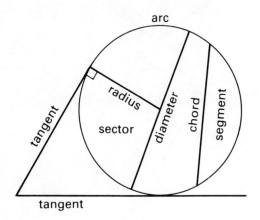

★The angle in a semi-circle

The angle in a semi-circle is a right angle.
This means that if you join the ends of a
diameter, AB, to any point, C, on the
circumference a 90° angle is formed at C.

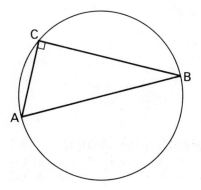

★★Angles in the same segment

Angles in the same segment are equal.
From A and B, lines are drawn to make angles
on the circumference at C and D.
These angles are equal.
Similarly the angles at A and B are equal.
Note that C and D cannot be on different sides
of the line AB i.e. they must be in the same segment.

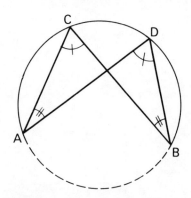

★★The angle at the centre

The angle at the centre is twice that at the circumference: lines are drawn from A and B to make angles at O, (the centre), and C. The angle at O is twice the angle at C. Here also, C and O must be in the same segment.

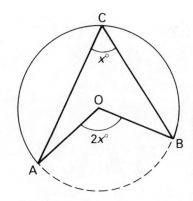

★★Cyclic quadrilaterals

A cyclic quadrilateral is the quadrilateral made by joining four points on the circumference of a circle.
Opposite angles add to $180° \Rightarrow A + C = 180°$
The exterior angle at B is equal to the interior angle at D
$\Rightarrow \theta_1 = \theta_2$

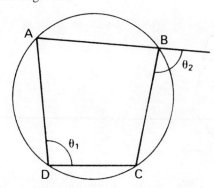

★Polygons

Polygons are plane shapes with many sides. They include triangles and quadrilaterals.
All the polygons considered here are regular i.e. all the sides are equal and all the angles are equal.

★Pentagon

5 sides   pentagon   5-gon
The sum of the interior angles is 540°.
The size of each angle is 108°.

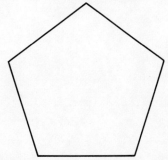

★Hexagon

6 sides   hexagon   6-gon
The sum of the interior angles is 720°.
The size of each angle is 120°.

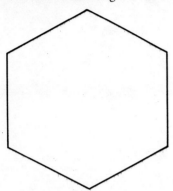

★Heptagon

7 sides   heptagon   7-gon
The sum of the interior angles is 900°.
The size of each angle is 128.6°.

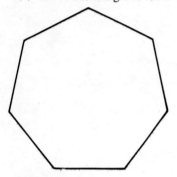

★Octagon

8 sides   octagon   8-gon
The sum of the interior angles is 1080°.
The size of each angle is 135°.

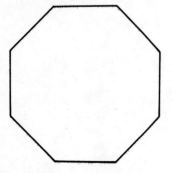

EXERCISE 10

★ **1**   Find *a*.

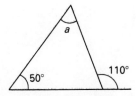

2   Find *b*.

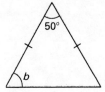

★ **3**   Find *c*.

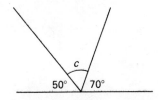

4   Find *d*.

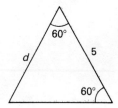

5   Find *e*.

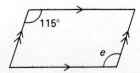

★ **6**   Find *f*.

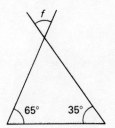

★ **7** Find g and $3g$.

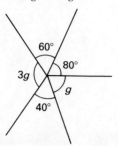

★ **8** Find h and i.

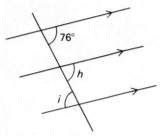

★ **9** ABCD is a rhombus.
Find all the other angles.

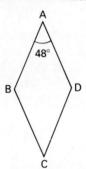

★★ **10** Describe the single transformation necessary to form a parallelogram from a scalene triangle.

★★ **11** Find j.

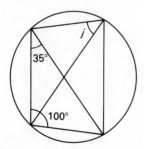

★★ **12**   Find k.
Is the quadrilateral cyclic?

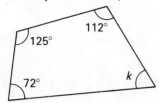

★ **13**   BD bisects $A\hat{B}C$. Find l.

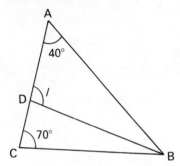

★★ **14**   AB is a diameter. Find m.

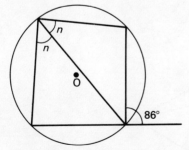

★★ **15**   Following on from question 10, explain why opposite angles of a parallelogram are equal.

★★ **16**   Find n.

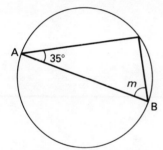

★★ **17**   Which single transformation will make a kite from a scalene triangle?

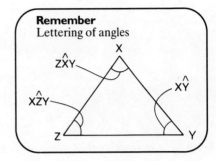

Remember
Lettering of angles

★★ **18**   Find p.

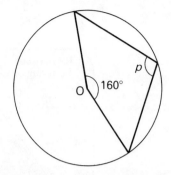

★ **19**   A **circumcircle** is one which passes through the three corners (vertices) of a triangle. Where is the centre of the circumcircle of a right-angled triangle?

★ **20**   Draw a regular hexagon and show all its lines of symmetry. Also state its order of rotational symmetry.

★ **21**   The diagram shows two sides AB and BC of a regular polygon.

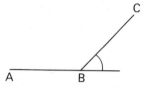

The marked angle is an exterior angle.
Find the size of the exterior angle of a regular pentagon and find the sum of all its exterior angles. Repeat for a hexagon, heptagon and octagon, all regular. Can you draw any conclusions?

★★ **22**   ABCDE is half of a regular octagon.
(a) Find the angles of △ADE.
(b) Name the shape ABCD,
      and give reasons.

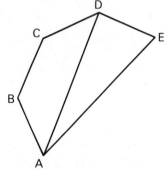

★ **23**   Calculate the exterior angle of a regular polygon with 15 sides.

★ **24**   ABCDE is a square and BCD is an equilateral triangle.
Find the angles of triangle ABC.

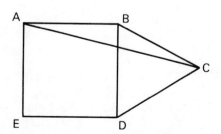

Solutions to exercises

SOLUTIONS TO EXERCISE 10

1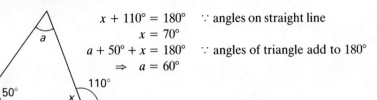

$x + 110° = 180°$ ∵ angles on straight line
$x = 70°$
$a + 50° + x = 180°$ ∵ angles of triangle add to 180°
$\Rightarrow \quad a = 60°$

> **NB** if you look at this carefully you can see that the exterior angle, 110° in this case, will always equal the interior opposite angles added together, 50° + 60° in this case: this is a geometrical fact which can be quoted and used.

2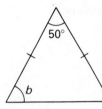

The third angle is also of size b ∵ triangle is isosceles
$2b + 50° = 180°$ ∵ angles of triangle
$\Rightarrow \quad b = 65°$

3 $50° + c + 70° = 180°$ ∵ angles on straight line
$\Rightarrow \quad c = 60°$

4   Two of the angles are each 60°
∴ the third angle is 60°   ∵ angles of triangle
∴ triangle is equilateral: all the sides are the same.
∴ $d = 5$

5 $e = 115°$ ∵ opposite angles of a parallelogram are equal.

6

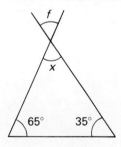

$x + 65° + 35° = 180°$ ∵ angles of triangle
$x = 80°$
$\Rightarrow \quad f = 80°$ ∵ $f = x$, vertically opposite

7 $3g + 60° + 80° + g + 40° = 360°$ ∵ 360° in one full turn
$4g + 180° = 360°$
$4g = 180° \quad \Rightarrow \quad g = 45°$ and $3g = 135°$

8 $h = 76°$ ∵ corresponding angles
$i = 76°$ ∵ alternate angles

9 $C = 48°$ ∵ opposite angles of rhombus (parallelogram) are equal
$B + D + 48° + 48° = 360°$ and $B = D$
$2B = 360° - 96° \quad \Rightarrow \quad B = 132°$

10

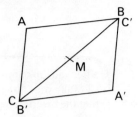

180° rotation about M, the midpoint of BC $\Rightarrow$ A'B'C'
$\therefore$ ABA'C is a parallelogram.

11

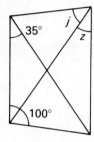

$z = 35°$ $\because$ angles in same segment
$100° + j + z = 180°$ $\because$ opposite angles of cyclic quadrilateral
$\Rightarrow \; j = 45°$

12 $72° + 125° + 112° + k = 360°$ $\because$ angles of quadrilateral add to 360°
$k = 51°$

$72° + 112° = 184°$

$\because$ opposite angles do not add to 180° the quadrilateral is not cyclic.

13

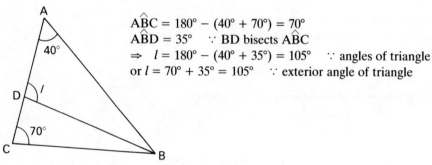

$A\hat{B}C = 180° - (40° + 70°) = 70°$
$A\hat{B}D = 35°$ $\because$ BD bisects $A\hat{B}C$
$\Rightarrow \; l = 180° - (40° + 35°) = 105°$ $\because$ angles of triangle
or $l = 70° + 35° = 105°$ $\because$ exterior angle of triangle

14   The unmarked angle is 90° $\because$ angle in semi-circle
$m + 35° = 90° \; \Rightarrow \; m = 35°$

15   The angles at A and A' are the same.
Angle B $\rightarrow$ B' and angle C $\rightarrow$ C'
$\therefore$ angles at B/C' and C/B' are the same.

16 $2n = 86°$
$\because$ exterior angle of cyclic quadrilateral = interior opposite
$\therefore n = 43°$

17

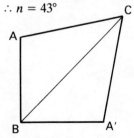

Reflecting ABC in BC gives A'BAC which is a kite.
$\because$ BA = BA' and CA = CA'

18

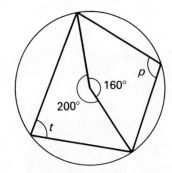

Reflex angle at O is $(360° - 160°) = 200°$
$p = \frac{1}{2} \times 200° = 100°$
∵ angle at circumference is half that at centre.

This question merits a careful study of the angles.
If we extend the diagram a little and make the angle t you must realise that p is half of 200° and t is half of 160°.

19 The midpoint of the hypotenuse.

20

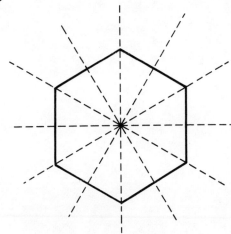

There are six axes of symmetry.
Rotational symmetry order 6: it can be rotated about its centre in 6 steps of 60° before it is back to its starting point and after each step we have the same shape in the same position.

21 The sum of the angles of a pentagon is 540°.
∴ size of 1 interior angle is 108°
∴ exterior angle = 72°
There are five exterior angles and their sum is $5 \times 72° = 360°$
Hexagon: exterior angle = 60° and sum = $6 \times 60° = 360°$
Heptagon: exterior angle = 51.4° and sum = $7 \times 51.4° = 360°$
Octagon: exterior angle = 45° and sum = $8 \times 45° = 360°$
Conclusion: sum of exterior angles is always 360° regardless of the number of sides.

22

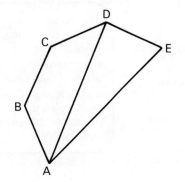

ABCDE lies on a circle with AE as diameter.
∴ A$\hat{\text{D}}$E = 90°   ∵ angle in semi-circle
Interior angle of regular octagon = 135°
∴ D$\hat{\text{E}}$A = 67½° and D$\hat{\text{A}}$E = 22½°

23   Sum of exterior angles = 360°

∴ 1 exterior angle = $\dfrac{360°}{15}$ = 24°

and interior angle = 180° − 24° = 156°

24

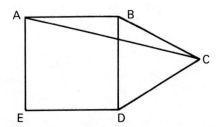

A$\hat{\text{B}}$D = 90°   ∵ angles of square
D$\hat{\text{B}}$C = 60°   ∵ angles of equilateral triangle
∴ A$\hat{\text{B}}$C = 150°
△ABC is isosceles   ∵ AB = BD = BC
∴ B$\hat{\text{A}}$C = B$\hat{\text{C}}$A = $\dfrac{180° - 150°}{2}$ = 15°

11 Similarity and scale drawings

In complete contrast to Chapter 10, the work in this chapter is practical from the word go. You are immediately plunged into questions and all the learning is done as you go along. It is essential that all questions and solutions are worked through thoroughly. By the time you get to the end of the chapter you will be at home with:

- **transformations**
- **similarity**
- **construction of 60°, 90°**
- **bisecting angles**
- **constructing perpendicular lines**
- **bisecting lines**.

★Transformations

We continue with our work on geometry by considering transformations again, but this time without using matrices. We shall again be using translation, reflection and rotation and combinations of these. The problems are invariably solved by drawing and great care is needed when doing these drawings.

★EXERCISE 11.1

1

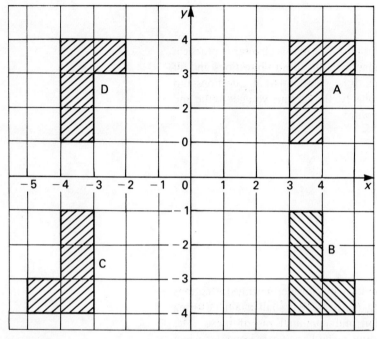

Complete the table:

Single transformation to make

from

	A	B	C	D
A	–	reflection in Ox		translation by $\begin{pmatrix} 7 \\ 0 \end{pmatrix}$
B		–		
C	rotation 180° about O		–	
D				–

2 A triangle is formed by joining the three points A (3, 4), B(4, 4) and C(3, 2). The triangle is then reflected in $x = 2$, and in $y = 1$. Draw a diagram to show the original triangle and the two reflections.

3 A is the point with coordinates (4, 1). Draw a diagram showing the point A and
(**a**) its reflection, A′, in $y = x$ and
b) its reflection, A″, in $y = -x$.
Try to form the rule which would give you the coordinates of A′ and A″ without drawing the diagram.

4

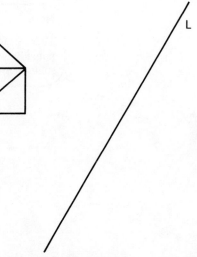

Copy the diagram, exactly, and reflect the shape S in the line L.
(Two methods are given in the answer but try to devise one of your
own first.)

5

O_×

Copy the diagram and show the image of S after a rotation of 70°
clockwise about O.

6   With X as the centre of enlargement enlarge the shape T by a scale
factor of 2.

New language and new
ideas here but have a go
before you turn to the
answer.

X ●

7   The diagram shows a part finished enlargement.

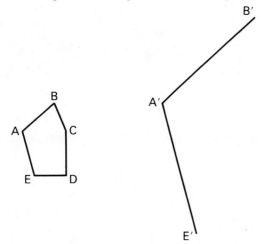

Note

There is an important note following the solution to this question.

Find the centre of enlargement and complete the diagram.

★★ 8   Using units of 1 cm on both axes, mark out the the x-axis from -8 to 11 and the y-axis from -5 to 7. Draw the triangle ABC where A is $(3, 2)$, B is $(3\frac{1}{2}, \frac{1}{2})$ and C is $(2, \frac{1}{2})$. Enlarge ABC by scale factor 3, centre the origin, to form $\triangle$A'B'C'. Also with centre of enlargement at the origin and with scale factor -2, form $\triangle$A''B''C''.

If the negative scale factor throws you a bit consider why you have been asked to draw the axes as you have done.

★★ 9   Consider the diagram in the answer to question 8.
   (a) What is the value of the three ratios AC : A'C', AB : A'B' and BC : B'C'?
   (b) How does the area of $\triangle$ABC compare with $\triangle$A'B'C'? How many times will $\triangle$ABC fit into $\triangle$A'B'C'?
   (c) Repeat parts (a) and (b) with the triangles ABC and A''B''C''.
   (d) What is the value of the ratio $\dfrac{A''B''}{A'B'}$?
   (e) What is the value of the ratio $\dfrac{\text{area } \triangle A''B''C''}{\text{area } \triangle A'B'C'}$?
   (f) Can you form some conclusion about the ratio of the areas of similar triangles compared with the ratio of the lengths of the sides?
   (g) If you can imagine similar three-dimensional shapes, how do you think the volumes would relate when compared with the sides?
       It might also help if you recall the units of volume and area.

★★ **10**

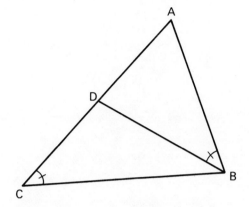

The marked angles are equal.
In the diagram there are three triangles. Two of them are similar. Which?
Which are the corresponding sides?

★★ **11**   A one-gallon bucket costs £1.50. A similar bucket has linear dimensions twice as big as the first. Compared with the smaller bucket how much material does it take to make the second bucket? How much does the second bucket hold, in relation to the first bucket? Find the cost of the second bucket if costs are proportional to
(**a**) diameter   (**b**) material required   (**c**) capacity.

★Similarity

Plans and maps are practical examples of the use of similarity. A plan has the same shape but is a different size from what it represents. Drawing plans and other scale drawings demands accuracy and skill in the use of instruments, and that is what we are going to look at now.

An instrument which is most useful but which is often overlooked is the **set square**. Set squares always have a 90° angle and *either* two 45° angles or a 60° and a 30° angle. By using the set square as a template we can quickly draw any of these angles. Used together with a ruler it is a simple matter to draw parallel lines (shown later in an example).

★EXERCISE 11.2

1   Mark two points, A and B, on your paper about two inches apart. At A draw an angle of between 30° and 80°. Using ruler and set square only, repeat the angle at B.

2

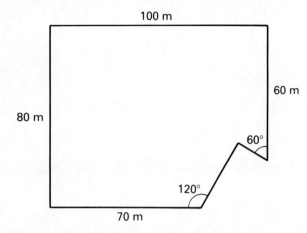

The diagram shows a rectangular car park with a bit cut out at one corner. Using a scale of 1 cm to represent 10 m and using a ruler and a (90°, 60°, 30°) set square only, draw a plan of the car park.

3 Make an accurate drawing of a triangle with sides of 3.5″, 2.8″ and 3″. Measure the angles of the triangle.

> You will need your compasses for this one.

4

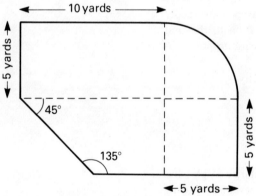

The diagram is a sketch from which a plan is to be drawn, scale 1 cm = 1 yard. Draw the plan.

5 ABCD is a rectangle in which AD = 16 cm, AB = 25.6 cm.

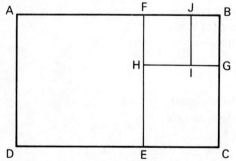

Draw the rectangle, full size. Work out $\dfrac{AB}{AD}$.

ADEF is a square. Draw FE. Measure CB and CE. Work out $\dfrac{CB}{CE}$.

HGCE is a square. Draw GH. Measure GH and BG. Work out $\dfrac{GH}{BG}$.

Carry on this process as long as possible, each time working out the ratio of the long side to the short side of the rectangle remaining.

★Ruler and compass constructions

We have already made several references to the angles of 60° and 90°. A further feature of these two angles is that they can be drawn very accurately using only a ruler and a pair of compasses.

Angles of 60°

Stage 1

Stage 2

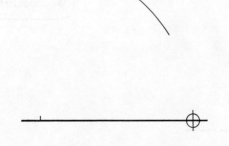

The compass setting must be kept the same throughout.

Stage 3

The compass point goes on the circled points.

Stage 4

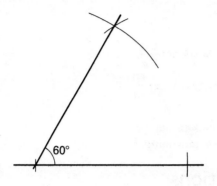

Now that you know how to draw an angle of 60° you should try to find out why this method works.

Angles of 90°
Stage 1

Stage 2

Increase the compass setting before going on to stage 3.

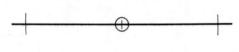

Stage 3

Stage 4

Why does this one work?

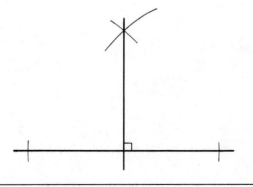

★Bisecting an angle

We are still using ruler and compasses only.

Stage 1

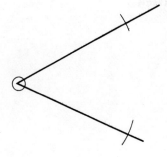

Stage 2

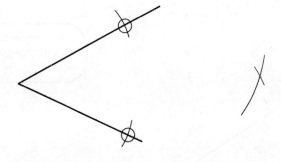

Stage 3

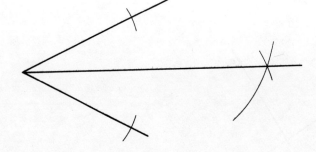

Why does this one work? To explain, add two extra lines to stage 3 and look for congruent triangles.

Now you know this, construction of angles of 45° and 30° becomes possible.

★Two further constructions

This is the usual name for ruler and compass only work.

I A LINE THROUGH A POINT, A, PERPENDICULAR TO ANOTHER LINE

Stage 1

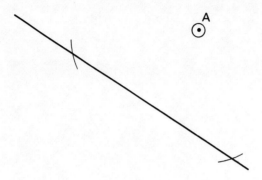

Stage 2

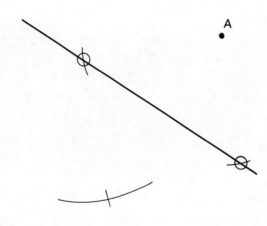

The compass setting may be changed to do stage 2.

Stage 3

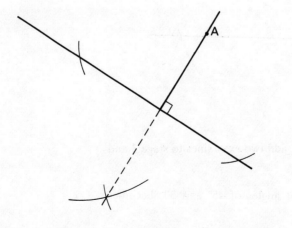

2   TO BISECT A LINE

Stage 1

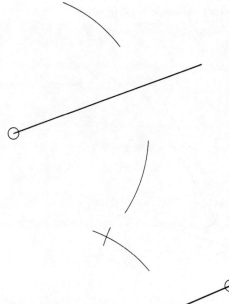

Stage 2

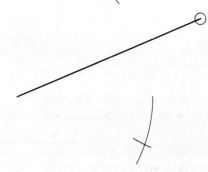

Stage 3

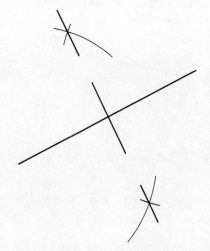

> The compass setting must not change throughout this construction.

> The final line not only bisects the first one but it is also perpendicular to it, and hence it is called the **perpendicular bisector**.

★EXERCISE 11.3

1   Using ruler and compasses only, construct a triangle XYZ in which XY = 3″, X = 90° and Y = 30°.

2   Construct the diagram shown here.
The diagram is not to scale.
Measure XY.

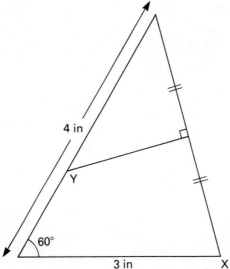

3   Using compasses, ruler and set square only, draw a parallelogram with sides of 10 cm and 6 cm and an angle of 75°. Measure the longer diagonal.

4   A trig. point A is 8 km from B on a bearing of 045°. Chimney C is on bearing 150° from B and 180° from A. Using a scale of 1 cm to 1 km, construct a plan showing the positions of A, B and C.
A straight path passes through the midpoint of AC and is at right angles to BC. It cuts the line BC at D. Find BD.

★★ 5   Construct the kite ABCD.

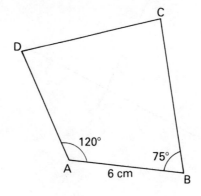

Solutions to exercises

SOLUTIONS TO EXERCISE 11.1

1 Single transformation
to make   from

	A	B	C	D
A	–	reflection in Ox	rotation 180° about O	translation by $\binom{7}{0}$
B	reflection in Ox	–	reflection in Oy	translation by $\binom{7}{0}$ followed by reflection in Ox
C	rotation 180° about O	reflection in Oy	–	rotation 180° about $(-3.5, 0)$
D	translation by $\binom{-7}{0}$	reflection in Oy followed by translation by $\binom{-7}{0}$	rotation 180° about $(-3.5, 0)$	

It is not possible to make D from B, or B from D, in a single transformation. Two are needed.

D from B: translation $\binom{7}{0}$ to A followed by reflection in Ox

or rotation 180° about $(-3.5, 0)$ to C followed by reflection in Oy.

2

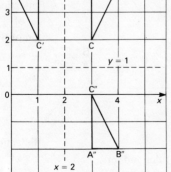

△A″B″C″ could also be obtained by rotating △A′B′C′ through a half turn about the point (2, 1).

3

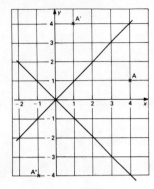

A′ is the point (1, 4).

A″ is the point (−1, −4).

(a) To reflect in $y = x$ exchange the coordinates: (4, 1) becomes (1, 4).

(b) To reflect in $y = -x$ exchange the coordinates and change their signs: (4, 1) becomes (−1, −4).

4   This question is made easier by the use of a set square.

Method 1

1   Place a set square on line L so that it also touches point A.

2   Place a ruler against the base of the set square.

3   Measure the distance from point A to line L.

4   Keep the set square in place and measure the corresponding distance along the ruler from the line L to the reflection of point A (A′). Mark the point.

5   Reposition the set square and ruler and repeat the process for the remaining points of the diagram.

6   Join up the reflected points using a ruler. The resulting diagram will be the reflection of the original diagram.

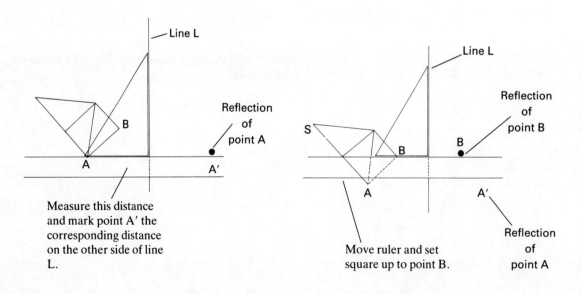

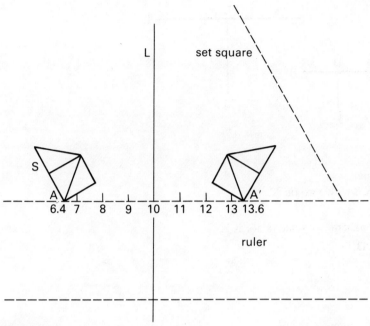

Method 2

Use tracing paper and on it mark line L and the ends of all the lines in S. Turn the paper over, place the tracing of L on L and mark the points of S.

5   Tracing paper is essential this time.

Add the line OA to the diagram.

Trace the diagram.

Using a protractor establish the line OB.

Use the tracing to complete the diagram.

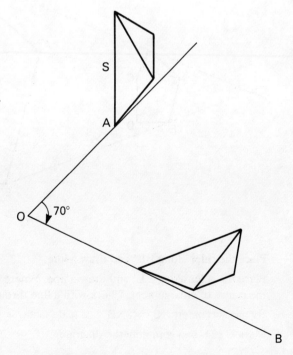

6

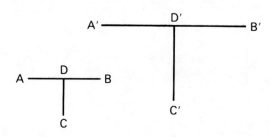

X●

Not a difficult technique.
Place the ruler along XA with zero on X.

NB: XA = 3.1 cm
⇒   XA′ = 2 × 3.1 = 6.2 cm   ∵ scale factor is 2.
Similarly for B, C and D.

Join up. Job done.

7

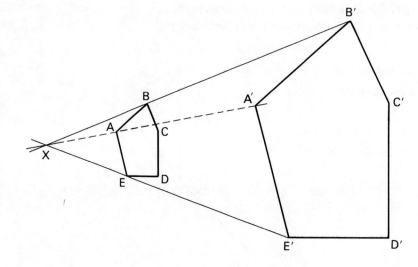

Place the ruler along BB′ and draw a line.

Place the ruler along EE′ and draw a line. Where the lines cross is the centre of enlargement. Check with a line through AA′.

By measurement, XB′ = 3XB   ∵ scale factor is 3.

Mark C′, D′ and complete the diagram.

Similar shapes

In the diagram for question 7, ABCDE and A'B'C'D'E' have the same shape but they are of different size. Consequently they are said to be **similar**: i.e. ABCDE and A'B'C'D'E' are **similar pentagons**.

Congruent shapes

If two diagrams have the **same shape** and the **same size** they are identically equal and they are said to be **congruent**.

> Similar shapes and congruent shapes defined.

8

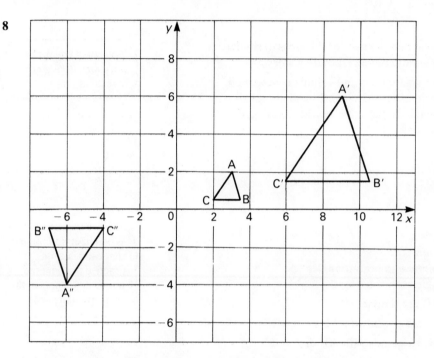

The diagram explains itself. Note all three triangles are similar.

9   (a) $1:3$

   (b) $1:9$ There are 9 of ABC in A'B'C'.

   (c) $1:2$ and $1:4$

   (d) $\dfrac{A''B''}{A'B'} = \dfrac{2 \times CB}{3 \times CB} = \dfrac{2}{3}$

   (e) $\dfrac{\text{area} \triangle A''B''C''}{\text{area} \triangle A'B'C'} = \dfrac{4 \times \text{area} \triangle ABC}{9 \times \text{area} \triangle ABC} = \dfrac{4}{9}$

(f) Now $\dfrac{AB}{A'B'} = \dfrac{1}{3}$ and $\dfrac{\text{area } \triangle ABC}{\text{area } \triangle A'B'C'} = \dfrac{1}{9}$

$\Rightarrow \quad \dfrac{\text{area } \triangle ABC}{\text{area } \triangle A'B'C'} = \left(\dfrac{AB}{A'B'}\right)^2$

Also $\quad \dfrac{AB}{A''B''} = \dfrac{1}{2}$ and $\dfrac{\text{area } \triangle ABC}{\text{area } \triangle A''B''C''} = \dfrac{1}{4}$

$\Rightarrow \quad \dfrac{\text{area } \triangle ABC}{\text{area } \triangle A''B''C''} = \left(\dfrac{AB}{A''B''}\right)^2$

And, $\quad \dfrac{A'B'}{A''B''} = \dfrac{2}{3}$ and $\dfrac{\text{area } \triangle A'B'C'}{\text{area } \triangle A''B''C''} = \dfrac{4}{9}$

$\Rightarrow \quad \dfrac{\text{area } \triangle A'B'C'}{\text{area } \triangle A''B''C''} = \left(\dfrac{A'B'}{A''B''}\right)^2$

This leads to the conclusion that the ratio of the areas of similar shapes is the square of the ratio of corresponding sides.

(g) Since area is measured in square units and volume is measured in cubic units, it would be reasonable to conclude that the ratio of volumes of similar solids is the cube of the ratio of the lengths of corresponding sides.

> You could check this out for yourself, as a mini-investigation.

10 In $\triangle ABC$ and $\triangle ADB$:

$\hat{ABD} = \hat{ACB} \quad \because$ given

$\hat{DAB} = \hat{BAC} \quad \because$ common to both triangles

$\hat{ADB} = \hat{ABC} \quad \because$ angle sum of triangle

So $\triangle ABC$ and $\triangle ADB$ are similar.

Then AB in $\triangle ABD$ corresponds with AC in $\triangle ABC$

$\qquad$ AD in $\triangle ABD$ corresponds with AB in $\triangle ABC$

and $\quad$ BD in $\triangle ABD$ corresponds with CB in $\triangle ABC$

or, to sum up in a concise way,

$$\dfrac{AB}{AC} = \dfrac{AD}{AB} = \dfrac{BD}{CB}$$

> When naming similar shapes, it is good practice to name the points or vertices in the corresponding order.

11 Material depends on area and

ratio of areas $\quad = \dfrac{2^2}{1^2} = \dfrac{4}{1} \qquad$ needs four times as much

ratio of volumes $\quad = \dfrac{2^3}{1^3} = \dfrac{8}{1} \qquad$ holds 8 gallons.

Cost depending on diameter $= 2 \times £1.50 = £3.00$

Cost depending on material $= 4 \times £1.50 = £6.00$

Cost depending on capacity $= 8 \times £1.50 = £12.00$

SOLUTIONS TO EXERCISE 11.2

1

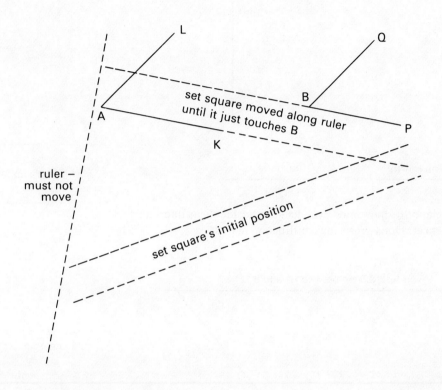

The set square is placed along AK.

The ruler is placed along the edge of the set square.

The ruler must not move.
The set square is slid up until it just touches B.

BP is drawn: BP is parallel to AK.

Repeat to get BQ from AL.

$Q\hat{B}P = L\hat{A}K$ $\because$ corresponding angles

2

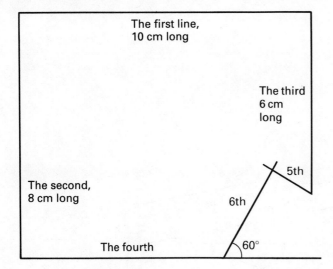

It is good technique to draw lines over length and let them intersect rather than just meet. Don't erase any construction marks.

3

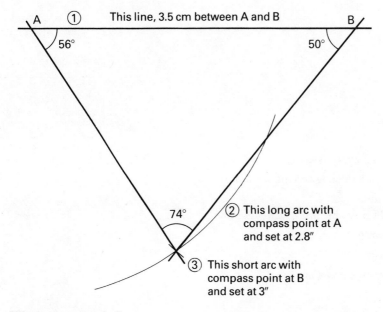

Where arcs cross is C.

Join AC and BC.

Angles are as marked.

4

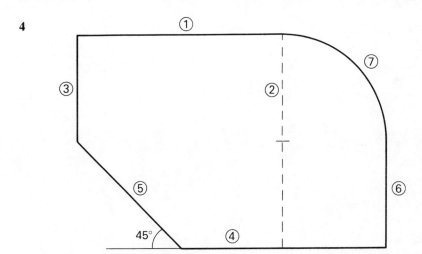

The numbers indicate the order in which the lines are drawn.
(5) can be drawn with a (90°, 45°, 45°) set square.

5   You should find the ratio always works out to be 1.6, i.e. the rectangles are all similar.

> Rectangles which have this property, i.e. long side/short side = 1.6, are known as golden rectangles and they are used a lot in Art and Architecture. You could carry out a good and interesting piece of coursework by researching them.

SOLUTIONS TO EXERCISE 11.3

1

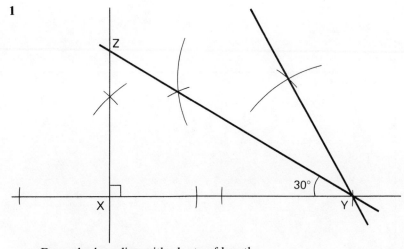

Draw the base line with plenty of length.

Mark off X and Y.

Construct angles of 90° at X and 60° at Y.

Bisect the 60° at Y.

Join up to the perpendicular to X, to find Z.

> **Important**
>
> All lines, arcs etc must be left on the diagram. Do not erase any marks.

2

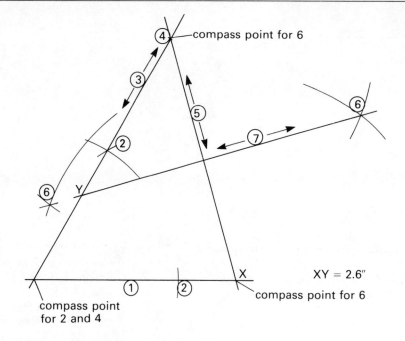

compass point for 6

XY = 2.6"

compass point for 6

compass point
for 2 and 4

The numbers indicate the order of steps.

3   A planning diagram is needed.

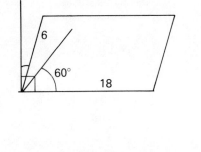

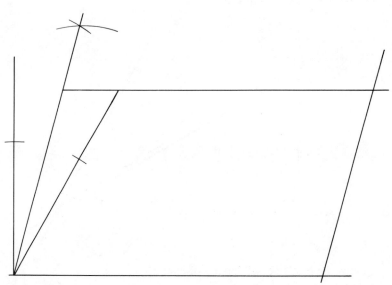

75° is the problem.

It can be done by constructing angles of 60° and 90° and bisecting
the angle between them. The parallelogram is completed by sliding
the set square along the ruler as shown in **Exercise 11.2**, question 1.

4

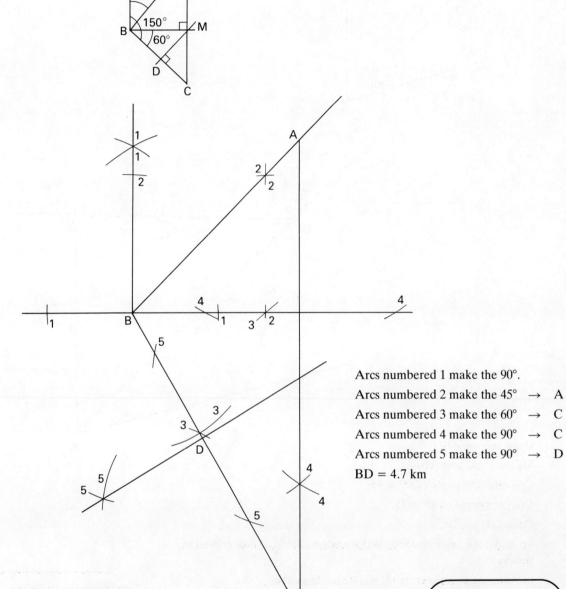

Arcs numbered 1 make the 90°.
Arcs numbered 2 make the 45° → A
Arcs numbered 3 make the 60° → C
Arcs numbered 4 make the 90° → C
Arcs numbered 5 make the 90° → D
BD = 4.7 km

Draw BA and BC first.

C is where BC and AC meet.

M is the midpoint of AC, found by using the ruler.

Join MD.

Note

A small rough diagram, from which you sort out what you are going to do, often helps.

5

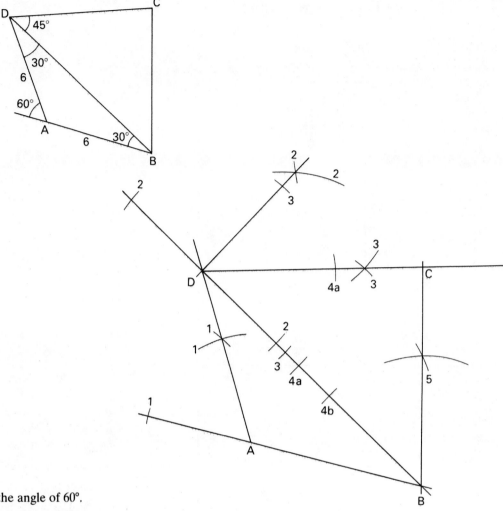

Draw the angle of 60°.

Measure AD and AB.

Construct the angle of 45° at D.

Copy the angle of 45° at B.

Draw DC and BC.

To make the angle of 45° at B the angle of 45° at D was copied in this way:

    Place compass point on D, mark arcs 4a and 4a.

    Do not alter compass setting; point on B and mark arcs 4b and 4b.

    Set compasses to distance across the two 4a marks.

    Place compass point on 4b mark on BD, draw 5.

    Draw BC.

Obviously, this is not the only way of getting an angle of 45° at B but this is a good and easy method: the method of **copying an angle**.

12 Revision papers

Revision paper 1

★ **1** Express these numbers in standard form ($A \times 10^n$).

(a) 57 900   (b) 0.005 41

★ **2** Find four consecutive integers which add up to 2.

★ **3** Use your calculator to evaluate this.

$$\frac{56.1 \times 0.93}{4.9 \times 0.004 \times 17.3}$$

4 This is a formula from mechanics.

$E = \frac{1}{2}mu^2 + mgh$

Find E when $m = 12$, $g = 9.8$, $u = 7$ and $h = 20$.

★ **5**

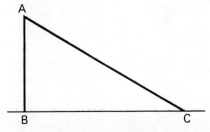

AB represents a TV mast.
BC is level ground and BC = 350 feet.
$A\widehat{B}C = 90°$ and $A\widehat{C}B = 27°$.

(a) Find the height of the mast.

(b) Find the length of AC.

★★ **6**

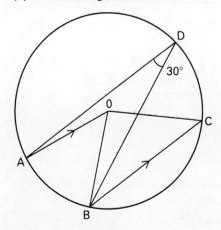

O is the centre of the circle, $A\widehat{D}B = 30°$ and AO ∥ BC.
(a) Find $A\widehat{O}B$ and $O\widehat{B}C$.
(b) Can you form any conclusions about the triangle OBC?

★ **7** John sets off at 9.00 a.m. on a leisurely bike ride. He covers 8 km in 50 minutes, then takes 40 minutes for a snack. Then he continues at 4 km per hour. Mark is a racing cyclist and he sets off at 11.00 a.m. riding at 36 kph.
Represent both journeys on a distance-time graph and find when and where Mark overtakes John.

★ **8** Pencils are bought at £35.00 per 1000.
They are sold at 6p each.
Find the profit on 1000 pencils and express this as a percentage profit.

★ **9** Two dice are rolled and the scores added. What is the probability of

(**a**) a total greater than or equal to 2

(**b**) a total which is prime

(**c**) a total which is prime and made up of prime numbers (1 is not prime)

(**d**) $8 \leqslant \text{total} < 12$?

10 Express $13\frac{5}{11}$

(**a**) correct to 2 decimal places

(**b**) correct to 2 significant figures

(**c**) correct to 1 decimal place.

Revision paper 2

★★ **1** For which range of values of x is $2x - 1 > 9$?

★ **2** Tony and Pam share £147 in the ratio 4 : 3. How much does each receive?

★★ **3** Simplify $\dfrac{p^{\frac{2}{3}} \times p^2}{p^{\frac{4}{3}}} + \dfrac{q^7}{q^{\frac{7}{2}} \times q^{\frac{5}{2}}} + (2r - 1)^0$

★ **4** A coin is spun five times and each time it shows tails. What is the probability of tails on the sixth spin?

★ **5** A survey of the houses of a class of pupils gave the following table.

Type	terraced	semi-detached	detached	bungalow	flat
Number	10	6	2	4	8

Illustrate this information on (**a**) a bar graph (**b**) a pie chart.

★ **6** The angles of a pentagon are $x°$, $(x + 20)°$, $(2x - 10)°$, $74°$ and $108°$.
Find the value of x and hence all the angles of the pentagon.

★ **7** The vector **a** has value $\begin{pmatrix} 4 \\ 3 \end{pmatrix}$ and **b** is $\begin{pmatrix} -3 \\ 2 \end{pmatrix}$.
Find **r**, given that $5\mathbf{a} - 3\mathbf{b} = \mathbf{r}$.

★★ 8 The cross-section of a triangular prism is an isosceles triangle with base 4 cm long and angles of 45°, 45°, 90°. The prism is 6 cm long. Using only ruler and compasses, construct its net.

★ 9 Draw the graphs of $y = x + 1$ and $2y + 3x = 12$ on the same axes, using values of x from 0 to 4. Write down the coordinates of the point where they intersect.
Is it possible to find another point with coordinates that will satisfy both equations? Justify your answer.

★ 10 In a cul-de-sac of 16 houses, 7 households had a dog, 5 had a cat and 7 had neither. Let n be the number of houses with both a dog and a cat and represent this information on a Venn diagram. Make up an equation containing n, and solve it.

Revision paper 3

1 Two sequences of numbers are:
(a) 2 4 8 16... and (b) 8 38 68 ...
Find the first number which is common to both sequences, excluding 8.

2 A dance team of eight girls has an average weight of 54 kg. The weights of seven of the girls are 52.5 kg, 55 kg, 54 kg, 50.7 kg, 56.2 kg, 58.9 kg and 53.7 kg.
Find the weight of the eighth girl.

★ 3 David spins a coin three times. Draw a tree diagram to show all the possible outcomes. Find P(two heads, one tail, in any order).

★ 4 A party goes by coach to the theatre. The hire of the coach is £100.
(a) Let the number of people in the party be n and write down the amount of each person's contribution to the hire of the coach.
(b) The cost of a theatre ticket is £8. Write down a formula for the amount C that each person has to pay.
(c) Find the cost per person if 34 people go to the theatre.

★★ 5 $f(x) = x^2$ $g(x) = x - 1$ $h(x) = \dfrac{3}{x}$
(a) Find $fg(x)$.   (b) Find $ghf(x)$.   (c) Find $h^{-1}(x)$.

★★ 6 Find the length of CD.

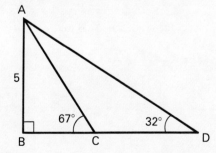

★ **7**

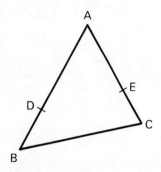

$\overrightarrow{AD} = 2\mathbf{a}$
$\overrightarrow{AB} = 3\mathbf{a}$
$\overrightarrow{AC} = 3\mathbf{b}$
$\overrightarrow{AE} = 2\mathbf{b}$

(a) Find $\overrightarrow{DE}$.   (b) Find $\overrightarrow{BC}$.

(c) What can you then say about the lines DE and BC?

(d) What can you say about the triangles ADE and ABC?

(e) What fraction of $\triangle ABC$ is the area DECB?

★★ **8**   Find the values of a and b.

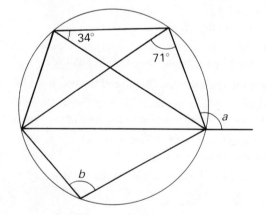

★ **9**   Construct the triangle ABC in which AB = 2.2″, BC = 2.5″ and CA = 1.75″.

Using ruler and compasses only, bisect the angles at A, B and C.
Can you draw any conclusions?

★★ **10**   Solve these equations. $5x + 2y = 23$
                                      $4y - x = 13$

Revision paper 4

★★ 1   After an examination the mark distribution was as follows:

Mark	0−9	10−19	20−29	30−39	40−49	50−60
Frequency	8	14	22	25	19	12

(a) Calculate the mean.

(b) Find the median, either by calculation or graphically.

(c) Draw the cumulative frequency curve.

★★ 2   If n is a positive integer explain why $n(n + 1)$ is always even.

★ 3   A kite is flying on the end of a string which is 80 yards long and at an elevation of 37°. Assuming the string is straight, find the height of the kite above the ground.

★ 4   The four aces are removed from a pack of cards.
Darren spins a coin and then chooses one ace from the four.
Show all the possible outcomes on a tree diagram. Find the probability of heads and a red ace.

★ 5   Find the single vector which would replace $2\mathbf{a} - 3\mathbf{b} + \mathbf{c}$
where $\mathbf{a} = \begin{pmatrix} 4 \\ 1 \end{pmatrix}$, $\mathbf{b} = \begin{pmatrix} 3 \\ -1 \end{pmatrix}$, $\mathbf{c} = \begin{pmatrix} 6 \\ 4 \end{pmatrix}$.
Show your results on an accurate diagram.

★★ 6   An engine has a fly wheel of diameter 28 cm and on the rim a fine timing mark is etched. The engine runs at 3500 revolutions per minute (rpm) for $2\frac{1}{2}$ hours and then 2000 rpm for 45 minutes.
Find, in km, how far the timing mark travels, to the nearest km.

★★ 7   The speedometer on a car has an error of +10%. Find the actual distance travelled when the car is driven for 1.5 hours with the speedometer reading 66 mph.

★ 8   Ravi and Jameel invest £2000 and £1800 respectively in a business, and they agree that the profits will be shared in the ratio of their investments.
The year's profits result in Jameel receiving £1530. Find the total profit the business made.

★★ 9   Find f(x) given this table of values.

x	1	2	3	4	5	6
f(x)	3	11	31	69	131	323

Find f(x) when $x = 7$.

The method of differences will help!

Question 9 is difficult: it will test your patience.

★★ 10   The equation $2x^2 - 5x - 2 = 0$ has a solution between 2 and 3.
Use an iterative method to find the root, correct to 1 decimal place.

Revision paper 5

★ **1** Make k the subject of the formula $t = \dfrac{k^2 - 1}{2}$.

Find the values of k when $t = 24$.

★ **2** The length of a rectangle is three times the breadth.
Its area is 48 cm².

(a) Find the area of a square which has the same perimeter.

(b) Find the area of a circle which has circumference equal to the perimeter of the rectangle.

★★ **3** Find the value of a and b if

$$\begin{pmatrix} a & 2 \\ 3 & 4b \end{pmatrix} \begin{pmatrix} 1 \\ 3 \end{pmatrix} = \begin{pmatrix} 7 \\ 27 \end{pmatrix}$$

★ **4**

P •

Use tracing paper to copy this diagram.
With centre of enlargement P, enlarge the figure by a scale factor of 3.

★★ **5** In the office car park there are 5 British Leyland cars, 3 Fords and a VW. The nine drivers finish work at the same time and the order in which they leave the building is random.

(a) Find the probability that a Ford will be first to leave.

(b) Given that a Ford is first, followed by two BLs, find the probability the VW is next.

★★ **6** The sum of Carole's age and Leon's age is 50 years. Three years ago Carole was three times the age of Leon.

(a) Let Carole's age be C years and Leon's be L years and form two equations, one for each of the above statements.

(b) Solve the equations simultaneously to find their ages now.

7 Find the value of $a^2 + b^2 - 2abp$ when $a = 5$, $b = 4$ and $p = 0.6$.

★ **8** A man earns £6.00 per hour for 40 hours work. Any overtime is paid at time and three-quarters. He works an average of 3 hours overtime per week.

(a) Find his average weekly gross wage.
He pays 6% in superannuation.

(b) What is the amount he pays in superannuation?

(c) Find his annual income after superannuation is paid.

(d) £4000 of his annual earnings are not taxed.
The rest is taxed at 25%. How much tax does he pay?

★ **9** Remove the brackets from this expression.
$(x + 1)(x + 3)(2x - 1)$

★ **10** Using ruler and compasses only, construct a triangle with angles of 67.5° and 52.5°, with the line opposite the 52.5° angle 6 cm long.

Revision paper 6

★ **1** The surface area of a cube is 69.36 cm². Find its volume.

★ **2** A man bought n watches at £p each. He sold m of the watches at £q each. Write down an expression for his profit. Find his profit as a percentage.
If he neither makes nor loses on the deal, find an equation linking n, p, m and q.

★ **3** From a full pack of cards the 3 of hearts is drawn. Find the probability that the next card drawn is
(a) a 3 **(b)** a 5 **(c)** a heart.

★ **4** The price of a TV set is £260.
For a cash sale there is a reduction of 10%. HP terms are £20 deposit plus twelve monthly payments of £24.

(a) Find the total HP price.

(b) Find the difference between the maximum and minimum prices which may be paid for the set.

★★ **5** Calculate the length of the longest stick which can be placed in a box which is a cuboid measuring 25 cm × 14 cm × 11 cm.

★★ **6** $gf(x) = 4x^2 + 1$ and $g(x) = x^2 + 1$.
Find $f(x)$.

★★ **7** On the same axes, draw the graphs of
$y = 5.5$, $x = 8.5$ and $y = 2x - 3$.
Shade the area which satisfies all the following.
$0 < y \leqslant 5.5$ $0 < x \leqslant 8.5$ $y < 2x - 3$

★★ **8** ABCDE is a regular pentagon inscribed in a circle, centre O. radius 10 cm.

(a) Find $C\hat{D}E$.

(b) Find $E\hat{C}D$ and hence find $B\hat{C}A$ and $A\hat{C}E$.

(c) State $A\hat{O}E$ and hence find $H\hat{O}E$ where $OH \geqslant AE$.

(d) Calculate OH.

(e) Calculate the area of △ OAE and hence the area of the pentagon.

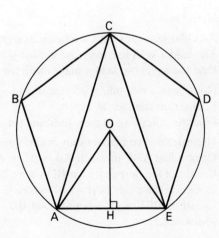

★★ 9   A pyramid has a rectangular base measuring 26 cm by 12 cm. Its perpendicular height is 18 cm. Calculate its volume.

★★ 10   Simplify the following, leaving your answers in surd form in each case.

       (a) $\sqrt{8} + \sqrt{18}$ **(b)** $\sqrt{75} + \sqrt{12}$

> **NB** A surd is the square root of an integer which is not a square e.g. $\sqrt{2}$, $\sqrt{5}$ but not $\sqrt{9}$ or $\sqrt{16}$.
>
> Hint: e.g. $\sqrt{72} = \sqrt{36} \times \sqrt{2} = 6 \times \sqrt{2} = 6\sqrt{2}$

Revision paper 7

★ 1   A lorry has a carrying capacity of 15 tonnes. It is fully laden with sacks of coal. The coal sacks are in two sizes, 50 kg and 25 kg. If there are equal numbers of both sizes of sack, how many of each are there?

★★ 2   Solve this equation. $x^2 - x - 20 = 0$

★★ 3   The triangle ABC, where A is (4, 3), B is (8, 3) and C is (8, 6), is transformed by the matrix
$$\begin{pmatrix} 0 & -2 \\ 2 & 0 \end{pmatrix}.$$
Find the coordinates of the new positions of A, B and C.

★ 4   ε is the set of whole numbers from 1 to 20.
A is the set of even numbers.
B is the set of multiples of 3.
Illustrate this information on a Venn diagram.

★ 5   Make y the subject of the formula $a = x + 2y + 3z$.
Find the value of y if $a = 5$, $x = 3$ and $z = 2$.

★★ 6   Simplify these expressions.

       (a) $3(2xy^3)^2(3x^2y)^3$

       (b) $\dfrac{x^{-1}y}{x^3y^2}$

       (c) $81^{\frac{3}{4}} \times 3^{-2}$

★ 7   A ladder leans against a wall with its foot on horizontal ground.
The ladder is 18 feet long and its foot is 7 feet from the wall.
Find the angle the ladder makes with the ground.

★ 8   Helen runs a five mile road race at a speed of 8 mph.
Louise runs the race at 7 mph.
Find the difference in their finishing times.

★ 9   Use ruler and compasses only in this question.
Draw a line ABC in which AB = BC = 4 cm.
Construct the perpendicular BD where BD = 8 cm.
Construct the angle BAE = 60° where E is on BD.
Construct $\widehat{BCF}$ = 45° where F is on BD.
Measure EF.

★★ **10**

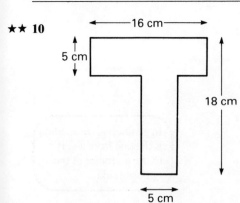

The diagram shows the cross-section of a steel girder 2 metres long.
Find the volume of the girder in **(a)** m³ **(b)** mm³.
Express both answers in standard form.

Revision paper 8

★★ **1**

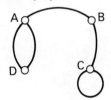

Draw up a one-stage route matrix for the diagram shown.

★ **2** A tractor has wheels which are 12 inches wide. It crosses a rectangular piece of ground, 60 yd × 100 yd, moving parallel to the 60 yd edge, 25 times. The wheels never cover the same ground twice.
A beetle has negligible size and it is asleep on the ground throughout. Calculate its chance of survival.

★ **3** Six people have a meal in a restaurant. Three have meals costing £6.75, two have meals costing £7.20 and one has a meal at £5.90. There is a service charge of 10% and finally VAT at 17.5% is added. Make out a bill and find the total cost.

★ **4** Solve this equation. $4(2x + 1) = 28$

★ **5** From Preston, Fleetwood is on a bearing of 310° and it is 75½ km away.
The bearing of Lancaster from Fleetwood is 044° and the distance is 21¼ km.
Using a scale of 2 cm : 5 km draw a diagram of the positions of Preston, Fleetwood and Lancaster. Find the distance and bearing of Lancaster from Preston.

★★ 6 For the equation $y = 4 + 3x - x^2$ draw up a table of values from $x = 0$ to $x = 4$.
Using 2 cm to 1 unit on each axis draw the graph of $y = 4 + 3x - x^2$.
Using the trapezium rule, with strips of width $\frac{1}{2}$ unit, find the area enclosed by the curve and the axes.

★★ 7 In the triangle, AM is a median and $AG = \frac{2}{3}AM$.
$\overrightarrow{CB} = \mathbf{a}$ and $\overrightarrow{CA} = \mathbf{b}$.

Find CG in terms of $\mathbf{a}$ and $\mathbf{b}$.

> In geometry, the median is the line from a vertex to the midpoint of the opposite side.

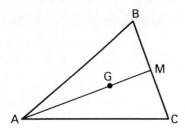

★★ 8 AB is a diameter.
Find **(a)** $C\hat{E}B$ **(b)** $C\hat{A}B$.

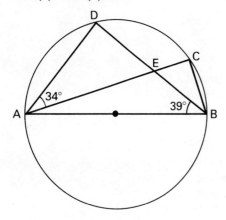

9 Within a square of side 3 cm make patterns which have
(a) one line of symmetry
(b) two lines of symmetry
(c) four lines of symmetry.
State the order of rotational symmetry in each case.

10 Find the exact value of $(\frac{1}{2} + \frac{2}{3}) \div (\frac{5}{6} - \frac{1}{4})$.

Revision paper 9

1   Arrange the following fractions in ascending order.

$$\frac{2}{7} \quad \frac{3}{11} \quad \frac{4}{17} \quad \frac{3}{13} \quad \frac{6}{23}$$

★ 2   Remove the brackets and collect like terms together in this expression.

$(3 - x)(x + 2) + 2x(x + 5)$

3   The rate of exchange on a particular day is 3.4DM to £1.
Draw a conversion graph with a scale from £0 – £10 on one axis and
0 – 34DM on the other.
Use your graph to convert the following amounts.

(**a**) £7.30 to DM   (**b**) 14DM to £
(**c**) £47 to DM   (**d**) 2750DM to £

★★ 4   Calculate the circumference of a bicycle wheel of diameter 27 inches.
Find how far the bike has travelled, in yards, when the wheel has turned 100 times.
If the gearing is in the ratio   chain wheel : sprocket = 11 : 4   how many turns will the pedals have made?
If this ride takes 40 seconds find the speed of the bike in
(**a**) yards per second (**b**) mph.

> This means the pedals go round 4 times for the wheel to go round 11 times.

★ 5

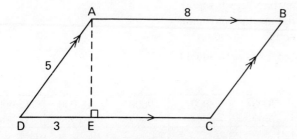

Use the theorem of Pythagoras to find
(**a**) AE   (**b**) the length of the diagonal BD.
Find the area of the parallelogram.

★ 6   The exterior angle of a regular polygon is 20°. How many sides has it?

★ 7   A row of four pairs of semi-detached houses is symmetrical, as is each pair of houses. Copy the diagram and show the transformations necessary to create a row of four houses. Show all details.

★ 8   Find the difference between 4^{-3} and 3^{-4}.

★★ 9 $A = \begin{pmatrix} 4 & -1 \\ 2 & 3 \end{pmatrix} B = \begin{pmatrix} 0 & -2 \\ 3 & -4 \end{pmatrix}$

    Find (a) **AB**   (b) **BA**.

★ 10   Solve this equation. $\dfrac{x}{4} + \dfrac{3}{8} = \dfrac{7}{8}$

Revision paper 10

★ 1   When screws are made by a particular machine they have a quoted length of 50 mm. The gauge through which they pass rejects screws with an error in length of more than 4%. What are the maximum and minimum lengths of screw that are accepted?

★★ 2   The motor dealers in a town issued a list of new cars bought according to price.

Cost (£)	4000 –4999	5000 –5999	6000 –6999	7000 –7999	8000 –8999	9000 –9999	10 000 –10 999	11 000 –11 999
Frequency	12	20	56	41	26	24	19	11

    Find
    (a) the mean   (b) the median   (c) the modal class   (d) the SIR.
    This question may be answered by calculation or by drawing the
    ogive (cumulative frequency curve).

    SIR is semi-interquartile range.

★ 3   Solve this equation. $\dfrac{2}{x} + \dfrac{1}{2} = 1$

★ 4   Draw the graph of $y = x^2 - 5x + 4$ for values of x from 0 to 6.
    Hence solve these equations.
    (a) $x^2 - 5x + 4 = 0$ (b) $x^2 - 5x + 1 = 0$

★ 5   A car leaves a junction travelling north-east at 40 mph. At the same time another leaves the same junction travelling south-east at 20 mph. Find the distance between them after 30 minutes.

★ 6   Find the gradient of the line joining A(0, −2) and B(6, 3).
Write down the equation of the line of which AB is a part.

★ 7   A rhombus has diagonals of lengths 10 cm and 24 cm. Calculate
(a) the length of the side of the rhombus
(b) the area of the rhombus.

★ 8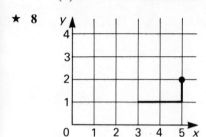

Draw the shape shown, and its image after reflection in the x-axis, followed by reflection in the line $y = -x$.
What is the single transformation which would have produced the same final image?

★ 9   Draw any triangle and construct the perpendicular bisector of each side. Can you draw any conclusions?

★★ 10   Two cubes have edges of 3 cm and 5 cm. Find
(a) the ratio of their surface areas   (b) the ratio of their volumes.

Solutions to revision papers

SOLUTIONS TO REVISION PAPER I

1 **(a)** $57\,900 = 5.79 \times 10^4$

(b) $0.005\,41 = 5.41 \times 10^{-3}$

2 Let the integers be: $n, n + 1, n + 2, n + 3$.
Then $n + n + 1 + n + 2 + n + 3 = 2$
$n + 6 = 2 \Rightarrow n = -1$
$\therefore$ integers are $-1, 0, 1, 2$.

3

Calculator sequence	Display
56.1	56.1
×	56.1
0.93	0.93
=	52.173
÷	52.173
4.9	4.9
÷	10.647551
0.004	0.004
÷	2661.8878
17.3	17.3
=	153.86634

A popular mistake on these two lines is to press × instead of ÷.

4 $E = \frac{1}{2}mv^2 + mgh$
$= \frac{1}{2} \times 12 \times 7^2 + 12 \times 9.8 \times 20 = 2646$

5 $\tan A\hat{C}B = \dfrac{AB}{BC} \Rightarrow \tan 27° = \dfrac{AB}{350}$
$\therefore AB = 350\tan 27° = 178.3 \text{ ft}$
$AC = \sqrt{(178.3^2 + 350^2)} = 392.8 \text{ ft}$

We could also have used sine or cosine to find x.

6 $A\hat{O}B = 2 \times 30° = 60° \because$ angle at centre $= 2 \times$ angle at circumference
$O\hat{B}C = 60° \qquad \because$ alternate angles, OA $\parallel$ BC
$OB = OC \qquad \because$ radii
$O\hat{C}B = 60°$
$\Rightarrow \quad B\hat{O}C = 60° \qquad \because$ angles of $\triangle$
$\Rightarrow \quad \triangle OBC$ is equilateral

7

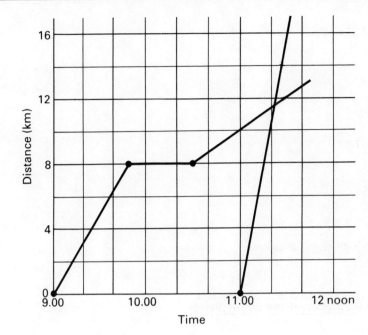

Mark overtakes John $11\frac{1}{2}$ km from the start at 11.22 a.m.

8   Selling price = 6p × 1000 = £60
Profit = £60 – £35 = £25
% profit $= \dfrac{25}{35} \times 100 = 71.4\%$

9   Refer to chart in probability section.
(a) P(total ≥ 2) = 1

(b) P(total prime) $= \dfrac{14}{36} = \dfrac{7}{18}$

(c) P(prime from prime numbers) $= \dfrac{4}{36} = \dfrac{1}{9}$

(d) P(8 ≤ total < 12) $= \dfrac{14}{36} = \dfrac{7}{18}$

10 $13\frac{5}{11} = 13.45$

(a) 13.45   (b) 13   (c) 13.5

SOLUTIONS TO REVISION PAPER 2

1 $2x - 1 > 9 \implies 2x > 10$ i.e. $x > 5$

2

Tony: $147 \times \dfrac{4}{4 + 3} = 21 \times 4 = £84$

Pam: $147 \times \dfrac{3}{4 + 3} = 21 \times 3 = £63$

3 $\dfrac{p^{\frac{2}{3}} \times p^2}{p^{\frac{4}{3}}} + \dfrac{q^7}{q^{\frac{7}{2}} \times q^{\frac{5}{2}}} + (2r - 1)^0$

$= \dfrac{p^{\frac{8}{3}}}{p^{\frac{4}{3}}} + \dfrac{q^7}{q^6} + 1$

$= p^{\frac{4}{3}} + q + 1.$

4   The sixth spin has nothing to do with any other spins.
It is independent.
P(tails) $= \frac{1}{2}$

5

Type	terraced	semi-detached	detached	bungalow	flat
Number	10	6	2	4	8

30 houses $\Rightarrow$ 1 house = 12° on pie chart

Angles	120°	72°	24°	48°	96°

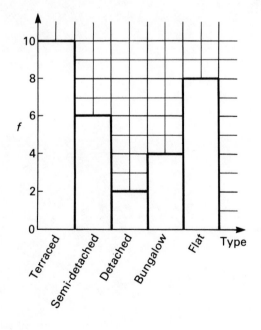

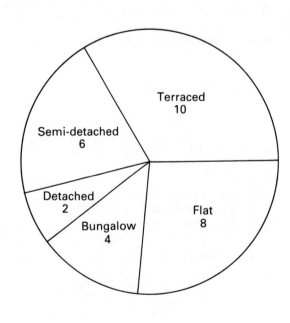

6 $x + (x + 20°) + (2x - 10°) + 74° + 108° = 540°$

                                 $\because 540°$ in pentagon

        $\Rightarrow\quad 4x + 192° = 540°$

                $4x = 540° - 192° = 348°$

                 $x = 87°$

$\therefore$ angles are: $87°, 107°, 164°, 74°, 108°$

7 $\mathbf{r} = 5 \begin{pmatrix} 4 \\ 3 \end{pmatrix} - 3 \begin{pmatrix} -3 \\ 2 \end{pmatrix} = \begin{pmatrix} 20 \\ 15 \end{pmatrix} - \begin{pmatrix} -9 \\ 6 \end{pmatrix} = \begin{pmatrix} 29 \\ 9 \end{pmatrix}$

8

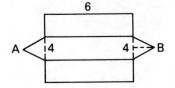

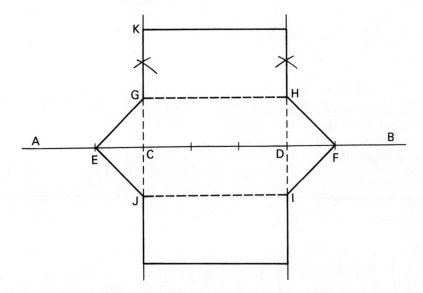

  1 Draw AB.
  2 Mark C and D.
  3 Construct E and F, CE = DF = 2.
  4 Construct $\perp$ lines at C and D.
  5 plot G, H, I, J, CG = 2.
  6 Construct GK = GE.

9

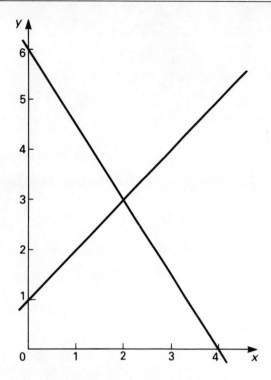

The lines intersect at (2, 3).
No other intersection points: they are only where lines intersect and two straight lines only intersect once.

10

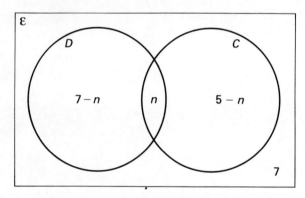

$7 - n + n + 5 - n + 7 = 16 \Rightarrow n = 3$
$\Rightarrow$ 4 houses have dog only, 2 have cat only, 3 have dog and cat.

SOLUTIONS TO REVISION PAPER 3

1 (a) 2   4   8   16   32 64   128
      (b) 8   38   68   98   128

$\Rightarrow$ 128 first common number

2 Total weight of team = $8 \times 54 = 432$ kg
      Weight of seven members = 381 kg
      Weight of eighth girl = $432 - 381 = 51$ kg

3

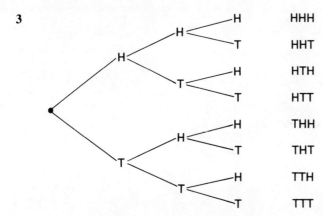

$$P(2H, IT) = \frac{2}{8}$$

4 (a) Each contribution $= \dfrac{£100}{n}$
      (b) Cost = ticket + fare $\Rightarrow$ $C = 8 + \dfrac{100}{n}$

      (c) $C = 8 + \dfrac{100}{34} = 8 + 2.94 = £10.94$

5 (a) $fg(x) = f(x - 1) = (x - 1)^2$
      (b) $ghf(x) = gh(x^2) = g\left(\dfrac{3}{x^2}\right) = \dfrac{3}{x^2} - 1$

      (c) $h(x) = \dfrac{3}{x}$

      $h(x)$ is formed by operating on x (1) reciprocate
                                              (2) $\times 3$
      h^{-1} is formed by   (1) $x \div 3 = \dfrac{x}{3}$

                                              (2) reciprocate $= \dfrac{3}{x}$ i.e. $h(x) = h^{-1}(x)$

6 $\tan 32° = \dfrac{5}{BD} \Rightarrow BD = \dfrac{5}{\tan 32°}$

$= 8$

$\tan 67° = \dfrac{5}{BC} \Rightarrow BC = \dfrac{5}{\tan 67°}$

$= 2.12$

$CD = BD - BC = 8 - 2.12$

$= 5.88$

7   **(a)** $\overrightarrow{DE} = \overrightarrow{DA} + \overrightarrow{AE} = -2\mathbf{a} + 2\mathbf{b}$

$= 2(\mathbf{b} - \mathbf{a})$

(b) $\overrightarrow{BC} = \overrightarrow{BA} + \overrightarrow{AC} = -3\mathbf{a} + 3\mathbf{b}$

$= 3(\mathbf{b} - \mathbf{a})$

(c) DE and BC are parallel and $\dfrac{DE}{BC} = \dfrac{2}{3}$

Parallel $\because$ both a multiple of the same vector $(\mathbf{b} - \mathbf{a})$.

(d) Triangles ADE and ABC are similar.

(e) Ratio of sides of ADE and ABC $= \dfrac{2}{3}$

$\therefore$ ratio of areas ADE and ABC $= \dfrac{2^2}{3^2} = \dfrac{4}{9}$

$\therefore$ DECB is $\dfrac{5}{9}$ of ABC. $= \dfrac{4}{9}$

8

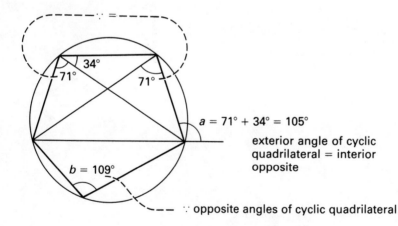

$a = 71° + 34° = 105°$

exterior angle of cyclic
quadrilateral = interior
opposite

$b = 109°$

$\because$ opposite angles of cyclic quadrilateral

9

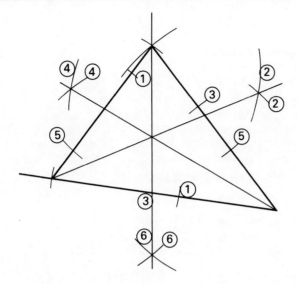

The angle bisectors all pass through the same point: they are **concurrent**.

The point they share is the **incentre**, the centre of the **inscribed** circle. The inscribed circle has the sides of the triangle as tangents.

10 $5x + 2y = 23 \quad \Rightarrow \quad 5x + 2y = 23$

   $4y - x = 13 \quad \Rightarrow \quad 20y - 5x = 65$

$\left. \right\} + \quad \Rightarrow \quad 22y = 88 \quad \Rightarrow \quad y = 4$

Substitute for y in either equation $\quad \Rightarrow \quad x = 3$

$\therefore$ solution: $x = 3, y = 4$

Remember to check your solution in the other equation.

SOLUTIONS TO REVISION PAPER 4

1

Mark	Midvalue m.v.	Frequency f	Cum. frequency c.f.	f x m.v.
0–9	4.5	8	8	36
10–19	14.5	14	22	203
20–29	24.5	22	44	539
30–39	34.5	25	69	862.5
40–49	44.5	19	88	845.5
50–60	55	12	100	660
		$\Sigma f = 100$		$\Sigma f \times$ m.v. $= 3146$

(a) Mean $= \dfrac{\Sigma f \times \text{m.v.}}{\Sigma f} = \dfrac{3146}{100} = 31.46$

(b) Mark   29   39

      c.f.   44   50   69

$$\underset{=\,6}{50-44} \qquad \underset{=\,19}{69-50}$$

$$\therefore \text{median} = 30 + \frac{6}{(6+19)} \times 10$$

             lower limit   class width

$$= 30 + 2.4 = 32.4$$

(c)

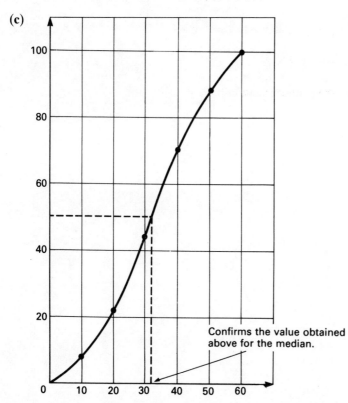

Confirms the value obtained above for the median.

2 A product is even if one of the factors is even because it will then
contain 2 × ...
If n is even
$n = 2 \times t$ and $n(n + 1) = 2 \times t \times (n + 1)$ – even
If n is odd
$n + 1$ is even, say, $= 2 \times r$ and $n(n + 1) = n \times 2 \times r$ – even
$\therefore n(n + 1)$ is always even.

3

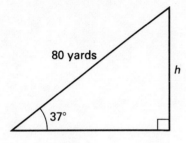

$\sin 37° = \dfrac{h}{80}$
$h = 80 \times \sin 37°$
$\quad = 48.1$ yards

4

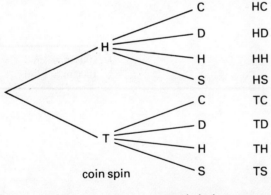

Red aces are H and D $P(\text{HD or HH}) = \dfrac{2}{8}$
$= \dfrac{1}{4}$

5 $2\mathbf{a} - 3\mathbf{b} + \mathbf{c}$

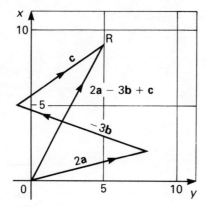

$$= 2 \begin{pmatrix} 4 \\ 1 \end{pmatrix} - 3 \begin{pmatrix} 3 \\ -1 \end{pmatrix} + \begin{pmatrix} 6 \\ 4 \end{pmatrix} = \begin{pmatrix} 8 - 9 + 6 \\ 2 + 3 + 4 \end{pmatrix}$$

$$= \begin{pmatrix} 5 \\ 9 \end{pmatrix}$$

6   In one revolution the mark travels $\pi \times 28$ cm

In $2\frac{1}{2}$ hours the wheel makes $3500 \times 60 \times 2\frac{1}{2}$ revs

rpm   mph   no. hours

$= 525\ 000$ revs

In 45 minutes the wheel makes 2000×45 revs

$= 90\ 000$ revs

Total revs $= 615\ 000$

Distance travelled $= 615\ 000 \times \pi \times 28$ cm

$$= 615\ 000 \times \pi \times \frac{28}{100}\ \text{m}$$

$$= 6150 \times \pi \times \frac{28}{1000}\ \text{km}$$

$$= 541\ \text{km}$$

> 100 cm = 1 m
> 1000 m = 1 km

7   Let the true speed be v.

Then $v + 10\%$ of $v = 66$

$\Rightarrow$ $v + \dfrac{v}{10} = 66 \quad \Rightarrow \quad \dfrac{11v}{10} = 66$

$v = 60$ mph

Distance travelled $= 1\frac{1}{2} \times 60 = 90$ miles

8   Ratio of share out $R : J = 2000 : 1800 = 10 : 9$

i.e. Ravi receives $\dfrac{10}{19}$ and Jameel receives $\dfrac{9}{19}$.

If total profit is P then $\dfrac{9}{19} \times P = 1530$

$$P = 1530 \times \frac{19}{9}$$

$$= £3230$$

9

f(x)		3		11		31		69		131		223
lst difference			8		20		38		62		92	
2nd difference				12		18		24		30		
3rd difference					6		6		6			

$\Rightarrow$ f(x) is cubic

x	1	2	3	4	5	6
Try x^3	1	8	27	64	125	216
Consider f(x) $- x^3$	2	3	4	5	6	7
Try $x^3 + x$	2	10	30	68	130	222
Consider f(x) $- (x^3 + x)$	1	1	1	1	1	1

$\therefore$ f(x) = $x^3 + x + 1$

> Method of inspection or 'trial and error'

10 f(x) = $2x^2 - 5x - 2$
f(2) = 8 $-$ 10 $-$ 2
   = -4
f(3) = 18 $-$ 15 $-$ 2
   = 1
$\therefore$ try f(2.8) = -0.32
    f(2.9) = 0.32
   f(2.85) = -0.005
$\therefore$ since f(x) goes from $-$ to + between $x = 2.85$ and $x = 2.9$ the root, to 1 d.p., is 2.9.

SOLUTIONS TO REVISION PAPER 5

1 **Operations**   1   squared
       2   -1
       3   $\div 2$

$\therefore \times 2 \Rightarrow 2t = k^2 - 1$
  $+ 1 \Rightarrow 2t + 1 = k^2$
  $\sqrt{} \quad \Rightarrow \sqrt{2t + 1} = k$
  $t = 24 \Rightarrow k = \sqrt{48 + 1}$
       $= \sqrt{49}$
       $= \pm 7$

2   If the width is x, the length is $3x$ $\Rightarrow$ $3x^2 = 48$

     $\Rightarrow$ $x = 4$

∴ perimeter of rectangle = 32 cm

(a) Side of square = $\dfrac{32}{4} = 8$ cm

     Area of square = $8^2 = 64$ cm²

(b) For the circle $2\pi r = 32$

     $\Rightarrow$ $r = \dfrac{32}{2\pi} = \dfrac{16^2}{\pi}$

     Area = $\pi r^2 = \pi \times \dfrac{16^2}{\pi^2} = \dfrac{16^2}{\pi} = 81.5$ cm²

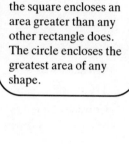

For a given perimeter the square encloses an area greater than any other rectangle does. The circle encloses the greatest area of any shape.

3 $\begin{pmatrix} a & 2 \\ 3 & 4b \end{pmatrix}\begin{pmatrix} 1 \\ 3 \end{pmatrix} = \begin{pmatrix} a + 6 \\ 3 + 12b \end{pmatrix} = \begin{pmatrix} 7 \\ 27 \end{pmatrix}$

∴ $a + 6 = 7$ $\Rightarrow$ $a = 1$

and $3 + 12b = 27$ $\Rightarrow$ $b = 2.$

4

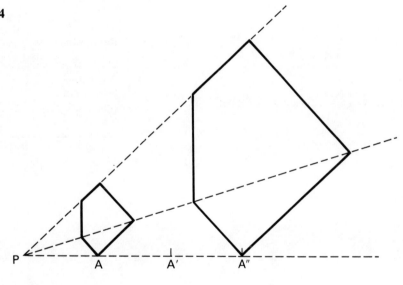

An accurate and efficient method:

   Draw the dotted lines, as shown, through the vertices.

   Place the compass point on P, set to PA.

   Do not alter the setting, place the point on A, mark A_1.

   Do not alter the setting, place the point on A_1, mark A_2.

Similarly for all the other vertices.

5 (a) P(Ford first) $= \dfrac{3}{9} = \dfrac{1}{3}$

(b) 1 Ford, 2 BL gone $\Rightarrow$ 2 Ford, 3 BL, 1 VW left

$P(VW) = \dfrac{1}{6}$

6 (a) If C is Carole's age and L is Leon's age,

$C + L = 50$

$C - 3 = 3 \times (L - 3) \Rightarrow C - 3 = 3L - 9$

$\Rightarrow C = 3L - 6$

(b) $C + L = 50$

$\therefore (3L - 6) + L = 50 \quad \because C = 3L - 6$

$\Rightarrow 4L = 56$

$\Rightarrow L = 14$ years, $C = 36$ years

7 $a^2 + b^2 - 2abp = 5^2 + 4^2 - 2 \times 5 \times 4 \times 0.6$

$= 25 + 16 - 40 \times 0.6$

$= 41 - 40 \times 0.6$

$= 41 - 24 \blacktriangleleft$

$= 17$

> Popular mistake at this step
> $= 1 \times 0.6 = 0.6$
> from $41 - 40$

8 (a) $40 \times £6 = £240$

$3 \times £10.50 = £31.50$

$\therefore$ gross wage $= £271.50$

(b) Superannuation $= 6\%$ of gross wage $= \dfrac{6}{100} \times £271.50$

$= £16.29$

> **Remember**
> Gross means before any deductions
> Superannuation – contribution to pension fund.

(c) Annual income after superannuation

$= 52 \times (£271.50 - £16.29) = £13\,270.92$

(d) The first £4000 is not taxed.

$\therefore £(13\,270.92 - 4000) = £9270.92$ is taxed at 25%.

Tax paid $= \dfrac{25}{100} \times £9270.92$

$= £2317.73$

(e) Take home pay $= £4000 + £(9270.92 - 2317.73)$

$= £10\,953.19$ p.a.

$= \dfrac{£10\,953.19}{52}$ per week

$= £210.64$ p.w.

> p.a. means *per annum* or per year

9 $(x + 1)(x + 3)(2x - 1) = (x^2 + x + 3x + 3)(2x - 1)$

concentrating on first two brackets

$= (x^2 + 4x + 3)(2x - 1)$

$= 2x^3 + 8x^2 + 6x - x^2 - 4x - 3$

$= 2x^3 + 7x^2 + 2x - 3$

10

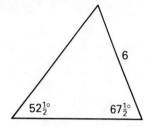

$52\frac{1}{2}°$ can be made from $22\frac{1}{2}°$ ($\frac{1}{2} \times 45$)
and $30°$ ($\frac{1}{2} \times 60$).
But with the angles given, the third angle is $60°$.
∴ the 6 cm line has $60°$ at one end and $(45 + \frac{1}{2} \times 45)°$ at other.

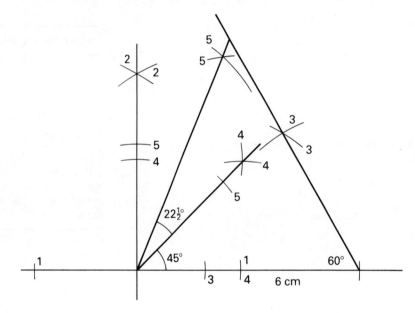

SOLUTIONS TO REVISION PAPER 6

1 Let the edge of the cube be x.

Then the surface area is $6x^2 = 69.36 \Rightarrow x^2 = 11.56$

$\Rightarrow x = 3.4$

The volume $= 3.4^3 = 39.3$ cm^3

2   Cost of watches = £np

Receipts from sale of watches = £mq

Profit = £$(mq - np)$

% profit = $\dfrac{(mq - np)}{np} \times 100 = \dfrac{100(mq - np)}{np}$

If the profit is zero then $mq - np = 0$

$$mq = np$$

3   **(a)** The 3 of hearts is taken out $\Rightarrow$ three 3s left

   P(2nd 3) = $\dfrac{3}{51} = \dfrac{1}{17}$

   (b) P(5) = $\dfrac{4}{51}$

   (c) 12 hearts are left $\Rightarrow$ P(heart) = $\dfrac{12}{51} = \dfrac{4}{17}$

4   Price of TV = £260

Cash discount = 10% of £260 = £26 $\Rightarrow$ Cash price = £234 (minimum price)

HP price = deposit + payments = £20 + 12 × £24 = £308 (maximum price)

So the difference between the maximum and minimum prices = £308 − £234 = £74

5

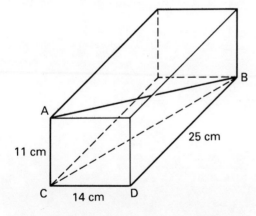

11 cm

25 cm

14 cm

AB is the longest stick that will fit in the box.

$AB^2 = AC^2 + CB^2$

$\quad\quad = AC^2 + CD^2 + DB^2$

$\quad\quad = 11^2 + 14^2 + 25^2$

$\therefore$ AB = 30.7 cm

6 $g(x) = x^2 + 1$ and $gf(x) = 4x^2 + 1$

But $gf(x) = [f(x)]^2 + 1$

$\quad [f(x)]^2 = 4x^2$

$\quad\quad f(x) = 2x$ or $f(x) = -2x$

> Study this carefully : it should make sense.

7

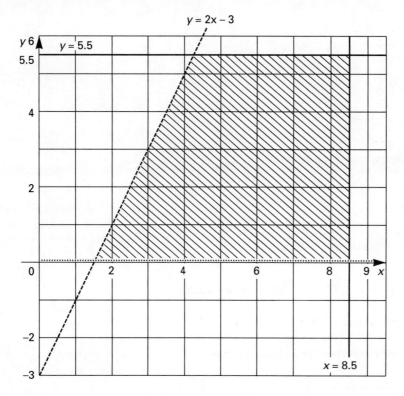

8 **(a)** The interior angles of a pentagon add up to 540°.
All the angles are equal. $\Rightarrow$ $C\hat{D}E = 540° \div 5$
$= 108°$

(b) $\triangle ECD$ is isosceles $\Rightarrow$ $E\hat{C}D = 36°$
Similarly $B\hat{C}A = 36°$
$A\hat{C}E = 36°$

(c) $A\hat{O}E = 72°$ $\because 2 \times A\hat{C}E$
OH bisects $A\hat{O}E$
$H\hat{O}E = 36°$

(d) $\dfrac{OH}{OE} = \cos36°$ $\Rightarrow$ $OH = 10\cos36°$
$= 8.1$

(e) Area $\triangle OAE = \frac{1}{2} \times AE \times OH$
$= OH\sin36° \times 8.1$
$= 47.6 \text{ cm}^2$ $\because AE = 10\sin36°$
Area of pentagon $= 5 \times \triangle OAE$
$= 238 \text{ cm}^2$

9 Let the volume of the pyramid be V.
$V = \frac{1}{3} \times \text{base area} \times \text{height}$
$= \frac{1}{3} \times 26 \times 12 \times 18$
$= 1872 \text{ cm}^3$

10 **(a)** $\sqrt{8} + \sqrt{18} = \sqrt{4}\sqrt{2} + \sqrt{9}\sqrt{2}$

$$= 2\sqrt{2} + 3\sqrt{2}$$

$$= 5\sqrt{2}$$

(b) $\dfrac{\sqrt{75}}{\sqrt{12}} = \dfrac{\sqrt{25}\sqrt{3}}{\sqrt{4}\sqrt{3}}$

$$= \dfrac{5}{2}$$

SOLUTIONS TO REVISION PAPER 7

1   Let there be n sacks of each size.

Then $n \times 50$ + $n \times 25$ = 15×1000

weight of   weight of   capacity of

50 kg sacks   25 kg sacks   lorry in kg

> Build up an equation.

$$75n = 15 \times 1000$$

$$5n = 1000$$

$$n = 200$$

2 $x^2 - x - 20 = 0$

$$(x - 5)(x + 4) = 0$$

$x - 5 = 0$ or $x + 4 = 0$

$\quad x = 5 \qquad\qquad x = -4$

> Quadratic – try brackets first

3   For **A** $\begin{pmatrix} 0 & -2 \\ 2 & 0 \end{pmatrix}\begin{pmatrix} 4 \\ 3 \end{pmatrix} = \begin{pmatrix} -6 \\ 8 \end{pmatrix}$

For **B** $\begin{pmatrix} 0 & -2 \\ 2 & 0 \end{pmatrix}\begin{pmatrix} 8 \\ 3 \end{pmatrix} = \begin{pmatrix} -6 \\ 16 \end{pmatrix}$

For **C** $\begin{pmatrix} 0 & -2 \\ 2 & 0 \end{pmatrix}\begin{pmatrix} 8 \\ 6 \end{pmatrix} = \begin{pmatrix} -12 \\ 16 \end{pmatrix}$

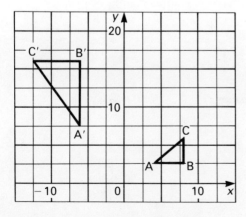

Rotation 90° anticlockwise about the origin and enlargement by scale factor 2, origin centre of enlargement.

4

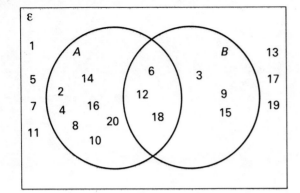

5 $a = x + 2y + 3z$

$a - x - 3z = 2y$

$$\dfrac{a - x - 3z}{2} = y$$

$a = 5, x = 3, z = 2 \Rightarrow y = \dfrac{5 - 3 - 6}{2}$

$$= \dfrac{-4}{2}$$

$$= -2$$

6   **(a)** $3(2xy^3)^2(3x^2y)^3 = 3 \times 4x^2y^6 \times 27x^6y^3$

$$= 324x^8y^9$$

(b) $\dfrac{x^{-1}y}{x^3y^2} = \dfrac{1}{x \times x^3} \times \dfrac{y}{y^2} = \dfrac{1}{x^4y}$

(c) $81^{\frac{3}{4}} \times 3^{-2} = \sqrt[4]{81^3} \times \dfrac{1}{3^2}$

$$= 3^3 \times \dfrac{1}{3^2} = 3$$

7

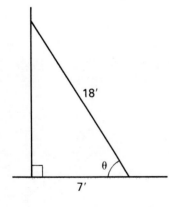

$\cos\theta = \left(\dfrac{7}{18}\right)$

$\Rightarrow \quad \theta = \cos^{-1}\left(\dfrac{7}{18}\right)$

$\quad\quad = 67.1°$

Calculator sequence	**Display**
7	7
÷	7
18	18
=	0.38888
inv	0.38888
cos	67.11462

8 Distance = speed × time

$\therefore$ time = $\dfrac{\text{distance}}{\text{speed}}$

For Helen: $t_H = \frac{5}{8}$ hours = $\frac{5}{8} \times 60$ minutes = 37.5 minutes

For Louise: $t_L = \frac{5}{7}$ hours = $\frac{5}{7} \times 60$ minutes = 42.9 minutes

Difference = $t_L - t_H$ = 5.4 minutes

9

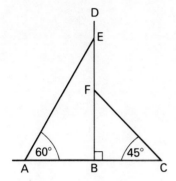

Draw ABC and construct BD.

Construct 60° at A and 45° at C.

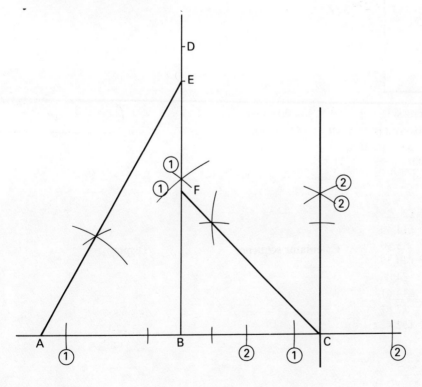

EF = 3 cm

10 Volume of prism = area of cross-section × length
    (a) $V = (0.16 \times 0.05 + 0.13 \times 0.05) \times 3$ m^3 = 0.0435 m^3
         $= 4.35 \times 10^{-2}$ m^3
    (b) $V = 0.0435 \times 10^9$ mm$^3 = 4.35 \times 10^{-2} \times 10^9$ mm^3
         $= 4.35 \times 10^7$ mm^3

> 1m = 1000 mm
> 1 m^3 = 1000 × 1000 × 1000 mm^3
> = 10^9 mm^3

SOLUTIONS TO REVISION PAPER 8

1

$$\text{From} \begin{array}{c} \\ A \\ B \\ C \\ D \end{array} \begin{array}{c} \quad\quad\quad \text{To} \\ \begin{pmatrix} A & B & C & D \\ 0 & 1 & 1 & 2 \\ 1 & 0 & 1 & 0 \\ 1 & 1 & 2 & 0 \\ 2 & 0 & 0 & 0 \end{pmatrix} \end{array}$$

2

100 yards

60 yards

Area covered in one crossing is $2 \times 60 \times \frac{1}{3} = 40$ sq yd
In 25 crossings area covered is $25 \times 40 = 1000$ sq yd
Area of field = $100 \times 60 = 6000$ sq yd

$$\text{P(splatt)} = \frac{1000}{6000} = \tfrac{1}{6}$$

and P(survival) $= \tfrac{5}{6}$

> $12'' = \tfrac{1}{3}$ yard

3

3 meals @ £6.75	£20.25
2 meals @ £7.20	£14.40
1 meal @ £5.90	£ 5.90
Subtotal (meals)	£40.55
Service @ 10%	£4.06
Subtotal (+service)	£44.61
VAT @ 17.5%	£7.81
Total	**£52.42**

4 $4(2x + 1) = 28$

$$2x + 1 = \frac{28}{4} = 7$$

$$2x = 6 \quad \Rightarrow \quad x = 3$$

5

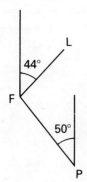

$5 \text{ km} \rightarrow 2 \text{ cm}$

$1 \text{ km} \rightarrow \frac{2}{5} \text{ cm}$

$27\frac{1}{2} \text{ km} \rightarrow 27\frac{1}{2} \times \frac{2}{5} \text{ cm} = 11 \text{ cm}$

$21\frac{1}{4} \text{ km} \rightarrow 21\frac{1}{4} \times \frac{2}{5} \text{ cm} = 8\frac{1}{2} \text{ cm}$

This N line is drawn parallel to the one at Preston using a set square.

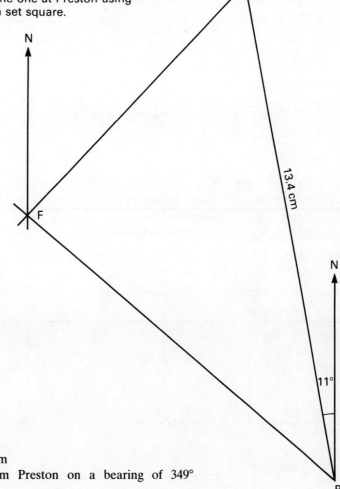

LP = 13.4 cm

$\quad = 13.4 \times \frac{5}{2} \text{ km} = 33.5 \text{ km}$

Lancaster is 33.5 km from Preston on a bearing of 349° (360−11)°.

6 $y = 4 + 3x - x^2$

x	0	1	2	3	4
y	4	6	6	4	0

For a better graph, work out the intermediate values – they are needed later anyway.

x	0.5	1.5	2.5	3.5
y	5.25	6.25	5.25	2.25

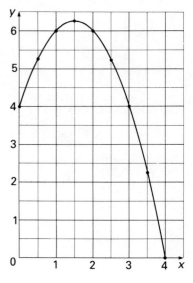

$A = \frac{1}{2} \times \frac{1}{2} \times \{4 + 0 + 2\,(5.25 + 6 + 6.25 + 6 + 5.25 + 4 + 2.25)\}$
$\therefore A = 18.5$ sq units

7 $\overrightarrow{CG} = \overrightarrow{CA} + \overrightarrow{AG}$

$\qquad = \overrightarrow{CA} + \frac{2}{3}\overrightarrow{AM}$

$\qquad = \overrightarrow{CA} + \frac{2}{3}(\overrightarrow{AC} + \overrightarrow{CM})$

$\qquad = \mathbf{b} + \frac{2}{3}(-\mathbf{b} + \frac{1}{2}\mathbf{a})$

$\qquad = \mathbf{b} - \frac{2}{3}\mathbf{b} + \frac{1}{3}\mathbf{a}$

$\qquad = \frac{1}{3}\mathbf{b} + \frac{1}{3}\mathbf{a} = \frac{1}{3}(\mathbf{a} + \mathbf{b})$

8 **(a)** $E\hat{D}A = 90°$ $\qquad \because$ angle in semi-circle
$\qquad \therefore D\hat{E}A = 56°$ $\qquad \because$ angles of $\triangle$
$\qquad \therefore C\hat{E}B = 56°$ $\qquad \because$ vertically opposite angles

$\quad$ **(b)** $C\hat{B}D = C\hat{A}D = 34°$ $\qquad \because$ angles in same segment
$\qquad \therefore C\hat{A}B = 180° - (39 + 34 + 90)° = 17°$

9 There are thousands of answers but examples are

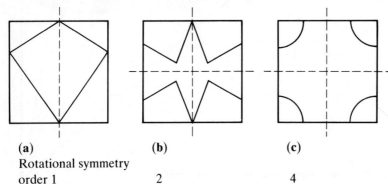

(a)
Rotational symmetry
order 1 $\qquad\qquad\qquad$ 2 $\qquad\qquad\qquad$ 4

(b) $\qquad\qquad\qquad$ **(c)**

10 $(\frac{1}{2} + \frac{2}{3}) \div (\frac{5}{6} - \frac{1}{4})$

$= \dfrac{3 + 4}{6} \div \dfrac{10 - 3}{12}$

$= \frac{7}{6} \times \frac{12}{7}$

$= 2$

> **Remember**
> The word 'exact' is telling you that you cannot use a calculator. On a calculator $\frac{2}{3} = 0.6666\ldots$ which is an approximation.

SOLUTIONS TO REVISION PAPER 9

1 $\frac{2}{7} = 0.286$
$\frac{3}{11} = 0.272$
$\frac{4}{17} = 0.235$ So the order is $\frac{3}{13}$ $\frac{4}{17}$ $\frac{6}{23}$ $\frac{3}{11}$ $\frac{2}{7}$
$\frac{3}{13} = 0.231$
$\frac{6}{23} = 0.261$

2 $(3 - x)(x + 2) + 2x(x + 5) = 3x + 6 - x^2 - 2x + 2x^2 + 10x$
$= x^2 + 11x + 6$

3

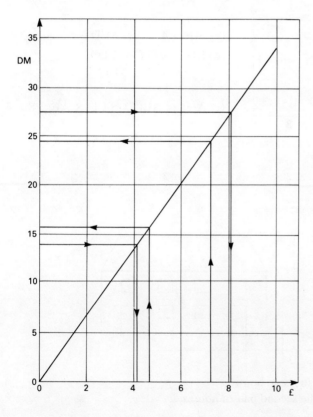

(a) 24.75DM   (b) £4.18

(c) £4.70 = 15.75 DM   ∴ £47 = 157.5DM

(d) 27.5DM = £8.10   ∴ 2750DM = £810

4 $C = \pi d = \pi \times 27 = 84.8$ inches

100 turns $\Rightarrow$ bike travels $\dfrac{100 \times 84.8}{36}$ yards

$\qquad\qquad = 235.6$ yards

Chain wheel : sprocket = 11 : 4

i.e. 4 turns of chain wheel = 11 turns of bike wheel

number of turns of pedal $100 \times \frac{4}{11} = 36.4$ turns.

(a) Speed $= \dfrac{\text{distance}}{\text{time}} = \dfrac{235.6}{40} = 5.89$ yards per second

(b) 5.89 yards per second$= \dfrac{5.89}{1760}$ miles per second

$\qquad = \dfrac{5.89}{1760} \times 60$ miles per minute

$\qquad = \dfrac{5.89 \times 60 \times 60}{1760}$ mph

$\qquad = 12$ mph

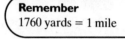

Remember
1760 yards = 1 mile

5

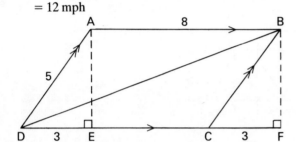

(a) AE = 4 $\because \triangle$AED is a 3, 4, 5 $\triangle$

(b) BD = $\sqrt{(\text{BF}^2 + \text{FD}^2)}$
$\qquad = \sqrt{(4^2 + 11^2)}$
$\qquad = 11.7$

(c) Area of ABCD = CD $\times$ AE = 8 $\times$ 4 = 32

6 Sum of the exterior angles is 360°.

polygon has $\dfrac{360°}{20°} = 18$ sides.

7

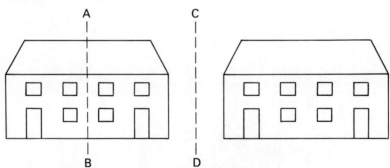

Firstly reflect in the line AB to get the first two houses.
Secondly reflect in the line CD to get the second pair of houses.

8 $4^{-3} = \dfrac{1}{4^3} = \dfrac{1}{64}$ $3^{-4} = \dfrac{1}{3^4} = \dfrac{1}{81}$

Difference $= \dfrac{1}{64} - \dfrac{1}{81} = \dfrac{81 - 64}{81 \times 64} = \dfrac{17}{81 \times 64} = \dfrac{17}{5184} \approx 0.003$

9 $AB = \begin{pmatrix} 4 & -1 \\ 2 & 3 \end{pmatrix}\begin{pmatrix} 0 & -2 \\ 3 & -4 \end{pmatrix} = \begin{pmatrix} -3 & -4 \\ 9 & -16 \end{pmatrix}$

  $BA = \begin{pmatrix} 0 & -2 \\ 3 & -4 \end{pmatrix}\begin{pmatrix} 4 & -1 \\ 2 & 3 \end{pmatrix} = \begin{pmatrix} -4 & -6 \\ 4 & -15 \end{pmatrix}$

10 $\dfrac{x}{4} + \dfrac{3}{8} = \dfrac{7}{8}$

  $\dfrac{x}{4} = \dfrac{7}{8} - \dfrac{3}{8} = \dfrac{4}{8} = \dfrac{2}{4}$

  $x = 2$

SOLUTIONS TO REVISION PAPER 10

1 4% of 50 mm = 2 mm $\Rightarrow$ maximum length = 52 mm
  minimum length = 48 mm

2

Cost (£)	Mid-value (m.v.)	Frequency f	Cum. frequency c.f.	$f \times$ m.v.
4000–4999	4499.5	12	12	53 994
5000–5999	5499.5	20	32	109 990
6000–6999	6499.5	56	88	363 972
7000–7999	7499.5	41	129	307 479.5
8000–8999	8499.5	26	155	220 987
9000–9999	9499.5	24	179	227 988
10 000–10 999	10 499.5	19	198	199 490.5
11 000–11 999	11 499.5	11	209	126 494.5
			Total	1 610 395.5

(a) Mean $= \dfrac{1\,610\,395.5}{209} = £7705.24$

(b) Median (105th) is in the 7000–7999 class

  Median $= 7000 + \dfrac{105 - 88}{129 - 88} \times 1000 = £7414.63$ ←——— This complicated fraction gives the place of the 105th vaule in the 7000–7999 class.

(c) Modal class: £(6000–6999)

(d) Quartiles can be worked out in the same way as the median.

  Lower quartile (53rd) $\Rightarrow$ $£\{6000 + \dfrac{53 - 20}{56 - 20} \times 1000\}$

    $= £6916.67$

  Upper quartile (158th) $\Rightarrow$ $£\{9000 + \dfrac{158 - 155}{179 - 155} \times 1000\}$

    $= £9125$

  SIR $= \dfrac{£9125 - £6916.67}{2} = \dfrac{£2208.33}{2} = £1104.17$

3 $\dfrac{2}{x} + \dfrac{1}{2} = 1$ $\Rightarrow$ $\dfrac{2}{x} = \dfrac{1}{2}$ $\Rightarrow$ $x = 4$

4 $y = x^2 - 5x + 4$

x	0	1	2	3	4	5	6
y	4	0	−2	−2	0	4	10

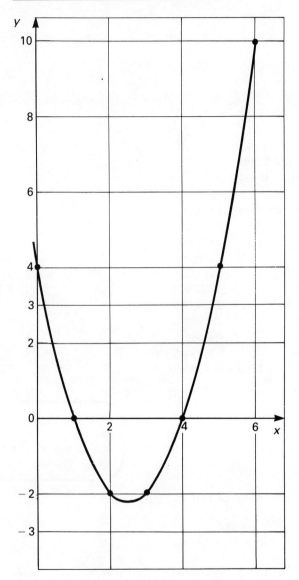

(a) $x^2 - 5x + 4 = 0$ when $x = 1$
   or $x = 4$

(b) $x^2 - 5x + 1 = 0 \implies x^2 - 5x + 4 = 3$
   $\implies$ finding values of x where the drawn function has the value 3.
   $\implies x = 0.2$ and $x = 4.8$

Remember

Make the LHS the same
as the drawn function.

5

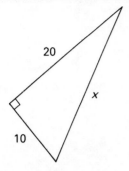

After 30 minutes the first car has gone 20 miles and the second car has gone 10 miles.

$x = \sqrt{(20^2 + 10^2)} = \sqrt{500}$

$x = 22.4$ miles

6

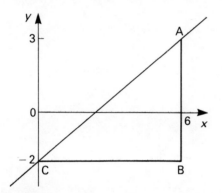

$\text{Gradient} = \dfrac{\text{AB}}{\text{BC}} = \dfrac{3 - -2}{6 - 0} = \dfrac{5}{6}$

The equation is of the form $y = mx + c$

$m = \frac{5}{6} \Rightarrow y = \frac{5}{6}x + c$

$(0, -2)$ is on the line $\Rightarrow -2 = \frac{5}{6} \times 0 + c \Rightarrow c = -2$

the equation of the line is $y = \dfrac{5x}{6} - 2 \Rightarrow 6y = 5x - 12$

7

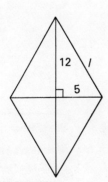

(a) $l = 13$ $\quad \because$ Pythagoras, 5, 12, 13 $\triangle$

(b) $A = 2 \times \frac{1}{2} \times 10 \times 12 = 120$ cm^2

8

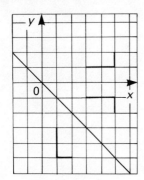

Rotation 90° clockwise about 0.

9

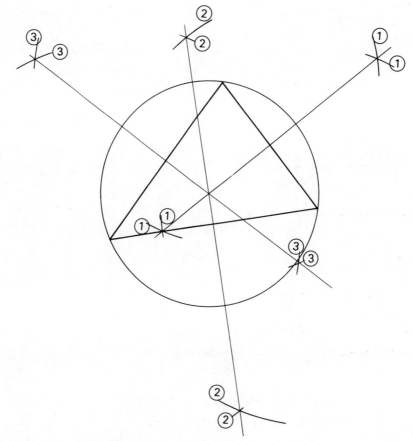

The bisectors of the sides of a triangle are concurrent i.e. they meet at the same point. This point is the **circumcentre**, the centre of the circumscribed circle, as shown.

10 All cubes are similar.

   (a) Ratio of surface areas = $3^2 : 5^2 = 9 : 25$

   (b) Ratio of volumes = $3^3 : 5^3 = 27 : 125$

Index